FRIULAN
Language and Literature

D. B. Gregor

Oh dolse Furlanìa
cussì verde in t'el sol!

Biagio Marin (gradese)

Un tappeto di smeraldo
sotto il cielo il monte par.

Carducci, In Carnia

THE OLEANDER PRESS

The Oleander Press
210 Fifth Avenue
New York   N.Y. 10010

The Oleander Press
17 Stansgate Avenue
Cambridge CB2 2QZ, England

Cover photograph: The Basilica of Aquileia

ISBN 0 902675 39 7

Printed in Malta by St Paul's Press Ltd

CONTENTS

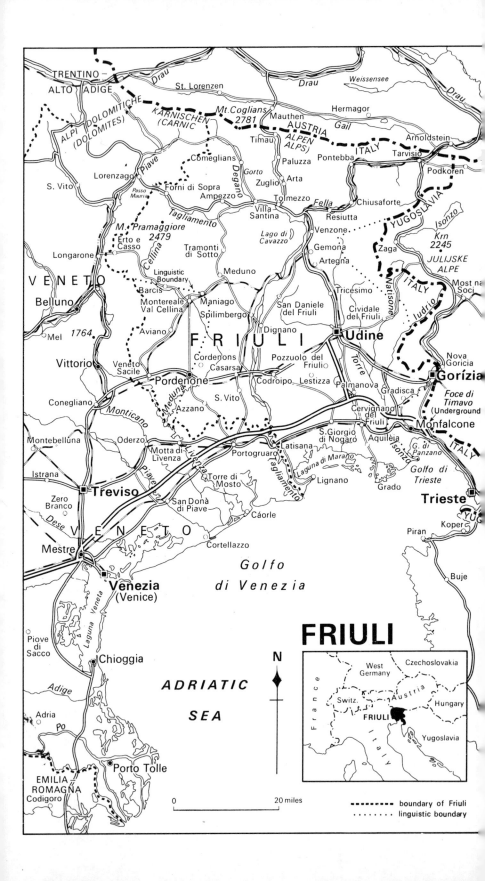

FRIULI

ADRIATIC
SEA

Golfo
di Venezia

N

········· boundary of Friuli
·········· linguistic boundary

0   20 miles

PREFACE

Whether Friulan is to be called language or dialect is a question that may well be asked;[1] and to answer it is both difficult and invidious: difficult, because a moment's thought shows that every language is also a dialect and every dialect also a language; invidious, because a dialect is felt to be in some way subordinate. It is important to understand in what this inferiority consists. It has nothing to do with the "dialect" as an instrument of human speech. The misunderstanding arises partly from the convention of describing a dialect as being "of" some other contemporary speech; but the phrase "a dialect of Italian" is a misnomer: the national language of Italy is simply that one of the forms taken by Vulgar Latin in Italy's various regions, Tuscan, which historical and literary factors caused to become the norm or koiné for the whole country. The other forms, such as Romagnol and Neapolitan, are not dialects of Tuscan, but, like Tuscan itself, dialects of Latin. They are Italian dialects only in the sense that they are spoken on Italian

---

1. As it was by the Friulan poet, G. Malattia della Vallata (1875-1948) in his poem: "Al Furlan èsel lenga o Dialet?".

soil. Thus the basic distinction is political rather than linguistic: a "language" is the official speech of a nation.[2] So true is this, that attempts to acquire autonomy for any regional form of speech are immediately felt by Government as a threat to national unity.[3]

There is one sphere, however, in which "dialects" can achieve equality with "languages": they can be the vehicles of a literature. Once they are used for literary

---

2. Vallata saw this:
     Lenga a è propi chel ch'a sierf
     Pal Governo e pai privâz.
   ("Language is really that which serves Government and individuals"). At the same time, the feeling that a dialect is of something is so strong that Welsh, for example, though serving no Government, is always called a language, because there is nothing it can be a dialect of. For a more linguistic criterion we may consider such morphological features as the ending in s of the 2nd person sg., the pronoun ur (to them) (a distinct improvement on the cumbersome non-conjunctive loro of Italian) and the regularization of the verb (Grammar §20). Hence we may adopt the definition of Gianfranco Contini (Letteratura dell' Italia unita, 1968): "il friulano partecipa piuttosto allo statuto scientifico d'una lingua minore, che d'un dialetto" ("not a dialect, but a minor language").

3. Vallata, for example, goes on to say that "German scholars call Friulan a language in order to sow a little discord between Friuli and Italy. Under Fascism priests were forbidden to preach in Friulan, and the poet-priest, Zaneto (G. Schif), could no longer publish his poems in a Catholic paper after 1933. Mistral's friend, Aubanel, denied that linguistic autonomy meant separatism (Il Tesaur, 1958, p. 9).

creation, they stand alongside national tongues with an equal claim on our interest. A fresh pipe has been added to the mighty organ of human song. And Friulan has been accumulating a literature for 500 years.

Literature alone, however, cannot guarantee the survival of a language. A writer needs a reader. There has to be a literate public capable of appreciating literary works; and if the presence of such a public can call a literature into existence, its disappearance can doom it. It is here that the power of the national tongue produces its fatal effect. Thanks to the mass-media, the language of the state penetrates into the inmost recesses of communities which, in earlier centuries, preserved intact every aspect of local life, including their speech: it becomes the sole bearer of knowledge and a chief source of entertainment. Thus the prestige of the official tongue is vastly increased, and the advantages of being proficient in it become more obvious and more tempting. The chances then of extending dialect literacy beyond the intellectual class (already hindered by lack of a "standard" orthography recognized as the norm[4]) grow less and less. Just when the metamorphosis from

---

4. On the importance of a koiné see p. 60.

dialect to language seems about to be achieved, it is
threatened with the reverse process of relapse from
dialect to _patois_. What happens is that the dialect loses
or fails to acquire snob-value.

   The process can be seen at work in Ireland, whose
language not only has a literature twice as old as
Friuli's, but is also one of the official languages of
the Irish Republic. A writer in <u>An t-Ultach</u> (The
Ulsterman) of June 1951 explains why Irish in County
Tyrone is losing ground: "Irish is synonymous with
poverty and social inferiority... Young people think it
is a sign of social inferiority if their parents speak
Irish, especially in the presence of a stranger[5]...
People think that to give up using Irish is equivalent
to turning their backs on the visible and audible signs
of poverty and backwardness." And thirteen years later
in the same magazine we read that people in the Gael-
tacht (Irish-speaking areas) "think they have risen in
your esteem when they speak English." The pathos and
horror of it! No wonder a Friulan writer, faced with the

---

5. I have myself heard and seen a Romagnol girl with
   tear-stained face upbraiding her father for speaking
   in dialect before the friends whom she had brought
   to the house.

same situation, has written:

> Certainly ignorance of or unwillingness to
> speak Friulan is not ethically a sin; but it
> is the unambiguous symptom of a whole com-
> plex of pitiable qualities: lack of principle,
> spiritual weakness, servility, mental incon-
> sistency, etc. It is the certain index of that
> widespread evil which makes men ashamed
> to be what they are and anxious to hide them-
> selves in a dress different from their own.
> It is the index of our gradual bastardization,
> of our moral decadence, of our perversity as
> a people ethnically distinct and autonomous.
> If we fail to apply a brake to this subtle form
> of cowardice we may as well give up any hope
> of a Friulan renaissance. [6]

Of course, Friulans conscious of their ethnic indi-

viduality and justifiably proud of the language enshrining

it are not going to let it slip from them without a strug-

gle. They see their sister-languages of the Grisons and

the Dolomites both enjoying a measure of official recog-

nition, the first indeed being Switzerland's fourth official

language, [7] and the second being protected by the Statute

of the Trentino-Alto Adige Region, receiving both

---

6. _Patrie dal Friûl_, July-Aug. 1950. D'Aronco (Il
   Tesaur, 1953, p. 14) points out the significant fact
   that Friulan is considered a language by the humble
   and a dialect by the better educated (except the
   experts, who know it is a language; cf. Contini
   quoted in note 2).

7. It can be heard broadcast in the 31, 48, and 75
   metre band on Saturdays and Sundays from 12.20
   to 12.30 GMT.

cantonal and governmental subsidies, and enjoying some

use in schools;[8] and they naturally wonder why Friulan,

whose greater homogeneity and considerable literature

entitle her to at least equal treatment, has to rely for

survival on the work of private Societies such as the

Società Filologica Friulana[9] or on the enthusiasm of

young writers such as founded the movement called La

Cortesele ("The little court") di Furlan and since 1948

have been publishing their work in a literary paper,

---

8. D'Aronco, I ladini si dànno la mano, in Il Friuli,
   30 luglio 1955. According to Patrie dal Friûl, lui-
   avost 1950, in the first year all explanations in Italian and German lessons are given in Ladin. From
   the 4th year there is one hour a week of Ladin (reading, writing, and history). The weekly $\frac{1}{4}$ hour
   broadcast is often prepared by the children. Only
   Ladin-speakers can be appointed to teaching-posts
   in the area. Adults are less fortunate: a Ladino can
   be President or Vice-President of the provincial
   Council only by claiming to belong to the Italian or
   German community (PdF, 16-31 zenar, 1953). Cf.
   Friuli, where Friulan-speakers could not register
   themselves as such in the census of 1971 (though
   they can do so in Switzerland, and 400 of them turned
   up in the Grisons in 1970) (Int furlane, jugn 1972).

9. Henceforth referred to as S.F.F. Its journal
   Ce fas-tu? (cf. Dante, de vulg. eloq. 1, xi),
   now annual, is the voice of Friulan scholarship.

Risultive (Source).[10]

There is no Society for the Prevention of Cruelty to Languages; but the extinction of a human tongue is no less a tragedy than that of an animal. We mourn the dodo and rally to the whale: is it nothing that Etruscan has vanished and Welsh is threatened? Let us look at Friulan and see how much richer the world is for its existence.

Northampton,   D.B.G.
England

---

10. See p. 50. Their reunions, called "sagrute", remind one of Romagnol trebbi.
    An encouraging sign of official support has been the recent introduction of Friulan culture and language into the Theological Seminary of Udine as a subject for study on the conclusion of the course (Int furlc‾‾, avril 1973).

ACKNOWLEDGEMENTS

The earliest stratum of this work owes much to the help
and encouragement of the late Dott. G.B. Corgnali, doyen
of Friulan scholarship and Director of the Biblioteca
Comunale of Udine from 1922-1954. Alas, that I cannot
thank him again for that and for the gift of an Estratto.
Alas too, that Sig. Arturo Feruglio cannot see the amp-
lified reprint of the extracts for which he waived copyright in 1965. At every stage of my studies I have
enjoyed the services of the Biblioteca Comunale of
Udine, as rich in Friulan treasures as enviable in the
splendid Palazzo Bartolini which houses them. To its
Librarian, Dott. Giovanni del Basso, and to his staff,
who found me many a dusty tome, I am very grateful.
To Dott. del Basso I am no less indebted for tape-
recordings, as I am also to Signorina Cornelia Foote
and Signor Giuseppe Micoli of San Daniele, and to Sig.
Mario Venturi of Artegna. I have been fortunate also
in the friendship of the Signorine Luisa and Lorenzina
Deganutti of Udine, who were always ready to find a book
for me or to supply information. The later stages of the
work benefited considerably from information gathered
for me by Dott. Giorgio Faggin, from discussion with
Avv. Nico Fabris, from consultation with Dott. A.
Comuzzi (all of Udine), from the mediation of Prof.
Angelo Bertolo of Portogruaro, from the publications
sent to me by the Clape Culturâl Aquilee, and from the
interest taken in it by Dott. Etelredo Pascolo, Editor
of the monthly Int furlane.

     To these, and to all those authors who have forgone
copyright, I express my best thanks.

The cover-photograph, showing the Basilica of
Aquileia, is published by kind permission of A. Cadel,
Trieste.

INTRODUCTION

1. The geographical and linguistic delimitation of Friuli

Until 1963 "Friuli", like "Romagna", was the name of an

area conterminous with neither a "Region" nor a "Prov-

ince" of Italy. On Jan. 31st of that year it became

Italy's fifth autonomous region, - a new unit covering an

area of approximately 3, 055 square miles, with a popu-

lation of about 1, 210, 000, called Friuli-Venezia Giulia,

with Triest as capital. [1] (Venezia Giulia had been the

easternmost of the three areas called Le Tre Venezie

and had consisted mostly of the territory ceded to Jugo-

slavia after the 2nd World War; but the name now

hardly covered more than the towns of Gorizia and

Triest and a few adjoining villages.) These two towns

and Udine were heads of Provinces; and to them in 1968

was added Pordenone, which, to its great indignation,

had been at first fobbed off with the status of circondario

(district). [2]

---

1. v. p. 4 n. 4.

2. A centre of light industry, "the Milan of Friuli",
Pordenone felt herself different and had already
cultivated her own private separatism - from
Friuli! (Cf. p. 14.)

The whole area lies framed within the natural boundaries of the Dolomite Alps on the west, the Carnic Alps on the north, the Julian Alps on the east, and the Adriatic on the south. In the north the boundary coincides with the national Austro-Italian frontier following the watershed of the Carnic Alps from Monte Croce eastwards to a point north of Tarvisio. Here the boundary turns south and follows the valley of the Fella to Gemona, whence it continues along the skirts of the Julian Alps to Gorizia and the mouth of the Timavo.[3] The southern boundary is formed by the coast from the Timavo westwards to the mouth of the Tagliamento (excluding Grado), follows the river inland as far as Villanova, and then continues westwards as far as Motta on the

---

3.   The mysterious underground river sung by Virgil (Aeneid iv. 7ff.). The traveller to Triest by road passes over it shortly after Monfalcone, and can see on his right Virgil's lines carved in the rock. The name occurs three times in Friuli: here; Timau in the Carnic Alps; and the Timavone near Maniago (where an altar to its deity from Republican times has been found). As all three rivers have the common feature of emerging from a rock, we are probably in the presence of an old pre-Roman and perhaps pre-Celtic (i. e. Venetan) word.

Livenza. This river as far as Sacile, and after it the

Cimiliana and the eastern watershed of the Dolomites up

to Monte Croce, form the western boundary. Anyone who

lives in this area lives in Friuli; but unfortunately he

will not everywhere hear Friulan spoken around him.

To have the linguistic frontier, we must withdraw the

boundary on the north-east to close to Gemona; on the

south-east from the Timavo to the Isonzo (thus losing

Monfalcone with its eastern Venetian); on the south (as

far as it is possible to fix it at all) we must exclude the

Venetian-speaking Portogruaro; and on the west the line

must curve in from Motta to pass between Pordenone and

Cordenons and follow the rivers Cellina and Cimiliana to

the Maniri Pass and thence reach Monte Croce. Even

then there will remain a few zones where Friulan is not

spoken: wedges of Slovene in the Julian Alps north of

Tarvisio, and islands of German in the Carnic Alps.

Linguistically, therefore, Friuli is an area of less than

3,000 sq. miles, with a population of 800,000, most of

whom speak Friulan.[4]

Between its most northerly point, m. Fleons, or its

highest point, m. Cogliano (2781 m) and its lowest and

most southerly, the beach at Lignano, Friuli includes

a considerable variety of scenery. Down from Carnia,

fed by rivers whose "canals", as the valleys are called,

furrow the mountains, comes the Tagliamento, flowing

from north to south to cut the Friulan plain in two and

"take possession of Friuli".[5] As this plain is less than

---

4. Cf. the other two Ladin areas: Grisons, 100,000,
    and Central Tyrol (Alto-Adige), 120,000, of whom
    about 40,000 and 23,000 respectively speak Ladin.
    D'Aronco estimated Friulan-speakers at 600,000
    in 1959 (Il Tesaur, 1960, p. 1). Faggin (La Panarie,
    June 1972, p. 21, note 7) thinks Marchetti's esti-
    mate of a million too high, but believes the great
    majority of Friuli-Venezia Giulia's 1,232,439
    inhabitants to be "friulanofoni". He points out that
    Friulan seems never to have been at home in Sacile
    and Monfalcone. On the other hand, according to
    the Gorizian De Gironcoli (v. p. 150), more Friulan
    is spoken in Gorizia than in Udine, because all the
    Slovenes of the area speak it, whereas few Gorizians
    speak Slovene. (Slovenes had been invited in by the
    Patriarch to repopulate the country after the Hungar-
    ian invasions of the 10th century; v. p. 12.)

5. See B. Chiurlo's poem No. 69. As Pliny's name for
    the river is Tiliaventum (Nat. Hist. 3,18,126), it
    must be only a coincidence that phonetic change has
    made the modern name describe its work of "cutting"
    Friuli in two. In fact, it is Celtic for "rapid
    devastator".

half the total area and has little or no mineral deposits,

Friuli has never been an economically well-endowed

area. The textile industry of Udine, the dockyards of

Monfalcone, and the breeding of silkworms by a special

technique have not been enough to absorb a labour-force

famous for its capacity for work.[6] The high figures for

emigration between the two wars tell their own tale.[7]

Even in 1950 its newspaper could lament its woes in an

article entitled "Furlanie, pais di miserie".[8] Such,

however, is not the impression made on the visitor,

who sees the fertility of the fields (corn and maize) and

the neatness of the villages, and who feels the mildness

of a climate which keeps the olive south of Zompitta and

Savorgnan del Torre (6 km. north of Udine), but

---

6. "Where a Friulan arrives, there the desert becomes a vineyard," said an Argentine minister to the Archbishop of Udine (Oggi, July 1963).

7. The Friulan colony of Buenos Aires alone numbered 100, 000 in 1928; and most of Brooklyn's masons in 1963 were reputed to be Friulans.

8. Patrie dal Friûl, July-August 1950.

encourages the production of several excellent wines.[9]

The smiling expanse of verdure is no more proof of

economic well-being in Friuli than it is in Ireland.[10]

Another thing the traveller will notice is the large

number of towns which seem to have grown up around

a castle. The most conspicuous feature of the Friulan

landscape is, in fact, the castle standing on its hill in

the middle of a cluster of houses, as at Gemona, Ar-

tegna, Tarcento on the roads leading south; and its

castle is the most conspicuous feature of Udine itself.

It will then perhaps also strike him that many other

towns are situated at the head of valleys. The

---

9.   e.g. "Verduzio" at Ramandolo (near Tarcento),
"Tocaj", "Picolit" (drunk with Cividale's special-
ity, the gubana, a puffed pastry stuffed with rais-
ins, nuts, and spices), and (reminiscent of
Romagna's "San Giovese") "Cabernet". Pucinum
(modern Duino) was famous for its wine in Pliny's
day (loc. cit. 127); in fact, the Empress Augusta
attributed her longevity to it (ib. 14, 6, 60). An
early name for Udine's central piazza was Piazza
del Vino. (See Introd. §4, p. 53 n. 43.)

10.   On Friuli's greenness see below, p. 53. Not for
nothing has Friuli the highest rainfall in Italy (cf.
N. Gladden, Across the Piave pp. 66-8, 90-1,
116), - another similarity to the "emerald Isle"
(cf. the quotation from Carducci on the title-
page). Cf. Poems Nos. 35, 39, 48.

explanation is the same for both phenomena: Friuli's

development was conditioned by its being in a highly

strategic position, and it was military necessity that

dictated where towns should arise. Aquileia at the

junction of the Via Postumia with roads from Illyricum,

Pannonia, and Noricum; Forum Iulii (Cividale) where

the Natisone emerges into the plain; Forum Iulium

Carnicum (Zuglio) on the Via Iulia Augusta in the valley

of the But - these were founded for the specific purpose

of guarding the approaches to Italy. Such military con-

siderations have been valid down to modern times:

Gradisca was founded in the last quarter of the 15th

century against the Turks; Palma a century later

against the troops of the Empire. Similarly the castles

represent advanced fortified positions close to road-

and river-crossings; and the road-system itself is

largely based on strategic needs. In this way Friuli

through the centuries has tried to fulfil its historic

function of covering the only approach to the peninsula

from the north-east. [11]

---

11. Cf. Patrie dal Friûl, 16-31 Jan., 1953: "In what
    condition would Friuli find herself? The one she
    always has done! The invaders...would pass straight
    through Friuli dealing out blows right and left upon
    the poor sentry who has always had to watch so many
    people of every sort pass through".

2. The history of Friuli

The history of Friuli shows us how the most diverse elements, split by alien encroachments and subjected to a succession of different masters, can, if geo-political conditions are favourable, develop a sense of unity and become a single homogeneous entity.

A degree of homogeneity is indicated for early times by the occurrence of names such as Carnia, Carinthia, Carniola (on the Upper Save), and Carnuntum (on the Danube east of Vienna), not to mention Caesar's Carnutes; and though the modern Carni are the Friulans of the Alps, both Pliny and Strabo state that the area inhabited by Carni extended to the coast and included Triest.[1] That these Carni

were Celts seems indisputable: an inscription records

the triumph of M. Aemilius Scaurus in 115 B. C. de

Galleis Karneis,[2] and many place-names contain

Celtic roots.[3] There may have been an infusion of

---

1. Pliny, Nat. Hist. 3, 18, 126 decima regio Italiae Had-
    riatico mari adposita...Carnorum haec regio. Stra-
    bo, Geog. iv. 206, 9 and vi. 292, places them in the
    area of Aquileia ($2\frac{1}{2}$ miles from the sea) and (vi. 314)
    calls Triest "a Carnic village". Their eastern
    neighbours, the Iapydes, also presumably reached
    the sea, because Virgil (Georg. 3, 475) calls the Riv-
    er Timavus, which flows underground till near the
    coast (see p. 2, n. 3), "Iapydian", and Pliny (loc.
    cit. 127) seems to make it run through or border
    Iapydian territory; and if Strabo (vi. 314) says that
    "Italy and the Carni are contiguous with Istria", that
    may be because the Iapydes, whom he has just called
    "a Celtic-Illyrian tribe" (313) can be loosely identi-
    fied with the Celtic Carni in contradistinction to the
    Illyrian Istri. Certainly these three peoples are reg-
    ularly named together, even if not in the same order
    (cf. Pliny 3, 5, 38 with Livy 43, 5, 3). In any case, the
    boundary between Italy and Istria was, until Augustus
    annexed Istria, the River Risano (Pliny's Formio),
    6 Roman miles east of Triest; and a Friulan dialect
    was once spoken in Triest (note 15 on p. 17). When
    Zaneto writes "tant in Cjargne che in Friûl" (Par
    prime Messe), it may be taken as poetic licence; but
    even Corgnali writes "né di Friûl né di Ciargne".

2. Unfortunately, there may be ellipse of et, in which
    case it would prove the opposite, or at least that
    contemporary Romans thought the Carni were not
    Gauls.

3. See p. 24, n. 3.

Etruscan blood, because Pliny (3, 20, 133) quotes a pecul-

iar theory that the northern neighbours of the Carni, the

Raeti, were descendants of Etruscans driven out by the

Gauls; and Etruscan artefacts have been found in the

Carnic Alps. It was against these Carni that the Veneti

appealed to Rome for help, and received it in the form

of a colony planted at Aquileia in 181 B. C. The site was

well chosen; for the name of Aquileia was destined to

dominate Friulan history for close on 2000 years. The

Carni are not mentioned among the 44 Alpine tribes

listed on the Tropaeum Alpium[4] as having been subdued

by Augustus or his generals in the years preceding 7

B. C. Probably they had been well-behaved since the

earlier foundation, perhaps by Julius Caesar (v. p. 25),

of two fortified towns: Iulium Carnicum in the valley of

the But (N. of Tolmezzo);[5] and Forum Iulii (whence the

---

4. Still partly standing near the town of La Turbie.
    Pliny fortunately quotes the inscription (3, 34, 20).

5. Among Roman remains found there are a fine statue-
    head and an inscription from the temple of the Celtic
    deity, Belenus, who was equated with Apollo (P. M.
    Moro, Romanità in Carnia: Zuglio). After Augustus
    raised it to the rank of municipium, one of its mag-
    istrates became procurator of Noricum (Rushforth,
    Latin Inscr. No. 90). See also the article of
    P. Sticotti, "Giulio Carnico", in Boll. della S. F. F.,
    1936.

name Friuli)[6] in the valley of the Natisone; or perhaps

they had been suitably impressed by Octavian's cam-

paign against the Iapydes in 35 B.C. and by that of his

stepsons against their northern neighbours, the Raeti

and Vindelici, in 15 B.C. Romanization proceeded nor-

mally, and under the Emperor Antoninus Pius (A.D.

138-161) the Carni received Latin rights. [7]

In the next reign (ca. 167) an invasion of the Marco-

manni was a foretaste of what was to come when Roman

defences crumbled. In 452 Aquileia was sacked by Attila

the Hun, and pre-eminence passed to Forum Iulii. The

Byzantine Narses had hardly had time (555) to recover

the area from the Goths, [8] when the Longobards arrived

from the north (568) and established a Duchy which lasted

for 200 years. Perhaps the most important result of

their rule was that they kept out the Slavs. In 776 the

Longobards made way for the Franks, when Friuli

became one of Charlemagne's vassal-kingdoms under

---

6. Whereas from the Forum Iulii of S. France came the
   name of the town Fréjus.

7. Dessau, Inscr. Lat. Sel. 6680.

8. Cf. the place-name Godia (and Godi in Romagna).

his son Pepino. [9] Eastern invaders were still kept out;

in fact Friuli became the centre of a vast area extending

eastwards to the Drave, with Cividale as its centre of

learning.   This brilliant epoch was terminated by the

Hungarian invasions of the 10th century.

Friuli next became a county in the March of Verona,

which was dependent on the Duke of Carinthia.   A seri-

ous result of this was the loss of unity through the intro-

duction into Friuli of what were really appendages of a

German kingdom.   Fortunately, at the same time the

Patriarch of Aquileia (then mostly resident at Cividale),[10]

thanks to his resistance to the Hungarians and the feudal

lords, established the temporal power of the Patriarch-

ate and thereby became the acknowledged champion of

Friulan independence.   In its "Ghibelline" period (1077-

1245), when the patriarchs belonged to families linked

to the Emperor, the Patriarchate was one of the largest

---

9.   Forum Iulii then changed its name to Civitas
      Austriae, whence its modern name Cividale
      (Friulan, Cividât).

10.   The title of Patriarch had been adopted by Mace-
      donius, Bishop of Aquileia, in 553, when he seceded
      from Rome, and it was retained after the end of the
      schism in 687.   Malaria had made Aquileia an
      unhealthy place of residence.

states in N. Italy.[11] A grave mistake was made, how-

ever, when in the eleventh century the Patriarch estab-

lished what was to be his legal representative in an

autonomous territory at Gorizia. He chose his relative

the Duke of Carinthia, with the result that the area of

Gorizia from then till 1916 remained a German enclave

inimical to Friulan unity.

In 1245 the invasion of Ezzelino, lord of Lombardy,

forced the Patriarch Pertoldo to seek the help of the

Guelph states; and in 1250 the Patriarchate passed from

German into Italian hands. In the 14th century Udine

rose to importance, and with her the family of the

Savorgnan, champions of the new commercial bour-

geoisie. A Parliament came into being and by 1400

was regularly meeting at Udine.[12]

The Patriarchs, first friends and then enemies of

---

11. About the year 1200 the German poet Walter von der
Vogelweide is at the Court of the Patriarch Vol-
chero. The name of the region, Patrie dal Friûl,
dates from this period.

12. The earliest document relating to Castrum Utini
is of A.D. 983, but the discovery of four graves
during excavation for air-raid shelters in 1944
shows that the hill on which Udine's Castle stands
(a kind of "Palatine") was inhabited much earlier
(Ce fas-tu?, Dec. 1944, pp. 237-240).

the Counts of Gorizia, repeated the process with the

Savorgnan; and taught perhaps by the murder of his

predecessor at the hands of the Count's party in 1350,

the patriarch Giovanni di Moravia in 1388 had his enemy

Federico Savorgnan assassinated, only himself to suc-

cumb six years later to the dagger of Federico's brother

Tristan. This feud was partly due to the fact that the

Savorgnan, doubtless in part for commercial reasons,

were drawing ever closer to Venice, mistress of Triest,

as was demonstrated in 1384, when Federico with his

descendants was admitted into the Venetian aristocracy.

In 1420 the inevitable occurred: western Friuli became

part of Venice.

The struggle was now between Venice and Austria,

master of eastern Friuli (Gorizia) and Pordenone. In

1511, owing to the treachery of Antonio Savorgnan,

Austria occupied the whole territory; but three years

later another Savorgnan, Girolamo, redeemed his fam-

ily's honour by an heroic resistance at Osoppo, [13] which

---

13. See note on Poem 11, and for an account of the
     fortress at the time Ce fas-tu?, 1944, pp.
     286-288. A later generation emulated this hero-
     ism during the Risorgimento (v. p. 48n and
     Int furlane, March 1974, p. 3).

gave the Venetians time to arrive, defeat the Austrians

at Pordenone, and recover Friuli. Later attempts to

seize the remaining Austrian possessions failed; but the

acquisition of Pordenone and Monfalcone, and the con-

struction of the fortress-town of Palma meant that Friuli

was in effect more united than it had been under the Pat-

riarchs. This was just as well; for on 6 July 1751 the

question whether Friuli was to be Venetian or Austrian

was finally settled by the suppression of the Patriarch-

ate, chief architect and bulwark of Friulan individuality.

In its place the Pope established two Archbishoprics:

Udine for Venice, and Gorizia for Austria.[14] The last

Patriarch died of a broken heart in 1762; and only its

splendid Basilica remains to remind us of the past glor-

ies of Aquileia (Poem 47).

Friuli now became a pawn in a larger game. In

1797 Napoleon put an end to the Venetian Republic and

defeated the Austrians on the Tagliamento; but he out-

raged Italian sentiment by ceding most of Venetian

---

14. It is significant that of the 15 Archbishops of Udine
     since then only one has been a Friulan. The title,
     "Patriarch of Aquileia", lives on as one of those
     borne by the Patriarch of Constantinople.

territory, including western Friuli, to Austria (Treaty of
Campofòrmido). The Friulan Parliament met for the
last time in 1805, shortly before Napoleon drove out the
Austrians and forced them to cede all Friuli to the
Regno d'Italia (Treaties of Pressburg and Vienna,
1808-9). With the fall of Napoleon in 1814 Lombardy
and the former Venetian provinces reverted to Austria,
under whom they remained till 1866. In that year
Friuli voted for union with the newly proclaimed
Kingdom of Italy.

The eastern frontier of Italy was now on the Judri,
not far enough east for Italian sentiment; and it was
only after Friuli had again seen Austria its master, for
one grim year (Oct. 1917 to Oct. 1918), that the frontier was pushed far back beyond the Julian Alps. In the
2nd World War Friulan partisans under a Savorgnan
made glorious again the name of Osoppo. But a price
had to be paid: part of the territory east of the Isonzo
had to be ceded to the Slavs, irredentist themselves
since 1919, and even Triest was nearly lost. Friuli,
however, was now a unified area of Italy; so much so
that its ancient spirit of independence stirred again and
brought forth a desire for regional autonomy. This

desire was finally satisfied on Jan. 31st 1963, when

Friuli-Venezia Giulia was established as the fourth

Italian "Region", though the joy of the separatists was

marred by the choice of non-Friulan Triest as regional

capital instead of Friuli's first city, Udine.[15]

---

15. The creation of the new Region was the work of a
centre-left Government (Friuli is predominantly
christian-democrat). The joy of the Triestines was
also marred, because they were in a minority on the
regional Council (24% of seats against Udine's 65%);
in fact, the mayor of Triest in 1963 was a Friulan
from Udine. Irritated by Triest's support of
Pordenone (see n. 2, p. 1), Friulans dreamed of
"friulanizing" Triest. Two thousand years earlier
the Carni had been "attributed" by Augustus to
Triest, and later admitted by Antoninus Pius to the
Triestine Senate and so to Roman citizenship
(Dessau 6680; cf. n. 7 above). But the Triestines
were themselves Carni then, whereas their descendants allowed their Friulan dialect to become
extinct in 1828. For socialist Triest, Friuli is a
reactionary priest-ridden area, which may not
have its own University (Int furlane, jugn 1972).

3. The language of Friuli

Friulan is in the paradoxical position of being a dialect of

Italy without being an Italian dialect. This, however, is

only another way of saying that, though spoken on Italian

soil, it does not belong to any of the main groups of

Italian dialects. Thus, being in the north, it might be

expected to belong to the Gallo-Italic group; but we find

at once that instead of the typically Gallo-Italic word for

"today", incú, it has uè; and the use of fradi for "bro-

ther" cuts it off not only from Gallo-Italic but from the

whole northern group of dialects, which are distinguished

from those of the south by their use of the diminutive

form in -ellu instead of the classical frater; so that in

this one archaism Friulan agrees with the otherwise

totally dissimilar southern dialects. The explanation can

only be that Friulan belongs to some other group of

Romance languages.

In 1790 the Slav J.R. Karli published his Delle

antichità italiche comparing Friulan with French and

discovering greater resemblances between them than

between Friulan and Italian. Such are the retention of

l in a final syllable (orele/oreille; voli/oeil; vieli/

vieil), plurals in -s, feminines in -e, the conjugation

of V̂ê (avoir) and L̂â (aller), the palatalization of c before

a (ciaf/chef), and such coincidences as soreli/soleil,

sur/soeur, nojàr/noyer (walnut-tree).[1] He then went on

to compare Friulan with the language of the Canton

Grisons in S. E. Switzerland, known since 1845 as

Romantsch. He translated the first verse of Genesis and

set it beside the same from the Romantsch Bible in the

version of Ingidiana Bassa:

Romantsch	Friulan
In il principi creer Deis il tichel e la terra; mo la terra era una chiaussa zainza fuorme e voede, e stürezar sur la fatscha del abiss; et il spiert de Deis s'muveiva sur la fatscha de las aguas.	In tal principij Gjo al crea il cjel e la tjare; ma la tjare e jere vuajde e cence fuarme, e pardut lis tenebris e jer in su la face de l'abis, e il spirt de Gjo al leve su lis aghis.

Eighty years were to elapse before scientific proof

of this intuition was given. Then in 1870, Ch. Schneller

studying the language of the S. Tyrol (the Alto Adige, the

Dolomites) and F. Rausch studying that of the Canton

Grisons (Grigioni, the Engadine) independently came to

---

1. G. G. Liruti (1689-1780), in his De lingua Foroiulianorum dissertatio (reprinted in Il Tesaur from
   1954 to 1956), actually derives Friulan from French
   on the ground of their invasions as Franks; and,
   like Karli, he compares it with the French version
   of the Strassburg Oath, of which a Friulan translation, probably his own, exists (D'Aronco, Ant.,
   p. 204).

one and the same conclusion: they and Friulan consti-

tuted a single linguistic family.[2] Three years later G. I.

Ascoli of Gorizia confirmed this conclusion and chris-

tened the family "Ladin", a term first appearing in 1560

in the Engadine to describe the language of their transla-

tion of the New Testament, and used there ever since.

(In Friuli itself it was only an adjective meaning

"fluent").

The chief characteristics of the group are: (1) pala-

talization of ca and ga; (2) conservation of l after occlu-

sives and spirants; (3) conservation of final s; (4) ie out

of stressed e, ue out of stressed o and o before two con-

sonants, ej out of stressed e and i.

Within this group, however, Friulan is distinguished

by several features not shared with the others. (1) Pho-

netically, it conserves l before consonants (cialde), d

between vowels (viodi), and qu both initially and after a

consonant (quarante, cinquante); diphthongizes stressed

---

2. Schneller calls the Romantsch branch "Churwälsch",
    Coira (Chur) being the capital of the area and wälsch,
    after the Romans supplanted the Celts, having shifted
    its Germanic meaning from "Celts" (from Caesar's
    Volcae) to "Roman" (La Panarie 16 June 1972, pp.
    7-20). The term "Raeto-romantsch" properly be-
    longs only to the western and central zones, Friuli
    not having been inhabited by Raeti.

e̲ (tiera); does not syncopate proparoxyton words (sdruc-

cioli) such as femine; has no sound u̲; and does not

change stressed a̲ to e̲. (2) Morphologically, it has dif-

ferent endings for the first and third persons plural, and

conjugates differently some irregular verbs (jessì, dâ).

(3) Lexically, it has many words peculiar to itself. It

can therefore be seen that Ascoli was right when he

wrote that "Friulan will have in the Ladin system an

independence hardly different from that of Catalan in

Provençal."

Its position may be represented schematically as

follows:

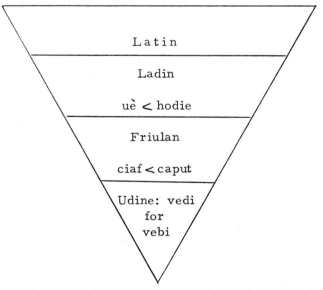

Friulan therefore poses a problem: how can it be

at once so similar to and so dissimilar from the other

members of the Ladin family, and how combine in such
measure Gallic and non-Gallic elements? To this "Ladin
question" various answers have been given.

Ascoli posited the splitting up of an originally single
area through the descent of Germans between the Grisons
and Raetia and the ascent of Venetians between Raetia
and Friuli. Carlo Battisti, for whom Ladinity was a
mere abstraction, considered each component an archaic form of the language of the neighbouring plain, so
that Romantsch represents archaic Lombardian, Tyrol-
ian Ladin and Friulan archaic Venetian. Most recently
Marchetti has suggested that Friulan evolved from the
rustic Latin of Aquileia untouched by the dialects of
central Italy, and spreading through the Alps. Each of
these theories contains an element of the truth.

Two questions are involved: (a) How can one family
be spread over three discontinuous zones? and (b) how
did Friulan originate within that family?

Firstly, research has shown that the germanized
zone north and south of the watershed of the Central
Alps covers an old Romance area linking the Swiss
Ladini with those of the Dolomites, and where Romance
is known to have been spoken down to the close of the

seventeenth century. Secondly, one feature common to

the whole area is mountain, and mountain-peoples often

develop a phonetic system of their own. Thirdly, French

evolved among Gauls; the Latin of Raetia was carried

there by Romanized Celts from the Po valley; and the

Carni who occupied the mountains around the Friulan

plain at the time of the Roman conquest were, as we

have seen (p. 9), probably Galli. Thus a second com-

mon element is present - a Gallic substratum.[2a] Fourth-

ly, never having been welded into a political unity and

lacking a literary language that could give one patois

preeminence over the others, the area was exposed to

infiltration both from the south and from the north.

Under such circumstances disintegration was only to be

expected.

As for the second question, several causes contrib-

uted to the formation of a special kind of Ladin in Friuli.

In the first place, the Raeti did not extend so far east

2a. G. Devoto (I dialetti delle regioni d'Italia, p. 49)
    prefers to speak of a Gallic "superstrato", supposing
    the "irradiation" of refined, gallicized Latin through
    the Swiss valleys in the last centuries of the Roman
    Empire. The one stratum does not exclude the other.

as to be in contact with the (Gallic) Carni.[3] Secondly,

Romanization was effected at different times and in dif-

ferent ways in the three zones. Whereas the Alpine reg-

ions and Raetia were not conquered till 14 B.C., when

they received their Latin from the legionaries of the Po

valley, Romanization in Friuli began early with the foun-

dation at Aquileia in 181 B.C. of a colony of discharged

soldiers to bar the path of invasion to the Celts and Illyr-

ians who lived beyond the friendly Veneti. Thirdly,

Friuli itself continued to receive infusions of Latin at

different times from different parts of Italy. The veter-

ans of Aquileia probably came from Samnium. The next

settlement seems to have been the winter-quarters of

three of Caesar's legions in the year 59 not far from

Aquileia at the town now known as Cividale (pp. 10 and

12); these men probably came from Cisalpine Gaul, the

main source of recruits after the Social War of 91-89.

---

3. See §2, pp. 8-9, note 2. Gallic are (i) place-names
    in -acco, e.g. Avosacco (Avesiacum) and -ago, e.g.
    Martignacco (Matriniacum); (ii) Isonzo (from Aeson-
    tius, containing the name of a Gallic divinity,
    Aesus); (iii) Monte Kern, reappearing in the Cornish
    for Cornwall, Kernwy; (iv) Cadore (from Cadubrium,
    i.e. Catubrig, "Battle Mountain"; cf. Welsh cad "bat-
    tle" and Gallic suffix -briga, e.g. Admagetobriga;
    (v) Tagliamento (see §1, note 5); and words like bar
    (clod), broili (orchard), and grave (gravel).

It may be supposed that when Octavian established a

Forum (market-town) here around 40 B. C. (calling it

Forum Iulii in honour of Julius Caesar), some of these

soldiers were among the new settlers. Another settle-

ment of Caesar's was a castellum on the road from

Aquileia where it enters the Carnic Alps. This too was

raised by Octavian to the status of a Forum and linked

with the memory of Caesar by the name Forum Iulium

Carnicum, which it still bears as Zuglio (p. 10). The

original settlers had probably been recruited in Latium.

At the same time other veterans were settled by Octav-

ian in a colony named after the pious hope of many

Roman Emperors, Concordia (south of Portogruaro);

and these were joined later by veterans of Antony.

The resultant amalgam, worked on by Carnic speech

and insulated from the rest of Italy by the extension of

the Veneti, was already in A. D. 350 so different from

official Latin that Bishop Fortunatianus of Aquileia then

thought it necessary to write in it a commentary on the

Gospels. Subsequent events preserved the seclusion of

the vernacular: the creation first of a Longobard Duchy

and then of a Patriarchate (p. 12) made it the language of

a distinct political entity; and while intermarriage with

the Veneti was modifying it in its own way, the inviola-

bility of the mountains of Carnia allowed the survival of

a more archaic form of the language.

Thus by the tenth century there had evolved in

"Friuli" a unique form of Romance, owed to a unique

set of circumstances. There was obviously never a

single, homogeneous Ladin language. If Friulan is akin

to Raeto-Romantsch dialects, it is because, like them,

it was spoken by once Latin-speaking Celtic mountain-

dwellers; if it is independent of them, it is because its

parents were earlier forms of Latin. [4]

The plain of Friuli, lying athwart the invasion-

routes, was not well situated for the preservation of

linguistic autonomy. It is remarkable that the absorp-

tion of Germanic and Slav words is not greater. Gothic, [5]

---

4. Similarly the Latin of Roman Spain is shown by
   inscriptions to be distinctive in its archaisms, pronunciation, and vocabulary. Characteristic of Friulan is the number of rustic words different from
   Italian: ciarpint (axle) from carpentum; glerie
   (gravel) from glaream; spadule (shoulder) from
   spatulum; taviele (cultivated land; v. p. 54) from
   tabellam; vuardi (barley) from hordeum; vat (ford)
   from vadum.

5. globa glove (forked branch); rukka rocje (distaff).

Longobard,[6] Frankish,[7] and Old High[8] and modern German have contributed to Friulan vocabulary hardly as
much as to Italian. Of Slav (Slovene) roots little more
than 100 can be surely identified. Modern conditions are
much more favourable to the infiltration of Italian; and
already some authentic Friulan words are threatened by
Italian synonyms.[9] The arch-enemy, however, is Venetian. That much of modern Venetia was once Ladin is
indicated by the use of the termination -s in the interrogative form of the Venetian 2nd person singular.
Grado on the coast was not long ago lost to Venetian,
and we have seen what happened to old Triestine

---

6. blajo bleon (sheet); braida braide (farm; v. p. 54);
   flap flap (flaccid); baizzjan paisse (ambush).

7. wachta uaite (guard); werra uere (war).

8. brute brut (daughter-in-law).

9. e.g. viarte or jessude (spring) by primevere, siarade or sorunviâr (autumn) by autun, scuedarin (tax-
   collector) by esator, vosâ or sberghelâ (to shout) by
   cridâ, fuars or vadi (perhaps) by forsi, impensâsi or
   visâsi (to remember) by ricuardâsi.

(p. 9 n. 1 and p. 17 n. 15).[10] It is to Venetian rather than to Italian that snobbery goes, "an outrage to good sense and beauty", as patriotic Friulans call it, knowing how different the Friulan character is from the Venetian, and how each is reflected in its language.

What sort of language is it then, this eighth Romance tongue?[11] Friulans are serious and reflective by temperament, and their language is therefore slow and measured. Perhaps this is what de Musset meant when he wrote[12] of the Friulan lover's "patois mélancholique". But Dante wrote[13] of the Friulans that they "orribiliter accentuando eructant" the words "Ce fas-tu?" (Che fai?);

---

10. See Ce fas-tu?, Dec. 1944, pp. 226-232. The dialect, called Targestine, to distinguish it from modern Triestine, has left one literary work: the Dialoghi piacevoli of G. Mainati (La Panarie, 16 June 1972, p. 12).

11. Counting Provençal and Catalan as the sixth and seventh.

12. Confession d'un enfant du siècle, 1, x.

13. De vulgari eloquentia, 1, xi.

and even the Friulan poet Bindo Chiurlo describes it as

"orrida di consonanti e di durezze foniche". The simil-

arity of this description to that made of Romagnol is

remarkable. It is true that both dialects multiply

pronominal subjects, are often monosyllabic, and have

other features reflecting a forthright, energetic soul;

but of aphaeresis and syncope, the two most character-

istic marks of Romagnol, the first has been much less at

work in Friulan;[14] and it is precisely the lack of synco-

pation in sdruccioli like femine that distinguishes Friu-

lan from the rest of the Ladin family. What further con-

tributes to give Friulan its highly individual physiognomy

is its predilection for certain prefixes (in-, dis-,

---

14. e. g. rivâ (to arrive), sassins (assassins), sut
(asciutto, dry), talian (Italian), Vanzeli (Gospel),
nemal (animal), strolic (astrologer), ligrie
(allegria, gaiety), vanzums (avanzi, remains).
Romagnol's characteristic ellipse of protonic vowels and their compensation by initial a is completely
lacking, unless the place-name Artegna (from
Retenia) is an example of it. There is, however, a
tendency in both to prefix a to some words and to
oscillate between a and o in pretonic position (especially before r); e. g. Altravis or Oltravis. Cf.
Phonology, 9.

mal-)[15] and suffixes (-ut, -at).[16] The reviewer of

Chiurlo's Versi friulani was right to find in these poems

proof that Friulan's "gentilezza di suono" enables it "to

express the most delicate gradations of feeling".

---

15. e. g. IN-: indurmidîsi (to fall asleep), inviâsi (to
     set off), inmalâsi (to fall ill), inacuàrzisi (to per-
     ceive), inneâsi (to drown). (In all these Italian
     begins with a prefix derived from ad). It is at-
     tached even to verbs already having a prefix:
     imprometi (to promise), improibit (prohibited).

   DIS-: disdurmidí (to wake up), disjerbâ (to
   weed), dispatussâ (to emerge from childhood)
   (patus being a twig or piece of straw), disverdî
   (to grow yellow), disutil (useless).

   MAL-: malpazient (impatient), malmadur (un-
   ripe), malegraziôs (rude). (Cf. French malheur-
   eux etc., and Esperanto prefixed mal-).

16. -UT is the regular diminutive (e. g. ciasut casina
     cottage) and may, like Italian -in- be used with
     adverbs: pulidut ("quite well").

   -AT, attached to nouns, corresponds to the
   Italian pejorative -accio, but it is seen more
   frequently because it may be added to adjectives
   just to emphasize a quality, and is also used to
   distinguish the male of the species (razzat
   "drake") or a person's local origin (Bujat
   "native of Buja").

4. The literature of Friuli

The first stirrings of Friulan within the chrysalis of

Latin become visible in a document of the mid-12th

century, the rotolo censuale (income-return) of the

Chapter of Aquileia, first published only in 1956;[1] but

they had been audible for many centuries. Why else

should Bishop Fortunatianus of Aquileia in A. D. 350

think it necessary to write a commentary on the gospels

in Friulan? The next extant document, of 1284, is also

concerned with the income of a religious body, this time

the monastery of Santa Maria in Cividale.[2] Later 14th-

century documents, still financial, deal with the expen-

diture of various communities, but now include secular

administration in Udine, Cividale, and Gemona. In the

earliest documents the Friulan element hardly consists

of more than a few words, especially proper names,

scattered about the Latin; but the later legal documents

---

1. G. Biasutti, Il più antico rotolo censuale del Capitolo
    di Aquileia (Udine, 1956); D'Aronco, Nuova Antologia
    della literatura friulana (henceforward "Ant. "),
    pp. 6-8.

2. G. B. Corgnali, Un documento friulano del 1284 (Ce
    fas-tu?, 1953, pp. 56-61); D'Aronco, Ant., pp. 9-
    12. It contains the word no, apparently from Latin
    annona (corn) but identified by Corgnali with avena
    (oats).

are entirely in Friulan (Prose-Extracts Nos. 1, 3, 4, 6,

9, 10) and when the School of Notaries in Cividale needed

to publish a Latin Grammar for Friulans some time

before 1400 (Prose-Extract No. 2a), we can say that

Latin was then officially recognized as a dead language

and that Friulan thereby received its birth-certificate.

It was indeed high time; for already there were in

existence two compositions which show Friulan as the

language of a literature. Both are ballads dating from

the first half of the fourteenth century, and one of them,

Piruç myo doç inculurit,[3] is clearly in the tradition of the

courtly lyric associated with Provençal. The other,

Biello dumlo di valor (Poem No. 1) is in the form of a

Contrasto.[4] The century ends with a sonnet, E la four

del nuestri chiamp, still considered too licentious for

---

3.   "My sweet rosy pear" (D'Aronco, Ant., p. 17).

4.   A dispute between two persons, usually a man and
     a woman. As such, they represent an intermediate
     stage between the zingaresche (sung by actor imper-
     sonating a gipsy) and drama. Cf. Poems No. 1,
     and the Contrast tra Carnevâl e Cresime (D'Aronco,
     p . 683).

publication,[5] using as it does the language of the vine-

harvest as an erotic metaphor in the manner of goliardic

songs. The following (15th) century seems to have been

a literary desert, yielding only one insignificant _frottola_

written at Cividale about 1484.[6]

It is not to be supposed, however, that the popular

muse was meanwhile silent. There must already have

been on people's lips the dance-songs and funeral

laments, the prayers (Orationes) and perhaps (for only

three are known)[7] the narrative poems which constitute

the earliest stratum of most western literatures; and it

was certainly not in Latin that babies were lulled to

sleep or children played their games (Poetry, Appendix

1, Nos. 1-6). The earliest dated documents of popular

poetry are two _Scongiuri_ (cf. App. 1, No. 4), one of

---

5. It was omitted from D'Aronco's Anthology (p. 48) by
   a last-minute expurgation; and an appendix of such
   poems promised both by him and by B. Chiurlo never
   appeared (G. Comelli in _Il Tesaur_, sett-ott. 1949,
   p. 23). The ms. is in the Museo Correr of Venice.

6. D'Aronco, _Ant._ p. 77. The _frottola_ is a kind of
   madrigal.

7. D'Aronco, _Il Tesaur_, luglio-ag. 1949, p. 14, and
   Ant. pp. 627 and 699-703.

1365, the other of 1431;[8] and many centuries were to

pass before the others were published. The same ap-

plies to the prose stories (fables and legends) which are

part of the patrimony of Europe and the East: they have

been committed to writing, with or without the deliberate

reworking of the artist,[9] only in modern times. In all

these spontaneous creations Friuli in no way differed

from the other regions of Italy; but there was to be one

form of popular art that Friulans could claim as their

own invention - the verse-form known as the villotta.

A single verse of four octosyllabic lines, with alternately

weak (usually unrhymed) and strong, rhymed endings, its

theme was always a state of mind, more often than not

melancholy. A particular source of this melancholy -

a characteristic of the Friulan soul (v. p. 28, n. 12

above) - is love; as a modern practitioner of the genre

puts it:

---

8. D'Aronco, Ant. pp. 34 and 70.

9. The first is in the Prose Section, No.
   18; the second in the Prose Appendix,
   No. 1.

La Vilota a è fate apuosta   The Villotta - Love's own metre,

  par ciantâ o vaî l'amôr!   be it song or sad refrain!

Liet a nâs cence fadia   Born the effortless repeater

da alegreze o da dolôr.[10]   of a heartfelt joy or pain.

Song it certainly was; for popular poetry being "an

indissoluble union of words and music", [11] the _villotta_

more than most was wedded to its musical accompani-

ment. According to D'Aronco, [12] this was vocal, not

instrumental: one singer (tenor or soprano) intoned the

melody, and then the others (including a bass) joined in,

singing in harmony; the mode was invariably major.

    The _villotta_, however, is not free from mystery.

The first problem is that of its origin, because it differs

in form, tone, and melody from the hendecasyllabic

strambotto which was the popular song in the rest of

Italy. [13] Someone has linked them with the melodies of

---

10. Malattia della Vallata. (_Liet_ is for _Lei_, she.)

11. D'Aronco, _Ant_. p. xii.

12. _Sull'origine della villotta friulana_, in _Atti del vii
     Congresso Nazionale delle tradizioni populari_, 4-8
     sett., 1957.

13. See below, Poetry App. 1, No. 10, note.

the Aquileian Patriarchate; another[14] has pointed out a

resemblance to the cancioncilla mozárabe of Spain;

another[15] sees the influence of Slovenia. In short, the

problem remains. Secondly, it has to be asked why

there are no examples of popular villotte before the sev-

enteenth century, whereas other lesser forms of popular

art are attested. The first known transcriptions date

from the second half of that century.[16] D'Aronco acutely

argues that conservative Carnia's abundant contribution

to the texts of villotte indicates a long tradition, and he

himself would assign the start of their "modern" form

to 1420.[17] Gaetano Perusini, who sees Friulan elements

in some Provençal poems and deduces the existence of a

Friulan literature earlier than the fourteenth century,

sees in the 13th-century Lament for the death of the

Patriarch of Aquileia, Gregorio di Montelongo, in 1269

---

14.   P. Toschi, "Rappresaglia" di studi di lett. pop.
       (Olschki, 1957), p. 205.

15.   G. Trinko, A proposito del canto popolare.

16.   B. Chiurlo, Valutazione psicologica e artistica dei
       canti popolari friulani (Rivista di sintesi letteraria
       1 (1934), pp. 322-360).

17.   See n. 12.

the same metrical schema as that of the <u>villotta</u>. [18] The

same critic suggests that the disappearance of typically

Friulan wind-instruments in the seventeenth century, by

reducing the possibility of musical accompaniment to

other songs, indirectly led to a new flourishing of the

<u>villotta</u>. [19]

What is certain is that the <u>villotta</u> first presents

itself under this name at the beginning of the nineteenth

century, in poems of Mariuzza and Zorutti. (Ermes di

Colloredo had used the same <u>quartina</u> in the seventeenth

century without naming it.) Dall'Ongaro quotes some in

<u>Nannetta</u> (1843), and a little later so does Percoto; but

the first collection was that made by M. Leicht in 1865.

Attention once directed to them, a vast store was discov-

ered. People were found in mountain-villages able to

recite 365 of them, and Achille Tellini in 1919 printed

---

18. <u>Il Tesaur</u>, sett.-ott. 1949, p. 10:
  Morz nos a tolt lo debonaire,
   lo pro patriarca Gregor,
  On avian fait lo(r) repaire
   tuit li bon aib e li mellor.
  ("Death has taken from us the good, the wise patriarch Gregorio, with whom had taken refuge all
  the good and the best qualities.")

19. See Poem 13, n. 3.

4, 491.[20]   Poets such as B. Chiurlo (Poem 34) began to
use the new-old form, and Friuli awoke to the fact that
its ethnic individuality had received the crowning attesta-
tion of a unique literary form.[21]

Meanwhile the sixteenth century had seen the literary language burst into life. Friulan then began to be,
as D'Aronco puts it, "consciously cultivated as a means
of poetic expression". The same author's apparent
self-contradiction in simultaneously praising the century's "gagliarda rusticità" and congratulating it on having emerged from the preceding "rustic circle"[22] is
doubtless a reflection of the fact that while the poet whom
he selects as the best of the century, G. B. Donato, cel-
ebrates the work and the fruits of the countryside in
"vigorous" georgics, other poets find their themes elsewhere: in personal introspection, like Biancone (Poem
2); in the eulogy of Friulan itself, like Morlupino (D'Aronco
95) or Sini (Poem 3), or in the treatment of external

---

20.   Il Tesaur de lenghe furlane, 5 fascicui in quart
      (with summaries in Esperanto).

21.   They have been likened to Heine's Lieder, but as
      the succinct crystallization of a mood they remind
      also of the Japanese hajku and tanka.

22.   Ant., p. 82.

events such as the Battle of Lepanto and the consecration

of a church by Philip II of Spain (No. 6). Similarly,

alongside an anonymous alphabetical satire on the country-

man, there are the sonnets of Strassoldo and an unknown

poet, to show that Friuli was in touch with literary currents

beyond its borders. The symbiosis becomes complete

when an anonymous sonnet of about 1571, apparently on a

rustic theme, proves to be an allegory of the Battle of

Lepanto.[23] An allegory of a different sort is an anony-

mous _frottola_ of the same year, which cloaks its erotic

theme in the guise of an invitation to a tournament, but

does it so unsuccessfully that it has to be banned from

the chaste pages of the Anthology - a fate shared by one

of a group of four contemporary _terzine amorose_.[24]

At the same time original literary prose is conspi-

cuous by its absence. What is literary is a translation

of one of Boccaccio's _novelle_ (IX.i) of about 1584;

---

23.   D'Aronco, _Ant._, p. 113. The merit of the discovery
      is Corgnali's (see his note 1 on p. 4 of his _Estratto_
      referred to below in n. 25). Students of Romagnol
      will note that one of the oxen in the poem is called
      Boo.

24.   D'Aronco, _Ant._, pp. 112 and 114.

what is original are a couple of letters (Prose Extract No.

11). Nor was the poetry all original: someone took it on

himself to test the language by producing a version of the

1st Canto of Ariosto's Orlando Furioso, and if the result

is a travestimento rather than a translation, the author

may at least be credited with a degree of originality.[25]

How far downwards literacy extended cannot be de-

termined; but an indication is given by a list of popular

proverbs from the middle of the century, and above all

by a letter written by a peasant-girl to her fiancé in

1561.[26]

The seventeenth century begins with the pleasing

spectacle of a group of young Udinesi forming a literary

coterie for the practice of Friulan poetry. Such a phe-

nomenon was nothing new in the history of poetry (wit-

ness Catullus and the neoteroi (younger poets) of Repub-

lican Rome in Cicero's day), and it was not to be the

25. Corgnali's edition was published in 1953 as an
Estratto from Ce fas-tu?, 1951-1952. On such
dialectal versions of famous poems the student
is referred to the companion-volume on Romagnol,
p. 15, n. 5.

26. D'Aronco, Ant., p. 84 and p. 88.

last in Friuli (below, p. 148). Presiding over the group
was Paolo Fistulario, to whom we owe the collection and
therefore the preservation of the work of eight of the
twelve poets (e.g. Poem No. 12).   The quality of the
poetry is high enough to justify the faith of these young
men in their native speech; but it was from outside the
group that the final patent of nobility was to come.

Ermes di Colloredo is the first great name in
Friulan literature. It is probably true to say that he
was the equal of any poet writing in Italy at the time;
and if our criterion is freedom from the vices of "secentismo" (the sentimentalism of the epigoni of Petrarch and
the artificiality of the followers of Marini), he can be
rated even higher. His verse reminds now of Horace,
now of Dafydd ap Gwilym. Diction and rhythm are perfectly fused; and the independence of his mind, as shown
in his dislike of court-life (Poem 10) is reflected in what
Chiurlo calls "a singular strength of expression". It is
regrettable that his influence was not felt in his lifetime,
all his abundant production having been published posthumously.

He was, however, not the only outstanding poet of
his day. Eusebius Stella, by the sheer force of the

personality which he stamps upon his work, has at last

broken through the prejudice excited by the uncompromis-

ing licentiousness of his verses, and been admitted to his

proper place in an Anthology.[27] It is significant that

when he repented of his youthful excesses, he chose to

express himself in Italian, and immediately sank to the

level of typical _secentismo_. The century ends with two

anonymous poems: a _canto carnascialesco_ of the type

made famous by Lorenzo il Magnifico, and a Contrasto[28]

similar to Poem No. 1.

In the eighteenth century Friulan seems to undergo

an eclipse, and the occulting body is Venetian, which,

being backed by the prestige of the Serenissima,

increased in snob-value and was responsible for the

fatal equation of Friulan with rustic speech (v. p. viii).

Only one major poet relieves the gloom - Gabriele

Paciani, and his most successful note is a resigned

melancholy (D'Ar. 199). Beneath the literary surface,

---

27. D'Aronco, _Ant._, pp. 129-130 and 143-150. Chiurlo,
    Ant. (1927), p. 225, relegates him to the promised
    Appendix (v. note 5).

28. D'Aronco, _Ant._, pp. 173 and 174 respectively.
    Chiurlo (p. 157) calls the first a _Cingaresca_.

however, the language was seething. Paciani himself

was concerned for its orthography;[29] and Giuseppe

Liruti produced the first serious study of the language in

his De lingua foroiulianorum Dissertatio[30] and the first

sketch of a history of Friulan literature.[31] The impulse

to measure the language against the classics (last exem-

plified by Fistulario's translation of Ariosto's O. F.; v.

above pp. 40-41) was also far from dead: G. Bosizio

translated the whole of Virgil; and if Friulan's richness

in agricultural terms renders it particularly suitable for

the Georgics, his choice of ottava rima (the "half-serious

rhyme", as Byron called it) affected the dignity of the

work and resulted in yet another parody of the Aeneid

(D'Aronco, pp. 187-193).[32]   Meanwhile Friulan

was still entrenched in the church - a position decisive

for the fate of a language, as the differing fortunes of

---

29. See below, p. 64, n. 50.

30. See p. 19, n. 1.

31. Notizie della vita e delle opere scritte dai letterati
    del Friuli.

32. Alongside the German one of Aloysius Blumauer
    (1784-1788) (translated into Polish in 1834), the
    Ukrainian of Kotljarevski (1798), and the Polish
    of Chotomski (1818).

Welsh and Irish sufficiently demonstrate; and what is
spoken in the pulpit, having usually been first written
down, can rise from the sphere of the colloquial and the
ephemeral to become a permanent contribution to literature. Such certainly is the sermon preached by the
Archbishop of Gorizia about the year 1760 (Prose
Extract No. 10).[33]

The hiatus of a century seems to have been a period
of gestation for the Friulan soul, for in the nineteenth
this brought forth a splendid harvest of poetry and prose,
in a quantity and of a quality such as to fulfil the highest
hopes of earlier years. Ushered in by the carnival-
songs of Florindo Mariuzza, the poeta-contadino, the
century soon produced one whose title of Friuli's greatest poet can be disputed only by Ermes di Colloredo.
Pietro Zorutti shares with Petrarch and Marini the distinction of having created a type of poetry and called into
being a horde of imitators who continued to write in his

----

33. Other sermons of his languish in the Library of the
    Seminary at Gorizia, as do thousands of other ser-
    mons in the Civic Library of Udine (v. Prose Ex-
    tract No. 16). The recent opening of Mass to
    Friulan has helped the language: "Perhaps God will
    hear us better in Friulan", as pre Checo Placerean
    put it in a sermon (v. p. 298).

manner long after the vein was exhausted. Starting point

for him, as it must be for all who live in that "little com-

pendium of the universe" (as Ippolito Nievo called it), is

Nature. To contemplate Nature as she unveils herself in

that magnificent landscape and to feel one's soul respond

to her varied moods[34] - that is the essence of what is

understood by "zoruttianismo". There is more to it than

this, however: equally characteristic of Zorutti is his

ability to see the comic side of things. It is the union of

these two capacities that enabled him to present a roun-

ded picture of human life, and thus to find an echo in

every heart. There are artistic defects in him, of

course, and he has been attacked for them;[35] and he has

---

34. It was in Friuli (precisely, in a field in Artegna)
     that I first understood how anyone could feel as
     Leopardi told Giordani he had felt (Letter of 6 March
     1820): aperta la finestra della mia stanza, e veden-
     do un cielo puro, un bel raggio di luna, ...mi parve
     di sentire un moto nel cuore, onde mi posi a gridare
     come un forsennato, domandando misericordia alla
     natura, la cui voce mi pareva di udire dopo tanto
     tempo. ("Opening the window of my room, seeing
     a clear sky, the bright moonlight, ...methought I
     felt a movement in my heart, which set me shouting
     like a madman, asking forgiveness of that Nature,
     whose voice I seemed to be hearing after so long
     an interval".)

35. e.g. by G. Marchetti in Il Friuli - Uomini e tempi
     (Udine, 1959).

even been criticized for apparently standing aloof from
the Risorgimento.[36] It is enough to reply with D'Aronco,[37] that "without the zoruttian tradition the poetic output of following generations would have been far less and
much less varied". Zorutti taught Friulans to feel
poetically.

Meanwhile Caterina Percoto was showing that Friulan prose also, in the hands of an artist, had a quality of
its own - that friulanità in style and syntax was something to be admired and cherished as the hallmark of an
independent literature. Her contemporary, Federico
Comelli, deliberately aimed at this recognition, with
such success that Chiurlo finds in his prose writings a
"distinct romantic personality" and a tone reminiscent
of the German Romantics and Tommaseo. All this time
the volume of authentic Friulan prose available to the
reader was being increased by the publication of successive collections of folk-tales: by Valentino Ostermann
("the father of Friulan folk-lore studies"), by the cousins

---

36. Such critics are well trounced by Meni Parut in
    Patrie del Friûl, lui-avost 1950, p. 1. ("Since when
    have poets had to write patriotic songs?")

37. Il Tesaur, 1959, p. 15 and Ant., p. 220, lines
    7-10.

Giovanni and Luigi Gortani, and by others (Prose Extract 18).

Even the theatre began to contribute its share of Friulan. Chiurlo thought[38] the Friulans too "inward-looking" to develop a dramatic sense (unlike the Venetians); and indeed Friulan had so far produced nothing more than a pastoral tale, Il Mago,[39] and Colloredo's "Dialogue of a hypocrite with her confessor" (Prose Extract No. 9), both of the seventeenth century. Now came some writers of comedies: F. Leitemberg, with subtle studies of village-life; G.E. Lazzarini, sometimes translating his own Venetian; F. Nascimbene, the most readable of them all.[40]

By the end of the century it was clear that sooner or later Friulan poetry was going to need renovation. The bridge to the new century was Piero Bonini, whose achievement in purging poetic diction of the prolixity and indiscriminate jocosity which are the besetting sins of regional poetry and keep it firmly "dialectal", was the

---

38. Ant., p. 167.

39. Another ms. still languishing in a library, this time the Guarneriana of San Daniele.

40. Extracts in D'Aronco, Ant., pp. 309-314.

indispensable first step. "With Bonini, " says D'Aronco,
Friulan dialectalism received a severe blow." Not that
the traditional metres and diction were immediately abandoned; far from it: there was still much excellent work
to be produced in the old forms. With Piero Corvat's
El Cuarantevot Friulan at last made amends for apparently ignoring the revolutionary struggles of 1848.[41]
Enrico Fruch is perhaps the most Romagnol of Friulan
poets, i.e. the one who most completely identified himself with his region and was moved by every aspect of
her scenery; who sang of her fauna and flora, and of the
history of her towns; who loved liberty and remembered
his happy boyhood. Akin to him are Emilio Nardini and
- our first poetess - Francesca Nimis-Loi. In Bindo
Chiurlo Friuli possessed a poet who was also an outstanding literary critic. Many of these poets have had
their works set to music; for Friulans have always been
a musical race and can claim the credit for inventing the
dance now known all over Europe as the "furlana". Many
of them were also active in, and even co-founders of,
the S.F.F. (p. x).

---

41. One could wish that his unfinished Difese di Osop
    (v. p. 14) might appear in print.

The renovation, when it came, was not the work of

youthful poets rebelling against an effete tradition: on

the contrary, the first sign of a break with everything

ottocentesco comes in the work of one whose birth took

place well within the nineteenth century. Francesca

Bàrnaba (b. 1877) was past middle age when she began to

write poetry, but as though by instinct she expressed

herself in verse which is thoroughly modern not only in

its free form, but also in its individual note of introspec-

tion. She may of course have been influenced by the

work of Lea D'Orlandi, who, though born later than she

(1890), came to poetry earlier and had published a book

of poems in 1924. Franco de Gironcoli too (b. 1892)

belonged to an older generation, when his Vot poesiis

suddenly revealed to the Friulan reading public in 1944

that Friulan poetry would never be the same again. This

should have been clear two years earlier, when Pier

Paolo Pasolini, then aged 20, published his Poesie a

Casarsa. The ridimensionamento of poetry was taken

up with enthusiasm by the new generation, and Casarsa

(21 miles SW of Udine) secured a place in literary his-

tory as the name of a poetic school. Among the mem-

bers of this "Academiuta", as it was called, were

R. Castellani (b. 1910), determined that Friulan should
be capable of the same stylistic excellence as its sister-
language French; D. Naldini (b. 1929), who added to the
symbolist and "hermetic" qualities of Pasolini his own
"decadent" morbidity; Ovidio Colussi (b. 1927); and Toni
Spagnol (b. 1930): all of whom had in Casarsa, not
merely the name of a poetic school, but their actual
birth-place or place of residence. Thus we see again in
Friuli a group of young men united in the practice of
poetry (above, pp. 40-41), only this time it is more like
that around Dante, with a <u>dolce stil nuovo</u> of its own.

Casarsa was not the only scene of poetic activity in
the freer style. In Triest there was Maria Gioitti del
Monaco (b. 1890); in Moreto di Tomba, near Udine,
Someda de Marco (1891-1970); in Cordenons, Renato
Appi (b. 1923) (all three, incidentally, also writers of
comedies). Then, as if to assert the claims of the centre against the periphery, there were the new poets
(Novella Cantarutti, Dino Virgili, Aurelio Cantoni)
forming the association called at first il Cortesele del
Furlan (above, p. x) but soon known by the name of their
first collective volume, "La Risultive" (1950), so called
because they aimed to return to the pure "source" of

friulanità. The replacement of the Academiuta by Risul-

tive was more than a change of name: it meant a return

to the koiné and a rejection of foreign influences in fav-

our of Friuli's own folk-poetry. The growth of the move-

ment coincided with Friuli's developing sense of a sep-

arate identity, which culminated in the demand for, and

the grant of, regional autonomy in 1963.

The new poets, determined to show that Friulan

could reflect modern trends, including incomprehensi-

bility (the "hermetic") as successfully as any language,

continued none the less to find inspiration in Friuli

itself. In this they invite comparison with their Rom-

agnol brothers. Like them, they are lovers of freedom

(19),   proud of their "patrie antighe di latins"[42] and

of its part in history (24), and dwell lovingly on every

aspect of its scenery. The two scenic backcloths have

much in common. Once again, towns and villages pass

before us: Aquileia (23, 24), Udine (7), Gorizia (17),

Gemona (27),   Gorizzo (10, 11), Osoppo (25, 27).

The vast plain is dominated by the Carnic and Julian

Alps (17, 23, 25, 27) and is traversed by the rivers that

---

42. P. Someda de Marco, Il mio zardin, p. 24.

flow from them, especially "the proud and terrible Tagliamento" (22, 25, 27, 33), the Natisone hastening through Cividale (p. 56), the Lisonzo (17), and the Torre (22). From the streams a mist rises, to be dissipated by the sun.

The flora and fauna hardly differ. The pine is still conspicuous (24, 25, 27); and for Nimis-Loi it is the pine-tree which raises its "green hair" to the sky and rises "like a sword" (Stàtuis and L'Ancòne). The poplar also continues to stand out (15, 33), and wins a poem to itself from Nimis-Loi (Un pôl). It is even linked again with a bell-tower (33), still a prominent feature of a landscape resounding with its bells (24, 25, 35, 38). The elm also enjoys the distinction of being addressed by Nimis-Loi, but as the victim this time of the ivy which strangles it (36). Our choice now brings in the acacia (42), chestnut (41), and fir (27). Of fruit-trees we meet here only the peach (49), the walnut (27), and the fig-tree, warned to beware of the axe (26).

The vineyard appears mostly by implication in references to the vintage (10), and to wine (18), but it is so much a part of Friuli (46) that a grape-

cluster has been the symbol of the region from the

eighth century.[43] Corn, as an essential element in

the scene (22, 25, 29, 41), evokes a paean (22).

Hedgerows there are (15, 16), but of the hawthorn

(may) and the clover we catch only l'odôr amâr de

blancespine that Lorenzoni liked (Sot sere). In compen-

sation we get roses (41, 49), cyclamen (25, 27), violets

(15, 21, 49), and geraniums (25). Particularly empha-

sized is grass (47), as well it may be; for the green

of Friuli's verdure ("la ligrìe di verd che viest i prâz",

as Nimis-Loi puts it) is a very special colour (22, 24).

Perhaps this owes something to the rain, evidently

more abundant up here beneath the Alps (35, 39, 48),

and eagerly drunk by the thirsty ground (15, 40).

---

43. e.g. on Roman funerary stelai, on the arch of
     the Longobard tempietto of S. Maria in Valle in
     Cividale (8th cent.), in Palma il Giovane's painting
     of Friuli and Venice (ca. 1600), in G.A. Porde-
     none's "La Madonna dell'Uva" (ca. 1525), on the
     tympanum of the main door of Udine Cathedral
     (14th cent.), etc.

And this fertile ground is a "stage for toilers":
the girls who hoe and rake and reap (29), the shepherd
striding behind his flock or rounding up his sheep (27),
the haymakers returning with the hay which smells so
good on the cart drawn by the panting oxen. Occasionally we catch a glimpse of the farm-yard with its dog,
its hens, and a goose.

Their typical tool is the sickle, hardly mentioned
without its inseparable companion, the hone (v. App. 1,
No. 7). We hear of this more often than of the plough,
though uarzine is as picturesque a word for it as Romagnol pardgher, and its work is constantly implied in
the equally quaint words for cultivated land, taviele (22)
and braide (Poem 49 and App. 3, 2).

Over this splendid countryside the usual birds are
flying: the swallow, unrecognizable under his new name,
cisile (49, 50), the lark (34, 38, 52), the cuckoo (11),
the sparrow (34), and others; but if we rejoice at the
absence of the huntsman's prey, the quail, we have to
grieve for the fate of the finch and the thrush (Carletti,
Sot la nape). Foremost place, however, now falls to the
nightingale (11, 24, 32). It is the leader of the orchestra

which Colloredo is laying on for his guests (11), in

which there will also be playing the other musicians

of the Friulan scene: the crickets (11, 30, 49) and

the frogs (11, 52). The star-studded, moon-lit Friulan

night (42) resounds with this music; and ushering it

in at dusk is the Avemaria of the bells (24, 33, cf.

38).

The sea, Friuli's southern boundary for so short

a distance, hardly comes into the picture. Here it

only provides the quiet background for a pilgrimage

to the sacred island of Barbana near Grado (24).

In the north the Carnic Alps tower over the plain

more awesomely than the Apennines over Romagna and.

rise more abruptly from it. Friulan poets are there-

fore more conscious of la ciadene des monz che t'in-

corone (Nimis-Loi, Miò Friûl) (38). "Ce quadri

immens! Ce spetacul dut chel Cercli di monz!" ex-

claims Fruch, doffing his hat in salute to "i païs de

nestre int" (Aquileia, 1). And perhaps because Friulans

so often look up at these mountains, the sky is also a

frequent part of the scene (25, 32), not so much for

its serene blue as for its clouds, whether bearing

rain or gilded by the sun at dawn or dusk.

No wonder all Friuli's poets are in a sense nature-poets. And every year they see this landscape vary its beauty in accordance with the seasons. Summer comes in for a special song (Mariuzza, Da l'istât); but the beloved season is spring (50) with its cool, gentle breeze (aiarut) (32), and that month of April which Nardini scolds for its fickleness, but which inspired Zorutti to one of his greatest poems.

It is the older poets who sing of all this with the greater passion. As memories lengthen and prospects shorten, the various sights of the countryside, such as a church (21) or a fountain, awake nostalgic thoughts and become symbols of a lost happiness (39), especially when associated with a remembered love. Exiled poets yearn for their Friuli (17); and the sermon of the log this time is on the transience of human life (Nardini, Il zôc). Friulan boys were no less happy than those of Romagna: gathering nuts (32), sailing to Barbana (23), swimming and fishing in the Natisone (Sul puint di Premariâs), going off to Carnia for a holiday (27). The last three memories all come from Fruch; and have we not called him the most Romagnol of our poets? But one must look

forward as well as back; and now Nature enters

their vision of the end just as it has coloured their mem-

ory of the beginning. Chiurlo wants to die in winter,

when the mountain-tops are capped with snow (34 iii);

Lorenzoni wants the sun to shine on his death-bed (35);

Someda de Marco wants to lie down for the last time

among the flowers; Adelgiso Fior hopes death will

come in a mountain-shelter (44). Sometimes life is

more to be feared than death (39, 53). More than once

a cemetery is a source of inspiration (30, 41); and

Nadia Pauluzzo asks for a grave on the top of a wind-

swept hill (53).

Meanwhile there is no dearth of poets. Domenico

Zannier (b. 1930) has two slim volumes to his credit,

characterized by what one critic calls "a baroque fever

of anthropomorphic metaphors". Galliano Zof (b. 1933),

who is also fond of metaphor, combines crude expres-

sionism with a painter's feeling for landscape. An even

greater sensitivity to the forms and colours of landscape

is revealed in the poems of Umberto Valentinis (b. 1938),

who writes in the aristocratic tradition and among the

classics finds Hölderlin and Leopardi most congenial to

his mind. But a social conscience was bound to seek
expression in poetry sooner or later. (The marxist
verses of Zuan Minut (1895-1965) had been a voice in the
wilderness in 1921.) In 1964 Leonardo Zanier's Libers
di scugnî lâ ("Free to have to go") took up the cause of
Friuli's emigrants; and in 1968 Renato Jacumin
(b. 1941), in his L'ultima stagion, sounded the note of
protest against all suffering caused by human injustice.
Finally, the work of Toni Colus (b. 1951), Requie par un
om, describes in hermetic language the horror of the
consumer-society in a world dehumanized by technology.

While poets and poetesses sing, Friulan has been
showing itself a mature language in prose also; in fact,
it is to poets that some of its prose-works are owed.
These may be plays such as the comedies mentioned
above (p. 47) (to which must be added those of G. Marioni, Anute Fabris, and S. de Marco (Prose Extracts
Nos. 16, 17); or serious dramatic works such as
L'Ultin perdon of R. Appi, which owes more to America
and Ireland than to Friuli; or short stories, such as the
"crudely realistic" dramatic ones of A. Cantoni (No. 21);
or even a novel, D. Virgili's L'aghe dapît de cleve ("The
water at the foot of the slope"). Most prose-writers

remained within the limits of the short story or the tale.

Outstanding among these are the Storiutis furlanis of

D. Zorzut, who combined a scholarly appreciation of

the folklorist's discipline with the skill of a literary

artist. Tales of another sort are those of A. Feruglio,

who also wrote plays and through his annual Strolic furlan

provided a platform for many other writers in Friulan,

such as Vico Bressan, Riedo Puppo (25), and Meni Parut.

The character of Tite Lalele which he invented as the

protagonist of his humorous adventures is also the picar-

esque hero of his longer story, Viaz a Vignesie.   In

the recently published work of Gino Cencigh, Aghe che

passe (1971) (26), we find prose and poetry successfully

combined.

Folk-lore has been the source of R.H. Cossar's

numerous tales, of which the best known is the fable of

the Three Oranges (18); and we have to thank the great

Pier Silverio Leicht, not only for saving from sup-

pression under Fascism the S.F.F., of which he was

President (as he was also Vice-President of the Acca-

demia dei Lincei), but for a series of legends of Civi-

dale.   One of the founders of the S.F.F., Ugo Pellis,

combined his linguistic studies with poetry, and was

innovator enough to give Friulan its only prose-poem (v.
D'Ar. 388) and to experiment with it in the classical metres of Carducci. Co-founder with him and another great
Friulan scholar, G. B. Corgnali, showed that he too was
a master of style (No. 14); and G. Marchetti, whose services to Friulan include the first modern Grammar, has
convincingly used the language on learned themes (No.
19). Thus tested and proved in science and philology,
Friulan has shown its powers in political and polemical
writing in the leading articles of Patrie dal Friûl (1946-
1965) and Int furlane. It remains to be seen whether it
will develop the technical vocabulary that is now part of
every western language; presumably it would require
nothing more than the adaptation of Italian, or possibly
other Romance, words to Friulan phonetics.

One precondition for such a development has apparently been satisfied: the provision of a common form
of the language, a koiné, to be used throughout the region for official and literary purposes. In Italy west of
the Livenza such a language was not forged without a
struggle, as is clearly shown by the space devoted to
the "Question of the Language" in histories of

Italian.[44] In Friuli dialectal fragmentation is less

marked than in the sister-region of the Dolomites (p.

19),[45] but the literary activity which is chiefly respon-

sible for this satisfactory state of affairs is inevitably

less influential than political centralization in securing

the recognition of one form of speech as superior to all

others. A sacrifice is required, and local patriotism is

strong. Is it not enough for a Cividalese to have to

speak in Italian, without being obliged also to write in

Udinese? Yet it was precisely a resident of Cividale,

Friuli's intellectual centre in earlier times (p. 31), the

eighteenth-century poet, G. Paciani, who chose to write

in a kind of koiné; and that this represents a deliberate

attempt to create a literary language is shown by his

being also one of the first Friulans to try to regularize

the orthography.[46] Zorutti and Percoto also used the

---

44. e. g. thirty pages in The Italian Language of
    Migliorini and Griffith.

45. Cf. G. Francescati, Premesse per una classifica-
    zione dei dialetti friulani in Il Tesaur 1955, pp. 17-
    20, and 1956, pp. 5-7; and E. Quaglia, Come si
    parla in Carnia, in Boll. della S. F. F., 1936,
    pp. 166-168.

46. Cf. his sonnet on the unlikely theme "Sore il mût
    di scrivi in lenghe furlane".

language of the Udinese[47] and thereby helped to make of

it "standard" Friulan.   Later in the century another

Cividalese, Guido Pedrecca (1860-1923) chose their

koiné for his annual Calendar; and he too busied himself

with orthography. Then, however, came the need to

"renew" Friulan poetry (p. 47), and an obvious short-

cut to the freshening of diction was to use the speech of

one's own locality. Pasolini, for example, used the dia-

lect of Casarsa (p. 49); De Gironcoli that of Gorizia;

Novella Cantarutti that of Navarons (NE of Maniago);

Appi that of Cordenons (v. p. 191), still today "an island

of Friulan in a sea of Venetian" (D'Aronco). This was a

dangerous tendency. To write in the dialect of a dialect

is to put oneself at two removes from world-literature.

If an Italian wrote in Neapolitan, he might be acclaimed

in Naples or in quel di Napoli; but it would have to be an

outstandingly excellent work if it was to be translated and

read even elsewhere in Italy, let alone beyond. Authors

---

47. According to D'Aronco, Ant., p. 557, a triangle
     whose base is the Tagliamento from Spilimbergo
     to Gemona and whose apex is Udine. This includes
     San Daniele, the so-called (and according to G.
     Faggin in his article quoted in note 50, miscalled)
     "Siena" of Friuli.

and poets surely write, perhaps subconsciously, for the

world, even though they know there is a language-barrier

to be overcome; and in the measure of their success in

doing so they create their country's literature. Aware

of their ethnic individuality and proud of the qualities

which seem to distinguish them from the rest of the

Peninsula, that is, of being deeply religious and

> int che fevele pôc, ame il lavor,
> ame la Patrie e cognòs ben l'onor[48]

> (Nimis-Loi, Testament)

Friulans should see in a unified language the best guar-

antee of their future as a race, and in an "autochthonous"

literature[49] the best means of winning the recognition

---

48. The "Fatherland" is of course the Patrie dal Friûl -
a reminder that in their more exasperated moments
Friulans speak of Italians as though they were for-
eigners (cf. Prose-Extract No. 22). On the
other hand, apart from the hard core who denounce
the Act of Union of 1866, they are also proud of
being Italians and grateful to il gran re che nus à fat
talians (V. Vittorello, La moral dai ciocs). The
parallelism with Wales and the Welsh is obvious.

49. The term occurs in D'Aronco's review of an Anthology of Catalan poetry (Il Tesaur, 1953, p. 16):
"Catalan poetry to be such must have an autochthonous value, a traditional lymph of its own; otherwise it is poetry translated from Castilian and
reveals lack of personality". Read "Friulan" for
"Catalan", and you have what D'Aronco himself
stated in La Panarie of 1949.

of the world for the eighth daughter of Latin.[50]

---

50. In his article significantly called "La lingua friulana
    e le sue 'chances'" (La Panarie 16, giugno 1972),
    G. Faggin stresses (p. 15) that there can be no lit-
    erature without a koiné, but that Friuli's must be
    purged of italianisms and receive a rational orthog-
    raphy (cf. above, p. 43 and below, p. 75). In an
    earlier number (Dic. 1971, "La letteratura ladina
    del Friuli negli ultimi trent'anni", he praises the
    "miraculous" Friulan of D. Zannier's poems and
    the "superlative" koiné of his novel La crete che no
    vai (published in instalments in the Patrie dal Friûl),
    in which Friulan appears as a fully mature lan-
    guage. Another novel written in a polished koiné
    is Prime di Sere (1971), the work of one of Friuli's
    intellectuals, Carlo Sgorlon, also known for his
    writings in Italian (e. g. Il trono di legno, 1973).

5. Folklore

Rural Friuli is a haunted place. All kinds of invisible

beings people it: the cialchiutt (incubus), which settles

on a sleeping person and prevents him from moving or

waking up; the aganis, naiads, who at Borgnan can be

heard washing their clothes on the banks of the Judri;[1]

and the striis, witches, who are no "secret, black, and

midnight hags", but a kind of angels, dancing, bathing in

fountains, and combing their blond hair.[2] According to

a proverb they are combing their hair whenever there is

sunshine and rain together;[3] and another warns that it is

better not to be born then,[4] though this may be because

the same phenomenon also means that the Devil is comb-

ing his tail.[5] Most numerous, however, are the spirits

1.   as told in C. Percoto's story, "Lis aganis di Borg-
     nan". The derivation from aqua (water) seems to
     me suspect; and they have in fact been described as
     cave-dwellers.

2.   Cf. Percoto, "Les striis di Germanie". They are
     "le fate" of Carducci's poem In Carnia.

3.   Se al plouf e al soreglea, a' si petenin lis striis.

4.   Al è mal nassi quan che si petènin lis striis.

5.   Puar chel ch'al nâs quan che il diaul al petène la
     code. Another proverb makes him do this when
     women fight.

of the dead; and since, even after the Council of Trent,

many of these are also damned, it behoves the living to

be on their guard. La gnot a' è d'altris, "the night

belongs to others"; and anyone walking abroad after

dark may expect to see a ghost, especially if his god-

father recited the Creed badly at his christening. So

priests and midwives should always be fetched by two

persons, because a priest with the Viaticum is particu-

larly vulnerable, but to three people nothing can happen.

So they say in the village of Giavons; and there in 1947

they were also telling the story of a boy who fell asleep

on the steps of a church, woke up to see a priest at the

altar, and helped him serve Mass. After three nights of

this the priest was never seen again: he had been a chap-

lain come back from the dead to hold promised Masses

and needing only a server. The same village also tells

of a woman drowned in 1948, who returned to suckle her

baby.

It is interesting to see how standard superstitions

are modified by the Friulan conscience. To the belief

that butterflies, moths, and ladybirds represent the

souls of the departed, Friulans add the detail that they

have come from Purgatory and are asking for our

prayers. The objection to the presence of a cat in a dying man's room is "rationalized" by the supposition that the cat, particularly if black, is the Devil himself. That the dead should not be bewailed is a belief as old as the Thracians of Herodotus; but Christianity in Friuli gives a peculiar twist to it by supposing that to do so increases their sufferings in Purgatory. "No sta vaimi pi, che tu mi slungis la pena, " says a ghost to her mother. A falling star is accepted without question as a soul; but there is some doubt as to what is happening to it, and so also some variety in the exclamations that must follow it. If you believe that it is a soul flying up to God you will say Giò ti lozi! (God give you lodging!); if you think it a falling angel you should say Giò t' aiudi! (God help you!); but those who take it for a lost soul will welcome the opportunity to save it from hell by uttering the prayer Giò ti salvi! (God save you!). In any case, the event must not be spoken of to others, and it is therefore better that children should not see it.

Another event that must not be divulged is the sight of a ghost. A boy who told the son of a dead man that he had seen his father is said to have died. This danger, however, does not deter many from wanting to see them;

and for them there is a method available. All they have
to do is to place their right foot on that of a priest; or it
might be enough merely to touch his stole. The same
device will enable one to see whether the soul of a dying
man is damned or not. Undesired ghosts may be exor-
cized in various ways, the commonest being that of sending them elsewhere - to the Red Sea, or 100 metres
underground, to rise up at the rate of one metre a year,
or beneath the hearth if they have been wicked, that they
may be consumed by the fire, or to the tops of mountains, there to spend their time, like the villains of
classical Tartarus, in carrying water in baskets and
sand in strips of cloth. Sometimes the spirit may be
allowed to choose his place of sojourn: a haunted house
was once freed when the ghost was conjured to betake
himself "sot dal seglar" (beneath the sink), as he had
chosen. There are times when ghosts are expected, as
on the eve of All Saints' Day, when souls return to their
homes to drink or even eat; and care is then taken to
have cisterns and larders full, and even a candle or
lamp at the window.[6] It takes courage to speak with a

6.   Cf. the Celtic story of St. Bridget's Eve in its
      Manx version (Coraa Gailckagh, Laa Boaldyn,
      1952).

ghost, but a man may find that he is rewarded by the dis-

covery of a buried treasure which the ghost has been set

to guard until the day of his liberation.

The boundary-line between religion and magic is thus

constantly traversed; indeed, in popular literature the

two are inextricably combined. The most innocent-

looking Lullaby or Nonsense-rhyme (App. 1, 1),

the most religious-looking Prayer (ib. 3), even a love-

lyric, may have originated as an incantation intended to

produce a certain effect, and may thus belong to magic

as much as the frankly magical scongiuri (ib. 4) and the

fairy-tale (fiaba) (App. 2, No. 1).[7]   Such fusion or

confusion made it easier to incorporate St. Peter and

even Jesus into the repertory of Friulan characters por-

trayed in popular narrative, where the moralizing ele-

ment is deliberately clothed in comic dress;[8] but it is

---

7. D'Aronco, Gli elementi magico-religiosi nelle forme
    d'arte popolare (Atti dell'Accademia di Scienze,
    Lettere e Arti di Udine, 1951-1954, Serie vi., Vol.
    xii., pp. 195-216), where he sums up the matter
    saying "Popular art means religious art; cultivated
    art involves deconsecration". Cf. his other article
    on Le Fiabe di magià in Italia in the same magazine
    for 1954-1957, pp. 49 ff. Hence the "epode" regu-
    larly appended to the Orazions.

8. Prose Section, No. 12.

significant that while these two are treated with a familiarity bordering on the blasphemous, the Madonna preserved her halo and is always mentioned with the greatest reverence.[9] (Even in ghost-stories she has a special place; for women who die in child-birth remain under her protection and are not judged for 40 days.) Friday of course, as in Romagna, remains a magic day: "He who sings on Friday will weep on Sunday", says the proverb; and if there has to be some significance in the simultaneous utterance of the same idea by two people ("when great minds think alike"), it is that then a soul has been released from Purgatory.

Finally Christianity is left behind, and we are back in the animistic age when the life of man is linked with that of trees and plants. At Moggessa they will tell you of the pinetree which overhung a ravine. A young man wanted to cut it down, but his mother was afraid of the danger and shut him up in a room. Then a voice was heard from the crag: "L'ore 'e ven e l'omp nol ven, l'ore 'e passe e l'omp al sta masse";[10] and the pine

---

9.   D'Aronco, La Madonna nella leggenda friulana (Ce fas-tu?, xxiii (1947), p. 16).

10.   "The hour comes and the man comes not, the hour passes and the man waits too long".

crashed down. When the mother entered her son's room

she found him dead. Similarly a peasant woman care-

fully waters a plant of rosemary, lest by dying it cause

the death of her master. Conversely, it can be danger-

ous to a household if one of its members plants a tree:

"If it flourishes, someone in the family will die within

the year", predicts the proverb; and the planting is

therefore best commissioned to an outsider.

Such beliefs die hard. In the last war, when Parti-

sans used to throw captured Cossacks into the River

Ledra (a tributary of the Tagliamento, on which Giavons

stands), one of these solemnly assured his captors:

"You throw me down now, but later many of you will

follow us." The local population is now convinced that

since then there have been far more cases of drowning

in the river.[11]

---

11. For other stories of the uncanny see Prose No. 24.
    Int furlane of September 1973 has an interesting
    account of the activities of a Poltergeist in the vil-
    lage of Mels (north of Udine) from June 17th 1872
    to September 15th 1873.

PHONOLOGY

1. The most important sounds peculiar to Friulan are: pre-palatal C, prepalatal G, guttural N, varieties of S, and sonant Z.

(i) Prepalatal C is a soft sound used where Italian has a velar (hard) C before a, o, u (cjase casa, cjan cane) or a T before i (j) (cjoli togliere, tanc' tanti, chesc' questi).

(ii) Prepalatal G is the sonant corresponding to the above surd. Hence gjambe gamba, gjat gatto; Gjò Dio, gjaul diavolo. It sometimes mistakenly represents Italian palatal G: gjorno giorno, cf. gjonde (gioia) giocondo, or is found instead of the surd: gjavâ cavare, vigjele vitello.

(iii) Guttural N is found (a) in the prefix in before another n (innidâsi annidarsi); (b) in the gerundial participle, with ellipse of T before a suffixed pronoun (Gram. § 22) (puartan'nus portandoci); (c) in the 1st Pers. Plur. Imperative before a suffixed pronoun (viodin'ju vediamoli).

(iv) S, when not sonant or representing ss, and when arising from an original hard C, is a sibilant fricative (plasê, dis, pâs from Latin placere, decem, pacem). The same sound arises from final s preserved from Latin Acc. Plur. ending -os: altris (alteros). But the sound is semi-dental (between surd s and surd z) when it arises from final s of Latin 3rd Decl. Acc. Plur. (lûs, vôs, crôs from luces, voces, cruces), or when altris is feminine.

(v) Sonant Z represents (a) the Italian soft G before a, o, u (zal giallo, zovin giovine, zuc gioco); (b) initial and medial palatal G (zimul gemello, strenzi stringe); (c) final palatal c (pastiz pasticcio); (d) medial hard G (uarzine organa plough, onzint unguento).

2. On the other hand, Friulan lacks Italian prepalatal liquid GL, using simple L (acolienze) or J or zero (mijor, miôr migliore), and the spirant SC before e and i, using simple S or, medially, SS (sienze scienza, passi pascere). Hence, when S happens to come before prepalatal or palatal C, both letters must be pronounced separately (s-cialdâ scaldare, dis-cioi scioglie, s-ciali scale).

3. Other consonants (incl. GN, GU, QU) as in Italian.

4. Words borrowed from Friuli's Slovene neighbours or enclaves are adapted as follows: Slovene initial h = c (cren from hren horseradish); final s = c (k) (madrac from modras

snake); initial v = f (frape from vrapa wrinkle); final š = s (cosse
from koš basket); initial s = sonant z ('zume from šuma copse);
intervocalic c and final č = surd z (razze from raca duck;
colazz from kolač cake). (See Introd., pp. 3, 4, 27).

5. Words of Longobard origin show the following changes: h
becomes g (gruse from hrudja crust, garp from harwi rough);
r becomes l (sglinghinâ from hringilon tinkle); w becomes v
(sbrovâ from breowan scald). (See also Introd., p. 27).

6. Celtic -acco in Place-names becomes -s (Ramanzas
Ramanzacco). (See also Introd., p. 24, n. 3).

7. VOWELS as in Italian.

8. DIPHTHONGS may arise (a) from short stressed o: UE (cuel
collo); before n - UI (cuintri contro); before r plus consonant -
UA (puarte porta). UA is retained in unstressed syllables of
verbs: puartâ portare. (b) from stressed e before r before consonant - IA (piardi perdere, tiare terra) or before two other
consonants - IE (biel bello, spietâ aspettare, piel pelle); (c)
from ellipse of intervocalic b after a - AU (peraule parola from
parabolam, taule tavola from tabulam); (d) from long o of 1st
Pers. Sing. Pres. of three verbs: doi, stoi (do, sto) and
voi vado through vo.

9. Further differences from Italian: D between vowels in some
Pres. Subj. (sedi sia); final surds (uf uovo, tart tardi, uarp orbo);
loss of soft G both initial and medial (int gente, lèi leggere, vilie
vigilia); frequency of J: for intervocalic hard C and G (zujâ
giocare, cjastijâ castigare); for initial L before e (jet letto);
before initial e or i (jessi essere, jarbe erba); to avoid hiatus
(ajar aria, cujetâ quietare); L preserved after occlusives (clamâ
chiamare, glesie chiesa, ploe pioggia), but lost initially (probably by confusion with Def.Art.; cf. for the opposite mistake
lesche esca) (odula allodola, ombul lombo) and finally (LL) (anei
anelli, taiadei tagliatelle); replacing Latin au before consonants
(gjoldi godere from gaudere, olsâ osare from ausare); omission
of final m after r (fer fermo); N for final m (prin primo), inserted
before k, g, t (duntrina dottrina), dropped after r when final (cuar
corno); GN initial before e, o, u, i (gnerf nervo, gnot notte, gnuf
nuovo, agn anni), from nge (agnul angelo), from initial L (gneur
lepre), from initial m (gnò mio); P after final m (omp uomo); R
for L (soreli sole from Lat. soliclum); V for intervocalic P (cjavel
capello), for intervocalic G (avost agosto), prefixed to initial o
(vot otto, voli occhio; cf. French aveugle blind), to initial semi-
vocalic u (vuardi orzo from Latin hordeum) (but this v is often
dropped (uardi), especially with words of Germanic origin beginning with gu- (uardâ guardare, uere guerra); fondness for pretonic
a: sapulî (seppellire), sancîr (sincero), sapuartâ (sopportare).

ORTHOGRAPHY

The satisfactory representation of Friulan sounds in writing would require considerable additions to the Italian alphabet; and Friulan authors are right in thinking that to drive such another wedge between the national and regional tongues (and between Friulan and the rest of the Romance family) would not be in the interest of their language.

Prepalatal C (Phon. 1 i) needs its own sign because of the large number of homographs that would result if it were not distinguished from the soft (palatal) C: e.g. ciale (cicada and looks at), cioc (log and drunk). Unfortunately, there is still disagreement as to the sign to be used: if çh is now obsolete, there is still contention between those who ignore the risk of occasional confusion by always writing ci (ciase house), and those who always write cj (cjale looks at; cjoc drunk).* Since the ques-

tion is not up for arbitration, this twofold spelling has

been maintained in this anthology; but where a word

involving prepalatal C is used for illustrative purposes,

the spelling ci has been preferred, chiefly on the ground

that whatever makes Friulan look peculiar is inimical to

its claim for outside recognition as a fully-fledged

Romance sister-tongue. (In glossaries and dictionaries,

however, words beginning with prepalatal C, however

spelt, are advisedly put in a separate group after those

with palatal C). In the final position, the sign is regularly

c' (duc' all).

 Prepalatal G (Phon. 1 ii) is likewise variously ren-

dered by gi or gj (giat or gjat cat).

---

* Cj and gj were introduced by G. Marchetti (v. p. 295),
who disagreed with the S.F.F.'s policy of "writing
Friulan as Italians" - a retrograde step after the 1st
edition of Pirona's Dictionary (1871), as the 2nd
edition (1935) showed. (Cf. Il Tesaur, 1953, 1-3,
p. 15 and Ce fas-tu? Dec. 1944, p. 350.) G. Faggin
(La Panarie 16, June 1972, p. 17) proposes a completely new system, which would clearly mark off
Friulan as belonging to Western Romance (French,
Spanish, Portuguese, Catalan). The use of the Czech
sign ⱽ, however, for palatal c before a, o, u or when
final and for sonant z, introduced by D. Zannier and
now appearing in Int furlane, gives the language a dis-
tinctly un-Romance look.

Guttural N (Phon. 1 iii) is distinguished by an apostrophe only in certain instances.

S: The sonant sound is distinguished only initially by a prefixed apostrophe ('Sef Joseph). No sign has been invented to distinguish the quality of the final s in masc. pl. altris from that in fem. pl. altris (Phon. 1 iv; Gram. §26). When s precedes prepalatal or palatal C (whether initially or medially), the two letters are separated by an apostrophe (presumably to avoid confusion with Italian spirant sc): s'ciars scarso, scarce; cis'ciel castello, castle (Phon. 2).

Sonant Z may be represented by 'z (recently ž, earlier ç) only when initial before a, o, u ('zal, 'zovin, 'zuc). Cf. zentil (gentile), zirin (girano).

In early Friulan palatalization was indicated by the letter g (e.g. cgiantaray in "Biello dumlo", Poem 1).

With vowels it was fortunately possible to separate homographs by the use of accents, though there is the usual disagreement as to whether they shall be acute or

grave (or replaced by a circumflex) in a given case.

Thus the word pes may be the equivalent of Italian peso

(weight) or pesce (fish) or per le (for the), but pês

stands only for peso with its long closed e. Similarly

tas may represent tace (is silent) or taccio (am silent)

or tasso (badger); nas - naso (nose) or nasce (is born);

pas - pace (peace) or passo (step) or pasce (feeds);

fas - fa (does) or faccio (do) or fatti (done, deeds) or

fascio (bundle); but a circumflex on the a will denote the

first meaning (and the 1st person sing. will then be

indicated by a grave accent (tàs I am silent, fàs I do).

Vis may be either avete (you have), viti (vines), vivi

(alive), viso (face); and the circumflex is found on the i

in both the first and the last. Similarly lei may stand for

legge (he reads), legga (he may read), leggere (to read)

and andai (I went), and only the last will have an accent

(lèi). The indication of stress by an accent is of consid-

erable morphological importance in the conjugation of the

verb: e.g. ciantàrin (cantarono, they sang), ciantarìn

(canteremo, we shall sing); jèssi (to be), jessî (to go

out).

The rule that qu is retained in words derived from

Latin, but that the same sound is represented by cu when

the u is part of diphthongized o (UA - v. Phon. 8) (i.e.

quant but cuarp) is not strictly observed. Cu-, however,

is always found in cujet (quieto) and cutuardis (quattordici),

because their u is vocalized.

A further orthographical complication arises when

an author chooses to write in his local dialect and spells

the words as phonetically as possible. But on the impor-

tance of a Friulan koiné see Introduction p. 60.

GRAMMAR

GRAMMAR

ACCIDENCE

1   The Definite Article

	Masc.	Fem.	Before vowel
Sing.	il	la	l'
Plur.	i	lis	-

Obs. i. l' (m. and f.) is not used before semivocalic u:
         la uere (war).

     ii. Fem. l' is sometimes used before other
          vowels and not used before a: la af (bee).

     iii. Friulan ignores impure s or z in the masc.
          sing. and plur.

     iv. Down to the 15th century the masc. sing. was
          lu, and the masc. plur. ju, and they are still
          used in certain areas.

     v.   Le is used for la in some areas.

     vi. El for il is due to Venetian influence.

     vii. The s of lis is sometimes elided, and some
          areas use las and les.

2   The Indefinite Article

              Masc.   Fem.

                un   une

Obs. i. No change is made in either before a vowel,
         z, or impure s.

                      Gender

The following nouns differ in gender from Italian:

    masculine[1]   feminine[2]

il nul   (cloud)   la bughê   (washing)
il palut   (marsh)   la flor   (flower)
l'aiar   (air)   la mont   (mountain)
l'incuin   (anvil)   la passare   (sparrow)
l'istat   (summer)   la sium   (sleep)
il glant   (acorn)   zobia   (Thursday)
il gneur   (hare)   la lum   (lamp)
il pulvar   (dust)   la mel   (honey)
il pulz   (flea)

---

1. The first five differ from Latin also.

2. The last two are from Latin neuters.

Obs. i. Nouns which in Italian form their plural in the
          feminine (with -a) remain masculine in Friulan:
          i cuars (horns), i lavris (lips), i dez (fingers),
          i us (eggs).

     ii. Trees are formed from a masculine suffix
          -arius: aunar (alder), fijar (figtree), orar[3]
          (laurel).

    iii. Greek neuters in -ma become feminine: la
          clime (climate), la steme (badge), la crisme
          (chrism).

     iv. Dí (day) is usually fem. in the sing., always
          masc. in the plur.

      v. Nouns borrowed from German may also change
          their gender: il crot (die Kröte, toad).

     vi. Gender may have a semantic value, allowing
          the same word to have two meanings:

          il tor   (bell-tower)   la tor   (tower)

          il sium (dream)   la sium (sleep)

    vii. A few nouns vary in gender according to
          locality.

---

3. For omission of initial l see above Phon. 9.

4   Number

Obs. i. The plural can assume a special meaning:

        la vilie   (eve)   lis viliis   (vigils, parties)
        l'ocjal   (monocle) i ocjaj   (spectacles)
        la fulugne (crowd)   lis fulugnis (confusion)

  ii. A singular noun, especially produce of the soil,
      may be used collectively:

        un zei di cevole   (a basket of onions).

5   Substantives

Latin 1st declension (-am) yields the ending -e; 2nd and
3rd declensions lose their ending and surdise final consonant. Words from Germanic and Slav conform.

6   Plural

The masc. plur. is regularly formed by the addition of s:

   cian, cians (dogs); boscs (woods); fradis (brothers).

So even monosyllables ending in a vowel: re, res (kings).

The fem. plur. changes -e to -is:

   ciase, ciasis (houses); fantate, fantatis (girls).

Obs. i. Subst. in -t change to a sound usually repre-
      sented by z, but which varies from -ts to
      sonant s (cf. li (i)):

      minut (minute), minuz; vit (vine), viz; giat
      (cat), giaz; citat (town), citaz.

  ii. Subst. in -s retain this letter or change to z to
      represent a more dental sound (cf xlv):

      la vos (voice), lis vos; la cros (cross),
      lis cros; la pes (fish), lis pes.

iii. Subst. in -z retain this letter to represent a
more surd sound:

la lez (law), lis lez; la pez (fir), lis pez
(cf. li (i)).

iv. Monosyllables in -f drop the f:

la af (bee), lis as; l'uf (egg), i us.

7   Exceptions to plural ending -s:

1. Subst. in -st form the plural in -sc' or s'c' (stʃ):

cronista (reporter), cronisc'; imprest (loan),
impresc'; forest (foreigner), foresc'.

2. Masc. subst. in -l form plural in i:

spetacul (spectacle), spetacui; pôl (poplar), pôi;
nul (cloud), nui; cuel (neck), cuei; popol (a people),
popui; mul (mule), mui.

3. Masc. subst. in -li form plural in -i (sometimes
-lis):

voli (eye), voi; pedoli (louse), pedoi; soreli (sun),
sorej or sorelis.

4. Masc. subst. in -nt form plural in -nc' (ntʃ):

dint (tooth), dinc'.

5. Irregular are:

agn[4] (years), umign[5] (men), bus (oxen) from
an, om, bue.

4. Also ains. (Agns is wrong; v. Phon. 9). A unique example of derivation from the genitive plural is agnorums
in the phrase Agn e agnorums indaûr (years and years
ago). Cf. Bacchelli, Il mulino del Po, 1, 212: "Il Po
morto che in anni annorum camminava per di lì".

5. Also oms, omps, omis.

8   Adjectives

Masc. sing. adjectives lack terminations and for the
plural follow the same rules as substantives:

ramaz nuz (bare branches) fantaz piarduz (lost boys)
biei timps (beautiful times) arbui imobii (motionless
cjavei bionz (fair hair)   trees)
voi zelesc' (blue eyes)   granc' nemis (great ene-
ciapiei gnus (new hats)   mies)
        lavors agricui (farm-work)

Obs. i. Irregular is pôs (few), plur. of poc.

   ii. Bon (good) yields boins, bogns, or bogn.
       (Cf. agn(s), note 4.)

9 Fem. sing. is formed by the addition of -e, which
   modifies the final consonant as follows:

   1. c becomes -cje: blanc, blancje (white)
      (Except a few such as cioc, cioche (ubbriaco,
      drunk) and learned words like gramatiche.)

   2. surdised sonants return: gnuf, gnove (new); uarp,
      uarbe (blind); piardut, piardude.
      (But -g takes a j: lunc, lungje; larc, largje.)

   3. final l remains unchanged after a lengthened open
      syllable: usual, zivil; but takes -e after a closed
      syllable or unstressed vowel: biel, biele; fàzil,
      fàzile.
      (Exceptions are: fedel, fedele; subtil, subtile.)

Obs. i. Present Participles in -ent may add -e or not.

   ii. Adjectives in -ri change to -re: legri, legre;
       neri, nere.

   iii. Adjectives in -i add -e: salvadi, salvadie
        (wild); strani, stranie.
        (Except: vieli, viele (vecchie old).)

   iv. Other original consonants may return: fer,
       ferme (stationary); prin, prime.

10   The fem. sing. termination -e also affects the
     preceding vowel:

   1. a stressed long vowel is shortened: frêt, fréde
       (cold); siôr, siòre (Mr., Mrs.).
       (Except: adj. in -s or -z: gris, grise; fals,
       false.)

   2. stressed and closed o and e are opened: vêr,
       vère (true); bessôl, bessòle (alone); sclét,
       sclète (frank). (But bon, buine.)
       (Except the suffix -on when used in the sense of
       a superlative, which lengthens without opening:[6]
       grandón, grandône.)

     Fem. plur. adjectives are formed in the same way
     as fem. plur. substantives: bielis flabis (beautiful
     fables); bisacis mitudis jú (knapsacks put down);
     sturiutis furlanis (Friulan tales).

     Obs. Fem. adj. in unchanging -l (see §9, 3 supra)
           either add -s: usuals, nazionals, zivils; or
           remain unchanged: (cf. the masc. pl. in -i:
           usuai, casuai).

           dopo lis primis domandis usual
           after the usual first questions

11   Comparison of Adjectives

The Comparative is formed with plui (more) or mancul
(less) followed by di or che (no) (than) according to need.

Irregular forms are: mijôr (miôr) (better) and (in non-
popular language) major (greater) and minor (smaller,
lesser).[7]

The Superlative is the comparative with the Def. Art.
unless the adjective follows a noun already articled:

  Lis flabis plui bielis   The most beautiful fables

6.   When the vowel is opened (broadened), the suffix has
     a pejorative sense.
7.   Pijôr (worse) is obsolete.

Obs. The absolute superlative is rendered in any of
three ways:

(i) By the suffix -on: grandón (grandissimo) (cf.
supra §10, 2).
This may be used even with verbs: plasonê
(piacere molto), fevelonâ (parlare molto).

(ii) By the locution une vore: une vore biel
(molto bello).

(iii) By the phrase tant - che mai.

12   The Comparative of Equality

Alongside come and sicu ("as") is the specifically Friulan
tanche:

tanche une fonghere   (like a mushroom)

Cumbinâ televisions di chê fate...al sares tan'che
fâ nassi une rivoluzion ("would be tantamount to")

Adverbs

13   1. Manner

Adverbs of Manner are formed by suffixing -mentri to
the fem. adj.:

profondamentri   deeply   finalmentri   finally

Obs. Typically Friulan is the suffix -vie, which may
even be used with nouns or other adverbs, the
word being usually introduced by a:

a stupitvie	stupidly
a frutvie	childishly
intor-vie	round about
sotvosvie	sotto voce
a contadinvie	like a peasant
artigjanvie	like an artisan
sotvie	underneath

Other Adverbs of Manner are:

bon ben	very well	juste	just, exactly
besclet)		mal	badly
besvelt)	quickly	pardabon	indeed
bielplanc	slowly, softly	pàrie	together
cussì	so	paromp	each (per man)
daurman	quickly, next	par ordin	gradually
denandaur	backwards	planc	softly
dibant	in vain	planchin	very softly
incorint	at the double	pulit	well

Adverbs compounded with a and di:

a dadis	intermittently
a colpo	suddenly
a cessecûl	backwards
a fuart	out loud
a giat	on all fours
a indopli	doubly
a ledros	back to front
a messede	together
a mismas	confusedly
a nivel	horizontally
a plomp	vertically
a sclip	in drops

di buride	in haste
di clap	astounded
di pueste	on purpose
di sbighez	aslant
di scuindon	secretly
(di) sotcoz	stealthily

14   2. Place

abas	below	dulinvie	everywhere
aduès	on	fur	outside
ator (intor)	around	incuintri	to meet
cà	here	indaûr	back(wards)
culi	there	insomp	at the top
cavie	here	jenfri	in the middle
chenti	there	jú	down
dacîs	nearby	lenti (-ci)	there (yonder)
dapît	at the foot	pardut	everywhere
daprûf	nearby	parentro	inside
daûr	behind	parmis	nearby
denant	before	parsore	
dentri	inside	sore	above
devant	in front	sorelûc	
disore	over	parsott	underneath
dongie	nearby	sú	up
dulintôr	roundabout	venti	there (yonder)

Compound Adverbs of Place:

di lunc-su	by that way up
in bande	on one side
in algò	somewhere (-whither)
in niò	nowhere
d'ogni dontri	from everywhere

3. Time

adore[8]	early
alore	then
anciemò (imò)	still
bielzà	already
cumò	now
cumòdenant	just (now)
daspò[9]	after
diduè	nowadays
dispes	often
dopomai)	
dopoinca)	for so long
in che volte)	
in(d)alore)	then
infratanto)	
intant)	meanwhile
ir	yesterday
maimodant)	
modant)	just now
nossere)	
orsere)	yesterday evening
ore presint	at the moment
passandoman	day after tomorrow
passe chi	henceforward
podopo	afterwards
prime	before
qualchi volte	sometimes
simpri	always
soresère	at dusk
uè	today
uedant	not long ago
usgnot	this evening
zà[10]	already
zaromai	now, henceforward

8. Italianism.

9. Obsolescent.

10. Especially in the sense "ago": zà un mes (a month ago); zà timp (some time ago) (= timp indaûr); cf. 'e son (Ital. or sono, but always preceding); nol è trop (not long ago). Cf. also par vinc' agn a lunc (for the last 20 years).

4. Degree

biel-aual)	
adimplen)	fully
almancul	at least
apene) cumpena)	hardly
avonde	enough
masse	too much
nome) dome)	only
poc	little
scuasi(t)	almost
soraplui	in addition
tant (par tant)	(just) so much
tropp	too much, much
un fregul) un ninin)	a little
un mont) une vore[11]) une vorone)	very a lot of

5. Negation

| nance | not even |
| non...fregul | not at all |

6. Interrogative & Relative

cemût?	how?
cetant?	how (much)?
dontri?	whence?
indulà, dulà?	where?
parcé?	why?
quan(t)?	when?

7. Sentence-adverbs

ancie	also
forsi) fuars) salacôr) vadi) impi)	perhaps
in pen) invezit)	instead
insumis	in short
nomo?	is it not?
nujemancul	no less
pardabon	really
pitost	rather
propit	really, just
ven a stai	in other words

---

11. See §11, ii.

8. Comparative

mancul   less

miei   better

plui)
)   more
pi)

pies   worse

9. Adversative

ma)
)   but
parò)

paratri   however

pidimancul   nevertheless

distes   all the same

10. Illative

parchel)
)   therefore
parchest)

duncje)
)   so
siceduncje)

15   Conjunctions

                          a. Co-ordinating

e   and   anzit   rather, indeed
ma   but
ni (ne)   neither
o (ben)   or   sedial... sedial   whether... or
poben   well   (§32)
sedi... che)
tant... che) both... and

                          b. Subordinating

Final		Temporal	
parché)	in order	biel[12] che)	while
a ciò che)	that	intant che)	
		fintremai che	until
Consecutive		quan(t) che	when
		prime che	before
cussì che)	so (in such	dispues che	since
in mût che)	a way) that		
tan... che)		Conditional	
Causal		se	if
		tanche se	as if
parce che)	because		
parvie che)		Concessive	
stant(e) che	since		
sicu	as, since	seben (che))	although
		cun dut che)	

---

12. Also used with the Present Participle; e. g.

S'impensàvial di ce ch'al faseve biel lant vie par
                                          Micotis?
Was he thinking of what he was doing while going
                                    away to M- ?

16   Prepositions

1. Place

a, ad[13]	to, at	
cja[14]	near	
da)		
di)[15]	of, from	
daûr	behind	
daûrvie	along	
denant di	in front of	
dongie	near	
fra (tra)[16]	between, among	
in t (te)	in	
insomp	on top of	
jenfri	among	
oltri	beyond	
parmis	beside	
parsore)		
disore)[17]	over	
sore	on	
sot	under	
su	on	
ret	near	
tor	around	
viars	towards	
visin	near	

2. Manner

compagn di)	
a us di)	like
cuintri	against
cun	with
par[18]	by
senze)	
cence)	without
seont)	according
secont)	to

3. Time

dilunc	throughout
dopo	after
fintremai te	until
prime di	before
vie par)	
intant de)	during

4. Possession

di	of

---

13. Sometimes a di: a di chê ore at that hour.

14. Now limited to a few place-names: Cja Blasut
     (near Biasutti).

15. Da and di are not distinguished.

16. Note tra (che)...tra (che) for "whether...or".

17. Frequently in the sense of "for"-in reference to
     price: Sore ce? (For how much?); sore nuje (for
     nothing, gratis); sore bêz (cash-down).

18. Used with languages ("in"): par talian (in Italian);
     voltat par furlan (translated into Friulan).

Prepositional Phrases

a taco di	beside
de bande di	on the side (part) of
parvie di	because of
traviars di	through, across
là di)) cà di)	at the house of
a ret di	on a level with
ador di	next to
a pet di	compared with
passe di	more than, over
a messet cun	among, together with
fale)) alinfur di)	except

17   <u>A, Di (Da), Par, Te, Cun, Su</u> are compounded
      with the Definite Article as follows:

	Masculine			Feminine	
	Sing.	Plur.	Sing.		Plur.
A	al	ai	'e (ae) or a la	'es (aes) or a lis	
Di (da)	dal	dai	de or da la	des or da lis	
Par	pal	pai	pe or par la	pes or par lis	
Te	tal	tai	te or ta la	tes or ta lis	
Cun	cul	cui	cu la	cu lis	
Su	sul	sui	su la	su lis	

Obs. i. In compound <u>di</u> the <u>a</u> or the <u>e</u> is used

indifferently (v. note 15 above).

ii. The shorter form of the fem. sing. is

preferred before consonants, <u>i</u>, and

semivocalic <u>u</u>: <u>prin de uere</u> (before the

war). The <u>a</u> of the longer form is elided

before vowels. In the plural the shorter

form is more usual.

iii. The preposition <u>te</u> may be preceded by <u>in</u>

in all forms.

iv. Cun takes a <u>t</u> before the Indefinite Article:

<u>cun t-un cian</u> (with a dog).

v. <u>Su</u> before the Indef. Art. often appears as

<u>sun t</u>'; before <u>chê</u> (that) as <u>sun</u>.

vi. <u>aes</u> is sometimes written <u>a'is</u>: <u>impiegât</u>

<u>adét a'is tàssis</u> (clerk concerned with

taxes); or <u>as</u> (<u>as 10</u>, at 10 o'clock).

vii. <u>nes</u> may be found for <u>tes</u> (Ital. <u>nelle</u>).

18   Verbs

                        (i) Regular

Tense	1st Conjugation	2nd Conjugation
Infin.	ciantâ, sing	tasê, be silent
Partic.	ciantant	tasint
Past P.	ciantat	tasut
Present	cianti	tas
Indic.	ciantis	tasis
	ciante	tas
	ciantìn	tasìn
	ciantais	taseis
	ciàntin	tàsin
Imperf.	ciantàvi	tasèvi
Indic.	ciantàvis	tasèvis
	ciantàve	tasève
	ciantàvin	tasèvin
	ciantàvis	tasèvis
	ciantàvin	tasèvin
Preter-	ciantài	taséi
ite[19]	ciantàris	taseris
	ciantà	tasé
	ciantàrin	tasérin
	ciantàris	taséris
	ciantàrin	tasérin
Future	ciantarài	tasarài
	ciantarâs	tasarâs
	ciantarà	tasarà
	ciantarìn	tasarìn
	ciantaréis	tasareis
	ciantaràn	tasaràn

19. A fusion of Latin Perfect (1st sg., 3rd sg., 3rd pl.) and Future Perfect (2nd sg., 1st and 2nd pl.).

3rd Conjugation	4th Conjugation
cioli, take	partî, set out
ciolint	partint
ciolt	partit

ciol	partis
ciolis	partissis
ciol	partis
ciolìn	partìn
ciòlis	partiis
ciòlin	partissin

ciolèvi	partivi
ciolèvis	partivis
ciolève	partive
ciolèvin	partivin
ciolèvis	partivis
ciolèvin	partivin

cioléi	partii
cioléris	partiris
ciolé	parti
ciolérin	partirin
cioléris	partiris
ciolérin	partirin

ciolarài	partissarài
ciolarâs	partissarâs
ciolarà	partissarà
ciolarìn	partissarìn
ciolareis	partissareis
ciolaràn	partissarìn

Tense	1st Conjugation	2nd Conjugation
Condi- tional[20]	ciantarés	tasarés
	ciantaréssis	tasaréssis
	ciantarés	tasarés
	ciantaréssin	tasaréssin
	ciantaréssis	tasaréssis
	ciantaréssin	tasaréssin
Present Subjunct.	cianti	tasi
	ciantis	tasis
	ciantí	tasí
	ciantìn	tasìn
	ciantàis	taseis
	ciàntin	tàsin
Imperf. Subjunct.	ciantàs	tasès
	ciantàssis	tasessis
	ciantàs	tasès
	ciantàssin	tasessin
	ciantàssis	tasessis
	ciantàssin	tasessin
Imper- ative	ciante	tas
	ciantìn	tasìn
	ciantàit	tasèit

Obs. i. Some verbs of the 3rd[21] Conjugation and many
irregular verbs have also a contracted form of
the 2nd Person Sing. Present Indicative; e. g.
ciols (ciolis).

---

20. From Latin Infinitive and the Imperfect
Subjunctive essem.

21. Although this conjugation has lost its characteristic
vowel (e) in the Infinitive, and has in many respects
been assimilated to the 2nd, it is convenient to
classify Friulan verbs in the order of the four
conjugations used in Latin.

3rd Conjugation	4th Conjugation
ciolarés	partissarés
ciolaréssis	partissaréssis
ciolarés	partissarés
ciolaréssin	partissaréssin
ciolaréssis	partissaréssis
ciolaréssin	partissaréssin

cioli	partissi
ciolis	partissis
cioli	partissi
ciolìn	partìn
cioleis	partîs
ciòlin	partissin

cioles	partìs
ciolessis	partissis
cioles	partìs
ciolessin	partissin
ciolessis	partissis
ciolessin	partissin

ciol	partis
ciolìn	partìn
ciolit	partît

ii. The 2nd Person Plural of the Pres. Indic. and the
Imperative of the 3rd Conjugation is sometimes
assimilated to the form of the 2nd;[22] e. g. cioleis
(ciolis).

iii. In the Future and Conditional of the 4th[23] Conjugation forms without the suffix -iss- are also found;
e. g. partirai, partires.

22. The 2nd Conjugation lost many verbs in Vulgar Latin
to other conjugations: e.g. tenere > tignî; vedere >
viodî; implere > jemplâ. Only a few were acquired:
e. g. podê < potere; savê < sapere; cjadê < cadere;
olê < volere.

23. The 4th Conjugation competed with the 1st for new
formations and for acquisitions from other conjugations: e. g. tradî < tradere. (See below §20, Obs. i).

19 (ii) <u>Irregular</u>

Infin.	vê, have	jessi, [27]be	stâ, be	lâ, go
Partic.	vint	jessint[28]	stant	lant
Past P.	vût	stât	stât	lat
Pres.	ài	sòi	stòi	vòi
Ind.	às	ses	stas	vas
	à	é[29]	sta	va
	vin	sin	stin	lin
	veis[24]	seis	stais	lais
	àn[25]	son	stan	van
Imperf.	vevi	jeri	stavi	lavi
	vevis	jeris	stavis	lavis
	veve	jere	stave	lave
Pret.	vei	foi	stéi	léi
	veris	foris	steris	leris
	ve etc.	fo	sté	lé
Fut.	varai	sarai	starai	larai
	etc.	etc.	etc.	etc.
Condit.	vares	sares	stares	lares
	etc.	etc.	etc.	etc.
Pres.	vebi[26]	sèi	stèi	lèi[30]
Subj.	vebis	seis	steis	leis
	vebi	sei	stei	lei
	etc.	etc.	etc.	etc.
Imperf.	ves	fos	stas	las
Subj.	vessis	fossis	stassis	lassis
	ves etc.	fos etc.	stas etc.	las etc.
Imper-	ve	jessi	sta	va
ative	-	-	stin	anin
	veit	jessit	stait	lait[31]

Obs. i. For the Pres. Subj. of <u>Jessi, stâ, dâ, lâ, fâ,</u>
Central Friuli prefers a form with inserted <u>d</u>
and closed <u>e</u>: <u>sédi, stédi, dédi, lédi, fédi.</u>

---

24. -<u>eis</u> is often contracted to -<u>es</u>.
25. <u>jan</u> after pronoun <u>a</u>' (cf. n. 29 below).
26. Udine prefers forms with <u>d</u>: <u>vedi</u>; or <u>t</u>: <u>veti</u> (p. 336).
27. Also <u>sèi</u> (rarer).
28. Or <u>sint</u>.
29. <u>je</u> after pronoun '<u>e</u>.
30. Or <u>vadi</u> etc.
31. Or <u>vait</u>.

dâ, give	olê,[32]wish	podê, be able	fâ, do, make
dant	olint	podint	fasint
dat	olût	podût	fat
dòi	uéi[33]	pues	fâs
das	us	pus	fas
dà	ul	pò[35]	fâs
din	olin	podin	fasin
dais	oléis	podéis[36]	faséis
dan	uelin	puedin	fàsin
davi	olevi	podevi	fasevi
davis	olevis	podevis	fasevis
dave	oleve	podeve	faseve
déi	oléi	podéi	faséi
deris	oleris	poderis	faseris
dé	olé	podé	fasé
darai	uelarai[34]	podarai	fasarai or
etc.	etc.	etc.	farai etc.
dares	uelares	podares	fasares or
etc.	etc.	etc.	fares etc.
dèi	uèli	puèdi	fasi
deis	uelis	puedis	fasis
dei	ueli	puedi	fasi
etc.	etc.	etc.	etc.
das	oles	podes	fases
dassis	olessis	podessis	fasessis
das etc.	oles etc.	podes etc.	fases etc.
dà	-	-	fas
din	olin	-	fasin
dait	oleit	-	faseit

ii. In the Imperf. Ind. and Subj. and 2nd plur. Imperative of stâ, lâ, dâ the root-vowel may be changed to e: stèvi, lèvi; stes, les; deit.

iii. The 2nd Sing. Pres. Ind. of Olê, podê, fâ, lâ has longer forms: uelis, puedis, fasis, vadis.

iv. The past part. stât is used for "last": il mes stât.

---

32. Prefixed v avoids hiatus.
33. u before e is semi-vocalic.
34. Or the Italianism orài, orés etc.
35. Or pues.
36. Or puedis.

20 It will be noted that in the above verbs the only
    really irregular tense is the Present. All Preter-
    ites are weak, all Futures end in -arài, all Pres.
    Subjunctives end in -i. Thus Friulan goes farther
    than other members of the Romance family towards
    the regularization of the verb. A few verbs, how-
    ever, owe their irregularities to phonetic causes:

Vignî (come): gn reverts to n in monosyllables; and
    vign- becomes vegn- when stressed. Hence the
    Present Tense: Vén, végnis, vén, vignìn, vignîs,
    végnin. So also the 2nd Sing. Imperative is Ven.
    The 2nd Sing. Pres. Ind. has also a contracted
    form: Vens. Otherwise the verb follows the 4th
    conjugation without the suffix -iss- (Fut. vignarài)
    and with Past Participle Vignût. Like Vignî goes
    Tignî (hold).

Durmî (sleep): Final m is dropped (Phon. 9) and stressed
    u may become ua. Hence Present Tense: Duâr,
    duàrmis, duâr, durmìn, durmìis, duàrmin.
    (Occasionally ua is found even in an unstressed
    syllable.)

Murî (die): stressed monosyllable becomes û; stressed
    penult becomes ue (before r: ua; cf. xviii). Hence
    Present Tense: Mûr, muéris, mûr, murìn, murîs,
    muérin. Past Participle: muart. The 2nd Pers.
    Sing. Pres. Ind. has also a contracted form: mûrs.

Scugnî[37] (have to): accords with both Vignî and Murî.
    Hence Present Tense: Scuen, scuegnis, scuen,
    scugnìn, scugnis, scuegnin. But scuegn- may be
    replaced everywhere by scugn- (e.g. Pres. Subj.
    scuegni or scugni); and scùgni, scùgne may
    replace scuen in the Pres. Ind. The 2nd Plural
    Pres. Ind. has also variants.

---

37. From Latin exconvenire. Note also: bigne it is
     necessary, one must; covente (personal and imper-
     sonal) is necessary (Ital. occorre, for which
     however ocôr is frequent).

Final sonants of course (Phon. 9) become surd: <u>mof</u> (I move) from <u>mòvi</u>; <u>viôt</u> (I see) from <u>viòdi</u>; <u>'o scrif</u> (I write) from <u>scrìvi</u>; <u>pant</u> (I reveal) from <u>pàndi</u>.

Obs. i. Only a few verbs besides Vignî, Tignî, Durmî, Murî follow the 4th conjugation without the suffix -iss. E. g. <u>Sintî</u> (feel): Pres. Ind. <u>Sint, sintis,</u> <u>sint, sintìn, sintîs, sìntin.</u> Future: <u>Sintarài</u> etc. Pres. Subj. <u>Sinti</u> etc. 2nd Sing. Imperative: <u>Sint.</u> Past Participle: <u>Sintût.</u>

ii. <u>Savê</u> (know) is unique in changing its root in the Pres. Subj.: <u>Sépi, sépis, sépi, savìn, savéis</u> (or <u>sépis</u>), <u>sépin.</u> Its Present Ind. is: <u>sai, sâs, sa,</u> <u>savìn, savéis</u> (or <u>savês</u>), <u>san.</u>

iii. <u>Viòdi</u> (see) and <u>Cròdi</u> (believe) have an alternative contracted form in the 2nd Person Sing. Pres. Ind.: <u>viôz</u> (<u>viódis</u>), <u>crôz</u> (<u>cródis</u>). In <u>Viodi</u> some subdialects modify initial <u>vi</u> to <u>j</u> (<u>jôt</u> for <u>viôt</u>).

iv. <u>Dî</u> (say) goes like <u>fâ,</u> and has an alternative 2nd Sing. Imperative <u>Di</u> for <u>Dis</u> and Future <u>dirai</u> for <u>disarài.</u> Past Participle: <u>Dit</u> and <u>dite.</u>

v. Examples of regularized 3rd conjugation verbs (incl. the Past Participle) are:

Infin.		1st & 3rd Pr.	3rd Pret.	Past part.
còri	(run)	cor	coré	corût
cuèi	(cook;pick)	cue	cué	cuet
difìndi	(defend)	difind	difindé	difindût
lèi	(read)	lei (Imp. lejeve)	leé (lejé)	let
mèti	(put)	met	meté	metût (mitût)
muàrdi	(bite)	muard	muardé	muardût
nàssi	(be born)	nass	nassé	nassût
rèzi	(direct)	rez	rezé	rezût
rìdi	(laugh)	rid	ridé	ridût
scrìvi	(write)	scrîf	scrivé	scrit
scuìndi	(hide)	scuind	scuindé	scuindût
spònzi	(prick)	sponz	sponzé	sponzût
vinzi	(defeat)	vinz	vinzé	vinzût
vìvi	(live)	vîf	vivé	vivût

So too 4th conjugation jèssi (go out): jes jessí jessût.

vi. A strong adjectival participle may survive beside the weak: <u>viart</u> (open), <u>viarzût</u>; <u>stuart</u> (twisted), <u>stuarzût</u>; <u>stre(n)te</u> (tight), <u>strenzût</u>; <u>maludet</u> (cursed, trans.), <u>maladet</u> (accurst).

vii. An Imperative is formed from the adverb <u>Ca</u>: <u>Ca</u>, pl. <u>càit</u> (give here).[38] (See §22, Obs. ii, and §24.)

Obs. Simple basic verbs combined with adverbs are frequent:

ciapâ-su	pick up
poja-jú	deposit
mèti-vie	replace
tirâ-vie	take off
para-vie	chase away
puartâ-ca	bring
butâ-là	get rid of
daj-seont	listen to, obey
vê-indiment	refer to
dî-su	recite

Sometimes they are real idioms: <u>dâ-dongie</u> prepare (a meal), produce (a book, a radio-talk);[39] <u>rivâ adore di</u> manage to.

---

38. Cf. colloquial Latin <u>cĕdo</u>.

39. <u>Lâ d'itori</u> (to lose oneself in the mountains) is said to contain Latin <u>adiutorium</u> (help).

21   Pronouns

| Subject | Pleonastic | Conjunctive | | Suffix | | Disjunctive |
		Acc.	Dat.	Acc.	Dat.	
jo	'o	mi	mi	-mi		me
tu	tu	ti	ti	-ti		te
lui	al	lu	i	lu	-j	lui
jê	'e	la	i	le	-j	jê
nô	'o	nus	nus	-nus		nô
vualtris	'o	us	us	-us		vualtris
		m. f.		m. f.		
lôr	'a	ju lis	ur	ju lis	-ur	lôr

Reflexive	si	si	-si	se

Particle	'ndi	-nt

Adverb	i	-j

Obs. i. The Pleonastic Pronoun is inserted between the
Subject-Pronoun and the verb, and may not be omitted unless the verb is preceded by a Conjunctive
Pronoun or by a Reflexive Pronoun other than the
2nd Singular: e.g. jo mi viot but tu tu ti viodis.

Dunce lui al è un fregul dificilot cu lis feminis.
So he is a little difficult with women.

Intant che jê 'e ciantave.   While she was singing.

Fi, tu tu ses simpri cun me.
Son, you are always with me.

Ur vuei ben a ducis doi.   I am fond of them both.

ii. After the preposition a the disjunctive 1st and
2nd sing. is mi and ti.

iii. Vô is used only in oldfashioned address to
superiors; noaltris may be used for nô.

iv. Unlike Italian, Friulan distinguishes gender in
the Singular of the Polite Form of address, using
lui for You masc. and jê for You fem., often combined respectively with siôr (signore), siore
(signora), paronzin (signorino), paronzine
(signorina). The Plural is lor for both genders,
the dative i:

      Paronzin, si dismentee lui.
      Master, you forget.

      Ariviòdilu (ArrivederLa).
      Au revoir.

Grazie, sior dotor, par Agnul lui al è stat plui
che no un pari e Agnul i voleve tant ben.

Thank you, doctor, you have been more than a
father to Agnul, and he is so fond of you.

Soi vignude ca a disturbâlu, sior dotor...
I have come here to bother you, doctor...

Oh! ise jé, siore comari; che veghi. La spietavi.
Oh, it's you, nurse; come in. I was expecting you.

v. The Reflexive Plural Pronoun is si for all
persons (§31).

vi. The suffix-pronouns may be used with the
adverbs daûr and intôr: daûrsi (dietro di sè);
intôrmi (intorno a me).

vii. In eastern Friuli the suffix-pronoun for the
3rd person singular is -gi.

viii. For emphasis the subject-pronoun may be
placed after the verb:

      'O vuei che tu deventis tu il paron.
      I want you to become the boss.

22   The Conjunctive Pronouns are suffixed to the

      Infinitive, Participle (Gerund), and Imperative,

      as in Italian (used here for illustration).

Obs. i.   The Participle (Gerund) drops its t before the

      suffix, and before -us and -ur inserts j (usually

      after an apostrophe): disin'jus (dicendovi),

      disinjur (dicendo loro). With nus the apostrophe

      always replaces j: disin'nus (dicendoci).

      (See Phonology 1, iii.)

      ii.   The 2nd sg. Imperative inserts i before the

      suffix, and this leads to the ellipse of final -e:

      clame (call), but clamilu (call him); viarzeinus

      (open to us); caimi[40] (hand to me).

      iii.   The 3rd pl. Imperative drops final t before

      the suffix: diseit (say), but diseinus (tell us).

---

40.   See §20, Obs. vii.

Accusative to Infinitive		to Participle	
cialale	(guardarla)	fermanlu	(fermandolo)
brusalu	(bruciarlo)	studianle	(studiandole)
ricevius	(ricevervi)	cialanti	(guardandoti)
		metinsi	(mettendosi)
		vedin'nus	(vedendoci)
faus	(farvi)	tigninjus	(tenendovi)
		portanju	(portandoli)

So also:

puartant	(portarne)
dint	(dirne)
vent	(averne)
fant	(farne)

(-nt with participle is rare)

pensaj	(pensarci)

to Imperative

clamilu	(chiamolo)
disinlu	(diciamolo)
cialailis	(guardatele)
capissimi	(capiscimi)
puartint	(portane)

E. g.

Chei no olerin savent di pajaju.
(Quelli non vollero saperne di pagarli.)

Se tu voressis vent une.
(Se tu volessi averne una.)

Lassainus jentra
(Lasciaci entrare)

Che no si rivoltin a sbranaus.
(Che non si rivoltino a sbranarvi.)

23 Dative to Infinitive   to Participle

dîmi (dirmi)   disinmi
dîti   disinti
dîi (dîj)   disintij
dînus   disin'nus
dîus   disinjus
dîur   disinjur

lâi daûr (andarle   langi daûr
         dietro)   (andandole dietro)

to Imperative

sing.   plur.

disimi (dimmi)   diséimi
disij   (digli, -le) diséj
disinus (dicci)   diséinus
disiur (di loro)   diséiur

E. g.   jo no sai ce dâi di mangiâ.
             (Non so cosa dargli da mangiare)

             al clame i amis par dîur.
             (Chiama gli amici per dir loro)

24   Conjunctive Pronouns combined

Preceding verb

Italian	lo	la	li	le	ne
me	m'al	m'e	m'ai	m'es	mi'nd m'an
te	t'al	t'e	t'ai	t'es	ti'nd t'an t'in
gli le	j'al	j'e	j'ai	j'es	j'an
ce	nus al	nus'e	nus ai	nus es	nus an
ve	us al	us'e	us ai	us es	us an
(loro)	ur al	ur'e	ur ai	ur es	ur an
se	si lu	si la	si ju	si lis	si'nd s'an s'in

Suffixed

Italian	-melo	-mela	-meli	-mele	-mene, etc.
me	-mal	-me	-mai	-mes	-mint
te	-tal	-te	-tai	-tes	-tint
gli le	-ial	-je	-ai	-es	-int
ce	-nusal	-nuse	-nusai	-nuses	-nusint
ve	-usal	-use	-usai	-uses	-usint
(loro)	-ural	-ure	-urai	-ures	-urint
se	-sal	-se	-sai	-ses	-sint

E. g.   Pieri j'al notave
         Peter noted it for him (glielo)

         Biel che ur al consegnavi
         While I handed it to them (lo... loro)

         Si'n lasse un
         One of them is left (Se ne)

         I uèi tan ben, e ance lui mi'nd ûl tant
         I am so fond of him, and he too is just
                                  as fond of me (me ne)

         A' vevin di pajâmal
         They were to pay me for it (-melo)

         Jò vuei mètimes
         I want to wear them (-mele)

Suffixed to Infinitive		Suffixed to Imperative	
		clamaimint	(chiamamene)
dîal	(dirglielo)	puartime	(portamela)
dînusal	(dircelo)	contial	(raccontaglielo)
dîuse	(dirvela)	dìmal or disimal	(dimmelo)
dîural	(dirlo loro)	diséial	(diteglielo)
dîint	(dirgliene)	faséimal	(fatemelo)
dîurint	(dirne loro)	domandàial	(domandateglielo)
dâmai	(darmeli)	tental	(tientelo)
dâialis	(dargliele)	càmal	(§20 obs. vii)

Obs. i.   Italianisms are found such as: mi lu,
                                          -milis etc.

      ii. The s in -sint is usually doubled: dîssint
                                               (dirsene).

     iii. Impersonal si ("one") (as in Spanish, but not in
           Italian) precedes the conjunctive Object-pronoun
           and has a singular verb always:

che robe là si la sune a une fantate   (one sings it)
si lu sintiva ta la sô vôs   (one heard it)
ce seradis... si lis pajave 30 centesins (one paid for them)
chei no son bêz che si ju tire-fûr   (one produces them)

Equally often the Object-pronoun is suffixed to the verb:

si sintivile	(one heard her)
si sintilis a sbàti	(one hears them)
la reputazion si difindile	(one defends it, the reputation)
si pò viòdilu	(one can see it)

It is always so suffixed when the verb after si "one" is reflexive (when Italian uses ci si):

si ciàtasi a jessi	(one finds oneself)
si consolisi a sintî	(one consoles oneself)
s'inacuarzisi	(one perceives)
s'inacuarzeressisi	(one would perceive)
si presentavisi	(one presented oneself)

iv. Conjunctive pronouns are rarely suffixed to the past participle, apart from the 3rd person sing. (with infixed i):

puartadij	brought to him	(portatogli)
ditial	it having been said to him	(dettoglielo)
contadiural	it having been told to them	(raccontatolo loro)

25   Demonstrative Pronouns and Adjectives

Singular			Plural		
masc.	fem.		masc.	fem.	
chest	cheste	this	chesc'	chestis	these
chel	chê	that	chei	ches	those

Obs. i. Chel etc. are often combined with altri etc., especially pronominally (§26):

chealtre   that one (fem.)

chealtris (m.)   those;   fem. chesaltris.

ii.   As a pronoun <u>stes</u> ("same") must be combined
with <u>chel</u>:

the same girl   chê fantate stesse   or   la stesse fantate
the same   chel istes

26   Indefinite and Negative Pronouns

     <u>Pronominal</u>   Adjectival

tal, tai   (such)
qualchidun(e) (someone)   qualchi   (some)
nissun   (no-one)   nissun   (no-)
nuje   (nothing)   tant, tante   (so much)
alc   (something)[41]   tanc', tantis   (so many)
alcaltri   (something else)
ogni(d)un   (everyone)   ogni   (every)
dut   (all)   dut   dute   )
                               duc' dutis)   (all)
ducidoi, m. (both)   duc' quanc')
chel altri, che altre (other) altri, altre (other)
chei altris, ches altris   altris, altris[42]
une vore (molti) (v. § 11)
                  (many)
poc (poco), pôs (pochi) (few)

Pronoun and adjective: trops (tross), tropis   (too) many
                        putrops, putropis   several

     Scriz par venit cun putropis peraulis furlanis

Obs. Pronominal "each" is rendered by the adverb
      <u>paromp</u> ("per man"):

      'e àn vut un 'denaro' paromp.

---

41. Also adverbially for "somewhat" (Ital. alquanto).

42. For the difference in pronunciation see Phonology
     1 (iv).

27   Possessive Pronouns

        Singular   Plural

Masc.   Fem.   Masc.   Fem.

il miò   la me   i miei   lis mes
(or gno)
il tò   la to   i tiei   lis tos

il sò   la so   i siei   lis sôs

il nestri   la nestre   i nestris   lis nestris

il vuestri   la vuestre   i vuestris   lis vuestris

il lor   la lor   i lor   lis lor

Obs. i. For the dropping of the article see Syntax (§38, 2).

       ii. The same forms are used for the Possessive
           Adjectives.

       iii. In the earlier language so may be found for
            lor; soi is an Italianism for siei.

28   Interrogative Pronouns

Cui?   (Who?)   Trop, trope?   (How much?)
Ce?   (What?)   Tros, tropis?   (How many?)
Qual, quai? (What? Which?) Cetant, cetante? (How much?)
                           Cetanc', cetantis (How many?)

   Tros chilos pesaràl?   How many kilos will it weigh?

   Trop mi daiso?   How much do you give me?

   Al à fat capî quâi che jerin i soi progjés.
   He made it clear what his plans were.

Obs. Cetant renders how before an adjective:

   A' podaran viodî cetant pizzul ch'al è il mont.
   They will be able to see how small the world is.

Relative Pronouns

Che   (who, which)   (See Syntax, §50)

Cui che   (He who)

Obs. i. An old form cu survives in a few fossilised
         phrases:

         chest an cu ven   (next year)
         a la miei cu sei   (at best)

     ii. The form cual with the Def. Art. is used less
         often than the Italian il quale.

29   Remaining forms of the Verb

                      The Perfect Tenses

Perfect   Pluperfect

'o ai ciantât   I have sung   'o vevi ciantât   I had sung
tu as ciantât   etc.
al a ciantât
'o vin ciantât   Future Perfect
'o veis ciantât
a jan ciantât   'o varai ciantât   I shall have
                                      etc.   sung

Dopo vêju ben cialâz in muse, ur à respuindût.
After having looked them full in the face, he replied
                                   to them.

Lis feminis lis vin lassadis a ciase.
We have left the women at home.

Obs. i. Friulan, in popular speech, uses a reinforced
         form of the Perfect form with the Perfect in-
         stead of the Present of Ve, thus having two past
         participles. The difference of meaning, if any,
         is that the vut suggests that an opportunity for
         performing the action of the verb was taken.
         E. g.

         'O ai vût ciantât   I have sung

         un ch'al veve vût lavorât di muridôr
         one who had worked as a mason

ii. The Past Participle usually agrees with
a following plural or feminine noun:

qualchidun al à copâs i servidors
someone has killed the servants

vevin mitudis jù lis bisacis
they had put down the knapsacks

il sassine al è crepât e lassade la sostanze a la massarie.
the murderer has died and left the property to the house-
keeper.

iii. Verbs of Rest and Motion take <u>Jessi</u>:

lor 'e son lâs   they have gone

30   The Passive Voice

Except in the Preterite and in compound tenses, Friulan
prefers to form the Passive with <u>Vignî</u> rather than <u>Jessi</u>:

E.g.   La some 'e jere stade mitude
The load had been put

16 milions 'a jerin stâz mitûz
16 million had been put

Bateit e us vignarà viart...Al sarà viart
a cui c'al bàt.
Knock and it shall be open to you...It shall
be open to him who knocks.

Obs. For the idiomatic use of the Past Participle after
<u>Olê</u> see §46.

31 <u>The Reflexive Verb</u>

Infinitive: cialâsi to look at oneself (each other)

Participle: cialansi looking at oneself

Present	Perfect
jo mi ciali	mi soi cialât
tu tu ti cialis	tu ti sês cialât
lui si ciale	si è cialât
nô si cialìn	si sin cialâz
vualtris si cialàis	si seis cialâz
lor si cialin	si son cialâz

Imperative: cialiti cialinsi cialàisi

Obs. i. The Pleonastic is usually omitted before the
Reflexive Pronoun, except in 2nd pers. sg.

Pauli si è distacât di lor   Paul left them

Si sin sentâz e 'o vin fevelât es feminis
che si erin dadis dongje
We sat down and talked to the women
who had assembled

But: tu ti butaràs partiere
you will throw yourself down

ii. Just as the Pleon. Pron. is sometimes omitted
(esp. in poetry), so it may be found even before
the Reflexive:

'a si son fâz batiâ   they had themselves baptized

dulà ch'o sin fermâz   where we stayed

iii. s may be written <u>ss</u> in the Infinitive and 2nd
pers. plur. Imperative (Phon. 1.iv):

Cui podaràl mai salvassi?
Who will ever be able to save himself?

Par l'amor di Dio, spiegàissi
For God's sake, explain yourself

iv. The Perfect is sometimes formed with <u>vê</u>
(cf. Spanish):

Jê si à mitût a vaî   she began to cry

32   The Interrogative Form

The Pleonastic Pronoun is suffixed to the verb to form
the Interrogative:

Present	Imperfect	Preterite
ciantio?	ciantavio?	-
ciantistu?	ciantavistu?	ciantaristu?
ciantial?	ciantavial?	-
ciantìno?	ciantavino?	ciantàrino?
ciantaiso?	ciantaviso?	ciantariso?
ciàntino?	ciantavino?	ciantàrino?

Future	Conditional
ciantarajo?	ciantaressio?
ciantarastu?	ciantaressistu?
ciantarajal?	ciantaressial?
ciantarino?	ciantaressino?
ciantareiso?	ciantaressiso?
ciantaràno?	ciantaressino?

Obs. i.   In the 1st and 3rd persons sing. an i is inserted
           before the suffix, whereby the preceding letter
           is affected as follows:

           (a) The ending -e is dropped: cialial? (is he
           looking?); savevial? (did he know?)

           (b) A long vowel is shortened: al dîs but disial?

           (c) Sonants and stem-consonants return:
           'o viot but viodio? (do I see?); al duâr but
           duarmial?; 'o pues but puedio?

           (d) S following a short vowel remains surd
           and is therefore doubled: al pas but
           passial?

           (e) The ending -n becomes -gn: 'o ven (I come)
           but vegnio?

ii. Final a may or may not be followed by j: sal or
     sajal (does he know?); àl or àjal (has he?);
     vignaral or vignarajal (will he come?). So final
     i of 1st sing. pres. may be dropped or changed
     to j: sao or sajo (do I know?); ao or ajo (have I?).

iii.   3rd sing. fem. suffix is e: ciantie (is she singing?);
      ciantaressie (would she sing?); dae or daje (is she
      giving?).

iv. There is no interrogative form for 1st and 3rd
     person sing. Pret. of 1st Conjug., and no interrog-
     ative Preterite at all in other Conjug., except jessi
     and vignî, which lack only 1st person: forial (was
     he?); vignirial (did he come?).

v. The Present Interrogative of Jessi is: Sojo? sestu?
    èsal? (Udine: îsal?) sino? sêso? sono?

Examples:

Cemût stastu?	How are you?
Cemût staial?	How are you, sir?
Cemût stae?	How are you, madam?
No erie ore?	Was it not time?
Indulà vastu?	Where are you going?
Vadial ben?	Is it all right?
Ce îsal?	What's the matter?
Sêso vignûz?	Have you come?
Cui mai puedial mangiâle?	Who on earth can eat it?
Ce diaul jerial lenti?	Who the devil was there?

33   The Subjunctive of Wish

Added to the Imperfect Subjunctive Active, or to the
Present Subjunctive of the verb Jessî, the Pleonastic
Pronoun creates an Optative:

Imperfect   Present

ciantassio!   seijo
ciantassistu!   sestu
ciantassial!   seijal (seal)
ciantassino!   seino
ciantassiso!   seiso
ciantassino!   seino

So savessio, partissio, ciolessio, fossio,
   vessio, puessio etc.

E. g.

            Seal benedet il vin di Rosazzis!
            Blest be the wine of Rosazzis!

34   The Negative Form

When the verb is negative, the Pleonastic Pronoun is
dropped except in the 2nd Person Sing., when it follows
the negative, and in the 3rd Person Masc. Sing., when it
is joined to it:

(jo) no sài   In the Interrogative Form the
(tu) no tu sâs   Pleonastic Pronoun remains:
(lui) nol sa
(je) no sa   no puedio?
(no) no savin   no mi crodistu?
(vualtris) no saveis   no duarmial?
(lor) no san   no podessino!

E. g.

      no' nd' ai   (I haven't any)
      no us cognòs!   (I do not know you!)
      no t'in ciatis un altre (You won't find another)
      tu no tu mi às judât   (You did not help me)
      e tu, se no tu partissis vie di cà.
      orestu neâmi che no tu sês stât a ciatâle?
      volê ben nol è peciat. (Loving is not a sin)

Obs. Negative Commands are expressed by a periphrasis
with the Imperative of Sta (with or without a following a):

no stâ jessi (do not be)   no stâ vê pore (do not be afraid)

no stâ spietami   (do not wait for me)

no stin disgustâlu   (let us not disgust him)

no stait a domandâmal   (don't ask me it)

35   There is, there are

Friulan omits the conjunctive adverb for "there":

    al è   (there is)

    nol è   (there is not)

    a 'nd'è   (there is some)

    no 'nd'è   (there is not any)

    Ind' èrial?   (Was there any?)

    no 'nd' ere stade   (there had not been any)

A plural subject may either be added with the preposition
di (a'nd'è ogni moment di gnûs); or put first for emphasis, leaving the verb singular:

    Laris and'è avonde su la tiare.
    There are enough thieves on the earth.

36   Interjections

Ariviòdisi	Arrivederci
Bondì	Good-day
Bon pro	Your health
Buine gnot	Good night
Buine sere	Good evening
Cje	Fancy
Cungiò	Adieu, Farewell
Diambar	The devil
Diluvueli	Would it were
Divuardi	Heaven forbid
Di'perdoni	The late....
Magaricussinò	More's the pity
Malafenò	In truth
Malafessì	On my honour
Mandi	Hallo; Good-bye
Ogniben	Your health
Osti	Good heavens
Po folc	But of course
Tute	Don't touch
'urcje	Come, come

Oaths:

(che il) folc ti trai.*

madocje

orcoboe

ostizie

ostrighe

sacrabolt

Obs. i. Cenonè is used in the sense of ecco (here is, suddenly): see Poem No. 14, p. 190.

ii. Mandi, possibly from m'arcomandi (Ital. mi raccomando) (Ce fas-tu?, Dec. 1944) is, like Ital. Ciao! and Spanish ¡Adios! both a greeting and a farewell. (See Poems Nos. 21 and 43.)

"Bondì, Berto, ce fàtu di biel?" j dîs Pieri.
"Oh mandi Pieri... Dulà vàtu?" j rispuint chel altri.

e lu salude: "Mandi, alore cemût vae?"

iii. requie, interjected after a noun, is equivalent to "the late":

la veve lassade to pari, requie,...

---

* Lit. "May lightning strike you!" and used also as a greeting! (Cf. German "Hals- und Beinbruch!".)

37   Numerals

                          1. Cardinal

un, une	vincjeun, -une	cent e nonantenuf
doi, dos	vincjedoi, -dos	dusinte
tre	vincjetre	tresinte
cuatri	vincjequatri	quatricent
cinc	vincjecinc	cincent
sis	etc.	sis-cent
siet	trente	sietcent
vot	quarante (corante)	votcent
nuv	cinquante	nufcent
dis	sessante	mil
undis	setante	mil e un
dodis	otante	mil e doi (dos)
tredis	nonante	etc.
cutuardis	cent	doi (dos) mil
quindis	cent e un	tre mil
sedis	cent e doi (dos)	vinc' mil
diseseit	cent e dis	cent mil
disevot	cent e vinc'	un milion
disenuf	cent e trente	un miliart
vinc'	cent e trenteun	doi miliarz

                          2. Ordinals

Only the first eight are authentically Friulan:

                  prin, prime; secont, seconde;
                  tiarz, tiarze; quart, quarte;
                  quint, quinte; sest, seste;
                  setim, setime; otaf, otave.

Obs. i. gjesime (diesime) (la decima, tithe)
          Setuagjesime (Settuagesima)

      ii. The others will, however, be met:
           e. g. gjesimenone 19th.

Months

Zenâr	Lui
Fevrâr	Avost
Màrz	Setembar
Avrîl	Otubar
Maj	Novembar
Iugn	Dicembar

Days of the week

domènie

lunis

martars *

miarcui (miarcus)

jòibe

vinars *

sàbide

Obs. miarcus stât   last Wednesday
(v. § 19, Obs. iv).

---

* An example of derivation from the genitive singular
(Martis and Veneris dies).

SYNTAX

38   1. The Simple Sentence

                        a. The Definite Article

Usage differs from Italian in a few respects:

1. It is omitted in a few stock phrases:

anìn a vore (andiamo al lavoro; let us go to work)

al è lât a braide (è andato al' campo; he's gone to the field)

al cricave dì (spuntava il giorno; day was dawning)

al va a mont soreli (tramonta il sole; the sun is setting)

sul lâ a mont soreli (sul tramontar del sole; at sunset)[43]

al sune gjespui (suonano i Vesperi; Vespers are sounding)

2. It is omitted in the plural of Possessive Adjectives
    with near relations:

    Sôs surs Giulie e Mignete la secondavin, siei fradis
    la ubidivin.

3. On the contrary it may be retained in the vocative
    of the Possessive Adjective Singular:

        Sint po', la me frute.

4. It is omitted before the Cognomina of men:

        Toni Parut, but Tunine la Parute.

---

43. For this use of a noun as subject to an Infinitive
     cf. Spanish.

39   b. The Indefinite Article

1. Un, invariable, is used before a numeral and a noun
    to mean "about" ("some"):

> Jacun al ere un sis ains che nol leve...
> It was some six years since J. had gone...

> un siet feminis   about seven women

2. une vore "many" takes a plural verb:

> une vore 'e son clamâz, ma pôs i pressielz
> many are called, but few chosen

40   c. The Pleonastic Pronoun

In the 3rd person this is used with a Subject-noun whether
the verb precedes or follows:

> Il Signor al nus judarà
> The Lord will help us

> Se al torni Atile
> If Attila returns

> Al jere cun lôr ance Toni
> Tony was with them too

> E' no balin plui lis striis
> The witches no longer dance

41   d. The Conjunctive Pronoun

1. More often than in Italian (cf. Spanish) the Conjunctive Pronoun is repeated after or introduces the
   noun-object:

   A mi mi à parut   It seemed to <u>me</u>

   Ce ch'al Signor i plas   What pleases the Lord

       Il puint che ai ciaradôrs di Ciargne ur faseve vignî
   i sudors frez nome a sintîlu a nominâ...
       The spot which made the Carnic carters break into
   a cold sweat merely at the sound of its name...

2. The ethic dative <u>ti</u> is frequent in narrative:

       Nol veve ancimò dite l'ultime peraule che ti entre
   une sflamiade...
       He had not yet said the last word, when (lo and
   behold) a flame enters...

       Ogni dí ti coreve a ciatâ il plevan
       Every day there he is running to find the vicar

       In chel 'e rive la massàrie, 'i slungie biel passant
   un comedon tes cuestis, e te lu distire lunc e distes
   sul concolat
       At that moment the servant arrives, gives him an
   elbow in the ribs in passing, and there he is flat on
   his back on the paving-stones.

42   e. The Infinitive

1. Is used after verbs of perception with a:

La vìn cialade a jevâsi   We watched her getting up
sintinmi a ciacarâ   hearing me talk
si viôt înt a cirî   people are seen seeking

Obs. i. So even in the passive:

'O soi stufe di sintîmi a maltratâ
I am tired of hearing myself slandered

ii. So ciatâsi a jessi meaning little more than
    "be":

si vìn ciatât a jessi   We found ourselves
si ciatave a sèi un giudiz   There was a judge

43

2. Is used with tal instead of a Gerundial Participle:[44]

Candide 'e ciantave in cusine tal messedâ i ris te padiele.
Candida was singing in the kitchen while stirring the rice
                                                    in the pan.

Tal lâ vie, un di chei doi viandanz al disé...
In going away, one of those two travellers said...

Tal strenzi al cur il so divin Bambin, lu preà...
In clasping her divine child to her heart, she begged
                                                     him...

...ur disé, tal giavâ fur la pinze.
...he said to them, taking out the cake.

Tal metilu vie, 'e bruntulavin.
While putting it away, they were grumbling.

---

44. Not that the Participle is not often found in the same
    sense: Al va pes ostariis, ciantant strofetis. (He
    goes round the taverns, singing songs). Al restà di
    clap viodint che erin sparis i soi bragons. (He was
    dumbfounded on seeing that his trousers had disap-
    peared).

44

3. When the Infinitive depends on the Preposition <u>a</u> after
another infinitive of a verb of rest or motion, the
conjunctive pronoun is attached to the first infinitive:

Al continuave a lâlis a ciatâ
He continued to call on them

Vignîmes a tacâ
To come and attach them to me

'O vevi propri timp di stâlis a contâ
I just had time to recount them

Si discôr di tornâju a mandâ
One speaks of sending them again

45

4. Is used after <u>Vê di</u> (da) in the sense of "must",
"have to":

Vìn di jessi boins
We must be good

Tu as di savê
You must know

La valise che à di lâ vie pe Germanie
The suitcase which has to go off to Germany

46   The Past Participle

(i) Is used with the 3rd person sing. and pl. of all tenses
     of Olê to express need, necessity:

                    vuelin metûz in muel
                    they need to be put to soak

Obs. i. The use is mostly impersonal:

                    Al ûl savût
                    One must know

                    Al ores cirût
                    One should seek

    ii. So too with mertâ (to deserve):

                    L'unic timp ch'al merte vivût
                    The only time worth living

        Cualchi volte a' mertin amâz, ma tantis voltis
                                a' mertin dismenteâz.
        Sometimes they deserve to be loved, but....

(ii) Is frequently made to agree with a following object-
     noun in gender and number:

            'e à presentade e votade la lec̆
            has presented and voted the law

2. The Compound Sentence

47   a. Indirect Question

Pronouns and Adverbs are often followed by an otiose che:

> Cumò us conti cemût che jè lade.
> Now I will tell you how it went off.

> Sastu cui che jè?   Do you know who he is?

> Ciale cetante înt che tu as fate fermâ.
> Look how many people you have caused to stop.

48   b. Indirect Command

Negative no precedes pleonastic tu when subject-tu is dropped:

Al à dit Checo che no tu vadis plui dongie di Liliane

49   c. Adverb Clauses

Final: Gigio po i veve fin metut tes orelis une rose di
       ciarte, par c'al pares plui bon ancemò.
       ("so that it might appear")

   Obs. The negative adverb comes between Par and che:

   Pieri j'al notave sul libri par no ch' al si dismenteas.
   Peter used to note it down so that he might not forget.

Consecutive:

Il buere sofle in mût che par quasi che gnaulin i giaz.
The storm blows in such a way that cats seem to be howling.

Causal:

Al voleve fermâsi anciemò, parcè che za 'e lusive la lune.
He wanted to stop even yet, because the moon was already
                                                    shining.

E par vie che ance lui al veve un ciamp.
And because he too had a field.

'E jè la tasse dal celibato parceche no tu sês sposât.
It is the bachelor-tax because you are unmarried.

Temporal:

Quan che la à ciatade, se la met su lis spalis.
When he has found it, he puts it on his shoulders.

Une domenie di sere, biel ch'e tornave di funzion, ...
One Sunday evening, while she was returning from
                                                   church, ...

Fintremai che no sune une campane, lis animis dai muars
                                                   'e zirin.
Until a bell sounds, the souls of the dead wander.

Conditional:

Se no tu lu sâs, t'insegni jo.
If you do not know it, I will teach you.

Ce saressial stât di me, se no ves podût sbrocâmi?
What would have become of me, if I had not been able to
                                                   let myself go?

Se fos pronte la ciase, chestis miseriis no si
                                                   viodaressin.
If the house were ready, these miseries would not be
                                                   seen.

Concessive:

Mi à plasût la to poesie, seben che l'argomento al sedi
                                                   grintos.
I liked your poem, though the subject is bad-tempered.

Obs.   The Indicative may be found when the reference is
       to a fact (cf. Spanish):
'e vignivin contentis seben che savevin di ciatâ
They came contentedly though they knew they would find

Comparative:

Cetanc' di lôr, e cetantis voltis, viazant bessoi,
   no si erino avicinâz cul cur in man al pas
   terribil, tanche se vessin vût di lâ a la muart
       ("as if they had had to go to their deaths")

50   d. Relative Clauses

1. The Pleonastic Pronoun follows the Relative Subject:

San Pieri, che al jere daûr,..   St. Peter, who was behind,..
chel ch'al dit il profete   what the prophet says
Barbe, tu che tu sês tant bon   Uncle, you who are so kind

So negative: il predi, che nol veve rivât adore,....
              the priest, who had not arrived in time,...

2. Instead of the dative, che may be used followed by
    the dative conjunctive pronoun:

        Chel che i è stât condonât di plui
        He to whom most has been forgiven

Lis quatri veciutis che ur è tociât il preziôs indument
The four old women to whom the precious garment fell

Obs. After a Preposition the forms of qual are used:

        Ju quindis Misteris di chest Rosari, in tai quai
        si conten la vite di nestri Signor   ("in which")

        (This form with in is seen less often because it may
        be replaced by dulà che ("where") (cf. French).

3. "What" (that which) is ce che:

        Rose, tu no tu sâs ce che 'o provi par te.
        Rose, you do not know what I feel for you.

4. Ce (what) is used after vê and the Infin. (Ital. da):

        No vin nuje ce dai   We have nothing to give him
        No à nuje ce piàrdi   He has nothing to lose

ANTHOLOGY

BIOGRAPHICAL NOTES ON THE POETS*

(The numbers refer to the poems)

LUIGI AMALTEO (fl. 1594), a notary at San Daniele, has

his name kept alive by a single sonnet.

Satire cuintri Filipo II   6

FRANCESCA BÀRNABA (1877-1960) discovered, or

revealed, her poetic gift late in life. Her one slim

volume, Flors di tale (1954), is however completely

modern in its verse-forms and only the disconsolate

nostalgia of its themes indicates the survivor from

an earlier age.

Crepecûr   39

ANTONIO BAUZÒN (1879-1952), cartoonist by profes-

sion, carried his gift of humorous description over

into his poetry.

LUIGI BERTOSSIO (b. 1908), artisan, realized his

poetic potential when he abandoned traditional forms

and gave free rein to his predominantly wistful thoughts.

---

* It has unfortunately not been possible to illustrate the
work of every author.

GIROLAMO BIANCONE (ca. 1515-ca. 1580), a lawyer,

was called by a contemporary the best Friulan poet

of the sixteenth century, so that one would have

expected more to be known about him, and more of

his work to have survived than two sonnets and

twenty-four stanzas of ottava rima, the first a des-

cription of a mild winter, the second a powerful

expression of the mood induced by the Counter-

Reform.

Povar Blancoon, ad i chest pas vignuut   2

PIERO BONINI (1844-1905), a lawyer turned man of

letters (he occupied the Chair of Italian Literature

in the Royal Institute of Technology in Udine),

garibaldine volunteer in the Trentino and Latium,

friend and translator of Carducci, "was determined

to elevate Friulan to the rank of language" (D'Aronco).

To the critics who consequently accused his works of

being "too studied" and "too Italian" he might have

replied that he was only following in the footsteps of

Ermes di Colloredo.

CESARE BORTOTTO (b. 1923), graduate in literature

and on the railway-staff of Udine, switched from

Pasolini's school to a more domesticated type
of poetry.

ALAN BRUSINI (b. 1923), artisan, showed in his first
published volume (Mans vueidis, 1957), that he is
one of nature's poets.

Mans vueidis   51

VITTORIO CADELL (1884-1917), artist, volunteered
for the air-force and was shot down on the Salonica
front in April 1917. In his poetry love for woman
alternates with or is fused with love for the countryside, both themes being treated with robust realism.

BERNARDINO CANCIANINO (1690-1770), priest turned
soldier, wrote his poems after retirement to the
peace of the countryside.

NOVELLA AURORA CANTARUTTI (b. 1920), a teacher

of Ital. Lit., is accorded a high place among those

who have adapted Friulan verse to modern taste. At

a ceremony to launch her Poesiis in 1952 the Italian

poet, Eugenio Montale, was present. Simple and

free of ornament to the point of dryness, her lan-

guage is perfectly in tune with her chosen theme of

communion with a pitiless Nature.

Planchinìn   46

AURELIO CANTONI (b. 1923), a clerk and in 1953

Editor of Patrie dal Friûl, finds inspiration, but

little comfort, in scenes of the countryside and of

city-life. In his prose-works this attitude takes the

form of an uncompromising realism (v. p. 338/9).

Ploe   48

GASPARE CARABELLO (fl. 1620), notary, was one of

the young brigade of poets grouped round Paolo

Fistulario.

Laudant iu poettis furlans   7

ERCOLE CARLETTI (1877-1946), accountant and

teacher of French, studied Friulan literature

alongside others, and then, like Bonini, eschewed

everything that smacked of "dialect" as opposed to

literary language. His basic theme is the pain of

knowing what might have been, for which D'Aronco

compares him to Gozzano and Carducci in certain

moods. His diction at its best achieves a perfect

harmony of feeling and language. With Corgnali

(q. v.) he revised Pironi's Vocabolario friulano and

for 25 years was active in the Società filologica

friulana.

CELSO CESCUTTI (Argeo) (1877-1966), land-surveyor,

used poetry (and music, to which he set some of his

verses) for the expression of his feeling for the mys-

tery of things. Pasolini rated him one of Friuli's

greatest poets. His best poem ensures that Friulan

shall not be without a specimen of "sepulchral" verse.

Gnot vagant   30

BINDO CHIURLO (1886-1943), professor of Ital. Lit.

in various Institutes in Italy and Czechoslovakia,

reserved for Friulan the first place in his affections.

Co-founder of the S. F. F. and Editor of its Revista

from 1920 to 1922, he was the first to produce a
comprehensive anthology of Friulan literature (1927),
which he had himself enriched with his own Versi
friulani in 1921. D'Aronco, his successor as critic
and anthologist, saw in him "the man who made
literary Friuli aware of itself".

'O ciantarài   32

Al Taiament   33

Vilotis   34

GIORGIO COMINI (1722-1812), most of whose poems
have been lost, is memorable for a Contrasto, in
which Mary Magdalene describes the entry of a
novice into a nunnery.

La monacaziòn   14

PIERI CORVAT (Pietro Michelini) (1863-1933), schoolmaster and later clerk, is particularly associated
with a long poem (reduced by himself from 400 to 80
sonnets), El Cuarantevot, dealing with events of the
year 1848; but only a few of its episodes achieve the
same standard of freshness and inspiration as his
occasional pieces.

Brindisi   18

Robis bielis, robis brutis   19

ENOS COSTANTINI (b. 1950) has just published as his first

book, Sgrisui ("Shudders"), the poems that won him the

prize awarded by the S.F.F. for the best Friulan verse

of 1973. The jury noted that his sub-Carnic speech suited

the "social inspiration" of a work clearly influenced by

foreign models (such as Bob Dylan) but original in tone.

ENRICA CRAGNOLINI (1904-1973) surveys Nature with the

calm gaze of the philosopher which she is by education; and

it is presumably this which is responsible for that "certain

nordic hardness" which D'Aronco sees in most of her work.

ANTONIO DE LUISA (b. 1906), schoolmaster, writes in

simple style and sincere affection of the persons and

things that make up his world.

GIOVANNI BATTISTA DONATO (1536-ca.1605), ille-

gitimate son of a Venetian patrician, combined a

succession of humble trades with a considerable

literary output, on the value of which Chiurlo and

D'Aronco differ. Chiurlo diagnoses poverty of

imagination, while D'Aronco finds him the least

bad of sixteenth century Friulan poets and selects

five poems as "of undoubted value".

COUNT ERMES DI COLLOREDO (1622-1692), page at

the Court of Tuscany, officer on active service in

the Thirty Years' War, captain in the Venetian army

in Dalmatia, courtier of Leopold I at Vienna, finally

settled down to spend the last 30 years of his life in

his villa at Gorizzo (near Codròipo). Here no doubt

most of his poetry was written. Posthumously pub-

lished, it showed at once that "Friulan poetry had

come of age" (D'Aronco). Though his style "smacks

of turned soil and of hay" (Chiurlo), he showed that

Friulan could be more than a rustic dialect. His

love-sonnets are probably his best work, being not-

iceably free from contemporary secentismo, though

he must have known of it from his contact with his

older cousin and fellow-poet in Italian, Ciro di Pers

(v. Fontanini). Some prefer him to Friuli's other

giant, the more spontaneous Zorutti.

CARLO FAVETTI (1819-1892), law-student and journal-

ist, had already been banished from his home for his

"liberal" ideas, before he was imprisoned for High

Treason by the Austro-Hungarian authorities who then

ruled his native Gorizia. After his release in 1867

he avoided a second arrest by voluntary exile in

Venice. Through him Friulan added an exile's voice

to her repertory, though economic forces saw to it

that it was not the last.

ADELGISO FIOR (b. 1916), clerk, used the dialect of

Verzegnis to infuse a "certain mountain freshness"

(D'Aronco) into his work.

PAOLO FISTULARIO (Turus) (1587-1631), lawyer,

gathered round him a band of 12 young Udinesi

(among them 2 lawyers, 2 notaries, 2 priests, and

a painter), who would meet from time to time and

recite their poems, - a pleasing reminiscence of

Catullus and his friends (p. 40), whose themes were
also the same - amorous, satirical, realist. It is
to Fistulario himself that we owe a collection of the
verses of eight of them, including himself, all con-
cealed under pseudonyms. He also translated from
Petrarch and Ariosto (p. 43).

GIUSTO FONTANINI (1666-1736), abbot, later archbishop, and man of letters eminent in Etruscology,
history (the Longobards), and literature (Eloquenza
italiana), owes his place in any Friulan anthology to
a sonnet on the death of Count Ermes addressed to
Ciro di Pers (nephew of Ermes' friend), who replied
with a sonnet using identical rhymes.

In muart dal Co. Ermes   13

ENRICO FRUCH (1873-1932), schoolmaster, was
strangely little appreciated in his own day. His
volume, Antigàis (1926), received only one mention,
and Chiurlo, though generous with quotations, vouch-
safed the briefest of introductory notes and for once
abstained from critical comment. Time, however,
brought an act of reparation: his poem in celebration
of the 9th centenary of the Basilica of Aquileia (1931)

did not receive the prize (a badly needed sum of

money), but was later chosen as the one to be

engraved in marble at the entrance to the Viale

dei Patriarchi nearby. Antigàis has been often reprin-

ted (last in 1949), and several of its poems set to

music.

GIOVANNI BATTISTA GALLERIO (1812-1881), priest

and for 40 years vicar of Vendoglio (near Colloredo,

where lived a friend of his and descendant of Count

Ermes), used his poetic vein for the moral edification

of his readers, but he is none the less a significant

poet in the use he made of traditional themes. His

elaboration of anonymous "popular" poetry is taken

as an illustration of the "ascending process", where-

by successive changes in traditional versions consti-

tute deliberate improvements made on artistic

grounds. Themes (humble things), diction (simple

words), metre (the ottonario of the vilote) put his

verses on the lips of ordinary men, and made them

eminently suitable for setting to music.

ANTONIO GASPERINI (1880-1944), gardener, found his

chief inspiration in flowers, but could handle other

occasional themes with skill.

FRANCO DE GIRONCOLI (b. 1892), surgeon, confirmed

the beginning of a new epoch in Friulan poetry by two

privately printed collections (1944 and 1945), in

which a complete break was made with the hendeca-

syllabic and rhyming tradition. He expresses his

feelings, mostly bitter, with an immediacy that may

owe something of its effect to the freshness of a more

archaic form of the language, and certainly owes

much to their untranslatable musicality.

Elegie   40

GIOVANNI LORENZONI (1884-1950), accountant turned

teacher and school-inspector, was another who

strove to animate the cultural life of Gorizia before

the first World War. His poetry is particularly

noticeable for attention to form and experiment with

new metres, in which the influence of Carducci is

evident.

Ciampanis   35

SOMEDA DE MARCO (1891-1970), notary, known also

for his writings in prose and in Italian, achieved

distinction as a poet only when he abandoned tradi-

tional forms. He too (cf. De Gironcoli) may owe

something to his dialect. His chief inspiration came

from the peace and beauty of the countryside in

which he lived.

FLORINDO MARIUZZA (1766-1841), peasant and shoe-

maker, was a latter-day giullare, writing poems to

be sung in the market-place to the accompaniment of

a guitar or a mandoline played by his brother. The

two were much in demand at every kind of rural

festivity (sagra). His favourite theme was an

invitation to enjoy the pleasures of love.

PIETRO MICHELINI: see PIERI CORVAT

NICOLÒ MORLUPINO (1528-1570), man of letters, is

the second name to break the anonymity under which

the earliest Friulan poems have reached us, and is,

oddly enough, a direct contrast with the first, his

older contemporary, Biancone. The "warm, vigorous

sensuality" (D'Aronco) with which Morlupino celeb-

rates wine and women befits the friend and imitator

of Berni; while the imitation leaves intact the essen-

tial friulanità of the man more used to country than

to town. It is interesting to see a man steeped in the

culture of the early Renaissance recognizing the

claims of Friulan.

SPARTACO MURATTI (1875-1937), lawyer, was led by

a private bereavement to switch from Italian to

Friulan poetry, perhaps because in his happier days

he had lived like a country-squire and shared in all

the activities of rural life at Tricesimo.

OTMAR MUZZOLINI (b. 1908), accountant, traditionalist

in form but modern in expression, can sound a hum-

orous or pathetic note with equal skill.

DOMENICO NALDINI (b. 1929), publisher's assistant,

is a poet of the school of his cousin Pasolini, i.e.

the sound has sometimes priority over the sense,

dark passions are hinted at, and the general attitude

is that of Montale and the Symbolists. His own are

the note of joie de vivre and the vivid portrayal of

the seasons.

EMILIO NARDINI (1862-1938), lawyer and journalist,

was in his sixties when he began to compose in

Friulan, but was at once acclaimed as of the first

rank. Introducing a collection of his poetry in 1934,

the President of the S.F.F., P.S. Leicht, remarked

on Nardini's achievement in combining delicate image-

ry with robust expression. His personal note is that

of a longing to escape to another land far, far away.

MARIA FORTE NICOLOSO (b. 1899), school-mistress,

was one of the first members of the association of

Friulan writers calling itself "La Risultive" (p. 50).

Nothing in Nature or the life around her was too

small to touch a chord in her heart; but the prevail-

ing note is that of melancholy resignation, as

D'Aronco saw when he called her "therefore the

special interpreter of Friuli". Her prose reveals

an amazing mastery of the language.

FRANCESCA NIMIS-LOI (1876-1959) was well-read in

Friulan literature before she began to compose.

Attached as she was to every part of Nature around

her, she shares the melancholy of her fellow-

poetesses. Some of her verses have been set to

music, and Ploe di rosis has been likened by

D'Aronco to a Japanese tanka.

GABRIELE PACIANI (1700-1793), lawyer, was the poet

laureate of Cividale, writing "official" poems for pub-

lic occasions. His real excellence, however, consists

in the rendering of melancholy consoled by oblivion.

PIER DI SANDANÊL: see PIETRO PASCOLI

PIETRO PASCOLI (Pier di Sandanêl) (1887-1955),

surveyor, wrote an emigrant's nostalgic verses of

appealing simplicity.

PIER PAOLO PASOLINI (b. 1922), thanks to a Friulan

mother, used to spend his holidays in Casarsa, and

Poesie a Casarsa was the title of his first book of

poems. Encouraged by the success of this venture, he

settled in Casarsa and devoted himself to founding a

new poetic school (Introduction p. 49). The Societat

Poetica Anti-zoruttiana (1944) aimed at creating a new,

vigorous Romance literature by subjecting what was

considered Friuli's own effete vernacular tradition to

the influence of modern French and Italian literature,

themselves needing to be refreshed by the example of

work in a new language. Such was his desire for a new

start that even the Friulan koiné was suspect, and he and

his school wrote in their own Casarsese. In 1949 he

moved to Rome, and his Academiuta di lenga furlana yiel-

ded to the association calling itself La Risultive (p. 50).

Avantgarde in one sense, Pasolini was nevertheless fun-

damentally Friulan in his attachment to the soil and in his

religious sense. G. Faggin finds in his poetry a note of

"aristocratico decadentismo" and thinks that his influence

delayed the appearance of social protest in Friulan verse

(p. 58). Most characteristic of him is a strongly visual

imagination - sign perhaps of the future film-producer.

'A planzin li' vis...   53

NADIA PAULUZZO (b. 1931), graduate in Ital. Lit. and

writer, sings of Nature with "an almost morbid" affec-

tion (D'Aronco). Her musical verse admirably succeeds

in expressing the mystery of man's ultimate destiny.

'ne piciule tombe   52

MARIA MOLINARI PIETRA (1853-1939), an authoress

in Italian, followed the example of Caterina Percoto

(p. 301) in writing in dialect also; but from her we

have poetry instead of prose. Her six sonnets perhaps

explain why Nardini and Chiurlo were her friends.

TOMASO SABBATINI (fl. 1583), nobleman and Italian

poet, wins a place in Friulan literature for 32 distichs

in praise of certain noble ladies. Friulan, therefore,

was never a despised patois.

In laude de zentildonis furlanis   4

GIROLAMO SINI (1529-1602), priest, orator, historian,

poet in Italian and Latin, and friend of cardinals,

owes his place here to a sonnet in praise of Friulan.

In laude de lenghe furlane   3

RENZA SNAIDERO (b. 1920), teacher, is a poetess of

disillusion.

L'ore dolze   47

TONUTI SPAGNOL (b. 1930), clerk, belongs, like

Naldini, to the school of Pasolini, sometimes

referred to as "the poets of Casarsa" (pp. 49-50),

where several of them happened to live.

EUSEBIO STELLA (1602-ca. 1665), lawyer, wrote

poetry in Italian, Spanish, Latin, and Venetian,

besides Friulan. He has been rated artistically

the equal of Ermes di Colloredo; but it will be

easier to judge of this when his exclusively erotic

poems are published in their entirety.

Ursula, vita mee   5

GIUSEPPE STRASSOLDO (ca. 1520-ca. 1597), priest,

wrote of the joys and sorrows of love, the sorrow

being particularly caused him by the obstinacy of

a certain Countess. Morally, therefore, earlier

than the Counter-Reform launched by the Council

of Trent (v. Biancone), he oscillates between the

petrarchismo of his predecessors and the secentismo

of his successors (p. 42).

DINO VIRGILI (b. 1925), schoolmaster, is inspired by

his beloved Friuli to write, not only poetry, but

Friuli's first full-length novel (p. 58). His poetry

sings of the twin beauty of Nature and Woman in a

language carefully purged of anything not genuinely

Friulan.

La vegle   49

PIETRO ZORUTTI (1792-1867), clerk and member of

a noble family fallen on evil days, shares with Ermes

di Colloredo the fame of being Friuli's greatest poet.

Chiurlo indeed puts him among Italy's greatest dialec-

tal poets, second only to the Milanese Porta. Poverty

forced him to the publication of an annual Calendar, the

Strolic furlan (cf. Feruglio, p. 59); but at least this guar-

anteed an uninterrupted output of poetry lasting 46 years,

and set the fashion as a method of publication. Typically

Friulan in his alternation of gaiety and melancholy, he

was occasionally guilty of excess in both; and then we

have prolix jocosity and querulous sentimentality. His

supreme excellence lies in the ability to fuse his own

state of mind with the scene before him; and hardly less

striking is the way in which he seizes on the comic ele-

ments in a situation and creates a little world of life-

like characters. Friend of men of letters such as Dall'

Ongaro and Nicolò Tommaseo, he counted Carducci

among his admirers: "Quant' è bella!" the great man

would say on hearing La Plovisine recited to him.

La plovisine   15

Il lôf di Lunciamp   16

ANONYMOUS

(<u>ca.</u> 1400)

1.   <u>Biello dumlo di valor</u>*

<u>Infant</u>   Biello dumlo di valor,
              Jo cgiantaraj al vuestri honor.

              Con cgio[1] soj in grant pinsi,
              Jo vul diray si vo voles,
              Chu zamay non pues durmi
              Mangia no bevi pluj d'un mes.
              Vo lu vedes ben apales
              Cgio muriraj par vuestri amor.

<u>Dumlo</u>   Si par me tu muriras
              Tu zamay non fos pluj gram,[2]
              alegro may no mi vedras;
              may el sarà pur lu to dan.
              Vacgint vio[3] chul malan
              E si cgin zir[4] uno altri flor.

---

* A <u>Contrasto</u> ("argument", usually between a lover and
his chosen; v. Introduction p. 32, n. 4). An early Italian
example is that of Ciacca dell'Anguillaia (<u>fl.</u> 1250). Earlier still is the mixed Provençal-Genovese one of Raim-
bautz de Vaqueiras (Dionisotti-Grayson, <u>Early Italian
Texts</u>, No. xv). Ours was found on the back of a parch-
ment used to cover a book written by one Simone di
Vittore in 1416.
    Our text is Corgnali's (<u>Ce fas-tu?</u> 1934, pp. 214-225),
not all of whose readings were adopted by D'Aronco in
his <u>Antologia</u> (pp. 19-21); but accents and punctuation
have been added and occasionally the word-division
altered.

---

1. ch'io.

2. for <u>gran</u> (equated by Chiurlo with <u>affatto</u>; but v.
   Corgnali, loc. cit.).

3. Vattene via.

4. Cèrcatene.

ANONYMOUS
(ca. 1400)
1. Gentle lady, fair to view

Youth   Gentle lady, fair to view,
              I shall sing in praise of you. *

              Since I am in anguish sore,
              listen please to what I state:
              it is now a month or more
              since I slept or drank or ate.
              So you see that at this rate
              I shall die for love of you.

Lady   If through me you die in vain,
              should you cease to be, I own,
              you'll not see me gay again;
              but the loss will be your own.
              Go away and elsewhere moan;
              any other flower will do.

---

* The introductory distich is repeated after each stanza,

the last word of which rhymes with it.

Infant   Biello dumlo inchulurido,
Chel nond' è al mont zardin
Chu se' flor chusì flurido
com vo ses sichu un flurin:
vo ses achel zintil rubin
ch'a Cividat arint[5] splendor.

Dumlo   Biel infant, va pur chun Dio
e no malamentri atentant,
Cgio mind'aj[6] un amador
Chu par me va pur cgiantant.
Si tu fos vignut inant, [7]
non curavo d'altri amador.

Infant   No mi stait achusì crudel,
Biello dumlo dolç chest siur. [8]
A vus soio fant fidel;
sirvit a vó simpri di bon cur.
Dio no mi lasat difur,
Cgio murires di chel dolor.

Dumlo   Lasimi stâ, si Dio cgiaiut![9]
Tu mi pars masse insurit.
Chom estu achi vignut
E parce estu tant ardit?
Si tu mi stas achi din pit, [10]
Tu poras avê remo. [11]

---

5. rende.

6. me ne ho (cf. nond'è above).

7. This line is missing in D'Aronco.

8. ? che sei sicuramente (Chiurlo).

9. che Dio ti aiuti.

10. invece.

11. rumore.

Youth   Gentle lady, fair and rosy,
there's no garden here below
that can boast of such a posy
as your own two cheeks now show.
With your noble ruby-glow
Cividale shines out too.

Lady   Comely youth, I pray, have done!
It is foolish to ignore
that I have already one
who will sing me and adore.
If you'd only come before,
I'd have been your mistress true.

Youth   Show me not such cruelty,
gentle lady, sweet as fair.
Faithful servant I shall be,
serving you, my only care.
In God's name, leave me not there;
such great grief I'd not live through.

Lady   In God's name, leave me alone!
You, methinks, are obstinate,
coming here with such a tone.
Why this bold and reckless state?
If in spite of all you wait,
You may have a quarrel due.

Infant Dio sa ben com mal content
    Un dî di vó tuel attentat. [12]
    Sufriraj peno e torment
    pluj ch'ogno altri inamorat.
    Vigno vus[13] di me pecgiat
    Di lasâmi in tant ardor.

Dumlo La to grant humilitat
    Mi scomenço[14] di pluj in pluj.
    El mi ven di te pecgiat
    D'abandonacgi par altrui.
    Veromentri t'es achului
    Chu sarà lu mio amador.

Fante Simpri mai jo disidraj
    Di vignî ad a chest pont.
    Sirvido vuestri saraj
    Fin cgio vivaraj al mont.
    Ben mi par cgio sei un cont
    Quant cgio viot lu vestri color.

Dumlo Biel infant, jo si cgi pry, [15]
    E sì cgi pry par curtisio,
    Chu tu no debis sì spes vigni
    Vagiçant[16] par chesto vio,
    Imperzò ch'altrui no dio
    Chu jo se' in desonor.

Fante Biello dumlo, al mio podê
    Lu vuestri honor si vuardaraj.
    Uno horo in di par vó vedê
    Per la contrado passaraj,
    Quant al balchon vus vederaj.
    Stacgi chun Dio, zintil tresor.

---

12. obscure (Chiurlo: "avenge myself").

13. Vi venga.

14. commuove (Corgnali).

15. ti prego.

16. vagheggiando, sc. facendo il vagheggino (Corgnali)

Youth   God knows how I shall be griev'd
if my pleading is in vain.
I shall feel myself bereav'd
more than any other swain.
O take pity on my pain,
left to burn as here I sue.

Lady   Such humility as yours
makes my resolution waver
and compassion now allures
to transfer to you my favour.
Yes, I choose you as the braver;
you shall be my lover new.

Youth   This was ever what my song
hop'd for more than anything.
All my life, however long,
faithful service I shall bring.
I am equal to a king
when I see your cheeks' fresh hue.

Lady   Comely youth, I now entreat
and beseech you: kindly, pray,
with your lover's ditty sweet
do not come so oft this way,
lest some neighbour start to say,
my dishonour I shall rue.

Youth   Gentle lady, I reply,
your good name is safe with me.
Once a day I shall pass by,
in the hope that you will be
standing on your balcony.
My sweet treasure, now adieu!

GERONIMO BIANCONE
(c. 1515-c. 1580)

2.   Povar Blancoon, ad'i chest pas vignuut!

Tant chi sai; si chi debi; e plui chi pues

Jo rengracij Signoor la too clementie

La quaal mi dà qualchi castijgh ben spes

E mi dà similmentri pacientie.

Frantumamj, Signoor, la charn'e i vues,

E faijt al moond dei miee pecchiaaz sententie:

Pur ch'in chel'ultijm dí par Gratie vuestre

Voo mi clamaas chui bogn de bande diestre:

Sal no baste chi pierdi lu vedee,

Sal no baste Signoor chi resti vuarp,

Marturizaami a boon vuestri plasee

In dute la persone in dut lu cuarp,

Chu dut lu straz che Voo farees de mee

Vite, mi sarà doolz, angh cal see garp:

Ed'accettarei sijmpri par segnaal

Dal vuestri grand'Amoor'ogni miò maal.

GERONIMO BIANCONE
(c. 1515-c. 1580)

2.   <u>Poor Biancone, come to this pass</u>*

As best I can, my debt to thee I own

and thank thee, Lord, for all thy clemency,

which oft chastises me, but while I groan,

gives me the will to bear it patiently.

Crush in me, Lord, the flesh and every bone,

and on my sins pronounce thy dread decree,

so long as through thy grace thou bidst me stand

one day among the good at thy right hand.

'Tis not enough that I am going blind?

'Tis not enough, Lord, that I shall not see?

Torture me as you like, I shall not mind,

wherever in my body it may be;

make of my life a woe of every kind,

its bitterness will still be sweet to me,

and every suffering borne beneath my roof

shall be of thy great love just one more proof.

---

* the last two of the 8 stanzas.

GIROLAMO SINI
(1529-1602)

3.   In laude de lenghe furlane

Al pâr al mont cu cui cu scrîf in rime

    al sei tignût a fâlu par toscan;

        sei pur cui cu compogn Napolitan,

Lombart o d'altre tiare o d'altri clime.

Jò l'ài par un abus parcè c'un stime

    cu chel cîl sôl sei ric e vebi a man

        dut chel di biel cu ciât in cûr uman,

ni cu ad altri Parnas mostri la cime.

Jò no soi di parê che in tal Friûl

    la frase sei miôr sint sparnizade

di Talian, Francês e di Spagnûl.

    Par chest l'istorie ven tant amirade:

lu mont è biel, avint par cui cu vûl

        tante varietât in sè siarade.

GIROLAMO SINI
(1529-1602)

3.   In praise of Friulan

The world believes that all who write in rhyme

    are bound to do it in the Tuscan tongue,

    though some in Neapolitan have sung,

or Lombard, or the speech of other clime.

I hold this wrong; I cannot think that Time

    has dower'd Tuscany so richly, strung

    her heart with all the chords whence beauty sprung,

as though she own'd Parnassus' peak sublime.

To me it also seems a bit absurd

    to think Friulan better if it proffers

the sprinkl'd French, Italian, Spanish word.

    What richness History stores within her coffers!

The world indeed is just to be preferr'd

    for all the sweet variety it offers.

TOMASO SABBATINI

4.   In laude di zentildonis furlanis (1583)

La siore Zanette Savorgnane

Non è bocchie chu s'aure, [1] chu no die
c'havees de Maiestaat e signurie.

La siore Ursine Savorgnane di Belgrat

Qual chu vali plui tas [2] io stoi suspees,
o la bellezze o la bontaat c'havees.

---

1. Italian apra.

2. tanc'

EUSEBIO STELLA
(1602-?1665)

5.   Ursula, vita mee

Ursula, vita mee,
Anime mee, coor gno, dolz il gno flaat,
s'amoor m'art il fiaat
e mi consuma il coor simpri par te,
parcè, crudeel, parcè
brammistu e vustu mo tu la mee muart?
Da Christian t'has tuart
a no m'amaa cumò, chi tu voraas
amâmi un dì, che, fors, tu no poraas.

TOMASO SABBATINI

4.   In praise of gentlewomen of Friuli*

Zanetta Savorgnan

All must admit, for it is clear to see,
your noble form, your radiant majesty.

Ursina Savorgnan

I cannot on one point make up my mind:
are you more beautiful than you are kind?

---

* Of 32 distichs written in honour of various ladies from
25 noble families of Friuli, who were present at a joust
in Udine during the Carnival of 1583, I select two pietatis
causa, a scion of the house of Savorgnan having been in
1943-45 the leader of a band of partisans, which called
itself "Osoppo" after the heroic resistance offered in
that town by an ancestor, Gerolamo Savorgnan, against
an Imperial army. (See Introduction, p. 14 and Poems
25 (iii) and 27.)

EUSEBIO STELLA

(1602-?1665)

5.   Ursula, my life

Sweet Ursula, say I,
you are my soul, my heart, my breath of life.
Love burns with red-hot knife,
and wastes my heart with an unending sigh.
Why, cruel one, O why
do you so fervently desire my death?
Not thus the Christian saith
'tis meet to do. The day may come again,
when you will want my love, and want in vain.

LUIGI AMALTEO

6.   <u>Satire cuintri Filip II</u>   (1594)

Cesar, chel grant Imperator roman,

  quant che dal traditor ij fo portât

  l'onorât chiaf, di lagrimis lu plat

bagnà, par squindi miei lu cûr di chian.

Filip des falsis Spagnis dur tiran

  une devote Glesie ha consecrât

  a Sent Laurinz, mostrant pure pietât,

par podê squindi miei l'anim maran.

La fabriche è ben dute signoril;

  ma fra lis maraveis mi parè

    in cheste sole havê intrigât iu pis:

vedei inzenoglât Filip humil

  in cheste glesie; mi parè vedê

    un guarp in cil e l'anime in abis.

LUIGI AMALTEO

6.   Satire against Philip II   (1594)

Caesar, that mighty Roman Emperor,

when some vile traitor brought the sever'd head

of his great foe, upon the platter shed

abundant tears, to hide the hate he bore.*

Philip, who keeps false Spain in durance sore,

has consecrated to Saint Lawrence dead

a noble church, and similarly said

abundant prayers, to hide his rotten core.

The building is indeed a noble pile;

but of its marvels there was none to me

more wonderful than this that now I tell:

To see this Philip kneeling in the aisle

in all humility, methinks I see

in heaven a body, and its soul in hell.

---

* Pompey's head was brought to Caesar in Egypt by the
sophist, Theodotos. Livy, Plutarch, Valerius Maximus,
and Eutropius believed Caesar's tears were sincere;
Amalteo seems to be following Lucan or Dio Cassius.

GASPARE CARABELLO

(fl. 1620)

7   Laudant iu poettis furlans

Sei benedet lu prin, ch'in viars furlans

comenzà poettant a faa leiendis

chu parecchis han fat dapò facendis

tant e quant, chu i lattins, e chu i toschans;

e chumò plui chu mai menin lis mans

e fazin par dij 'l veer chiosis stupendis,

sugietz chussì cumplijz, chu senze mendis

plui prest han dai divins, chu dai humans.

O Friuul vinturaat legre lu voli,

e tu citaat da Udin gratiiose,

chum' è timp chu'l to non par du'l mont svoli!

Lu floor dai biei inzens in viars e in prose

son in te, nissun plui ti pora tioli

ch'a paar d'ogn'altre tu no seis famose.

GASPARE CARABELLO
(fl. 1620)

7   In praise of Friulan poets

Blest be the man who first Friulan chose

to write his poems in, and launch'd a line

of poets whose production from that mine

equals what Rome and Tuscany compose;

and still the stream of poetry onward flows,

till we must truly stand amaz'd, how fine

their workmanship, how perfect their design!

God's handiwork is here, one could suppose.

O fortunate Friuli, bright of eye!

And thou, fair Udine, my city dear,

now must thy name around the planet fly!

The sweetest flowers of prose and verse are here

in thee; henceforth can no-one e'er deny

that thou art every famous city's peer.

ERMES DI COLLOREDO
(1622-1892)

8.   L'orloi

Chel tic-e-toc, cu conte ogni moment
    ju pàs, che il timp misure in nestri dan,
    e velôz trapassant dal mês a l'an,
cun chei pàs nûs condûs al monument,
Polìmie, pense pur, che a chel concent
    ancie i flôrs dal to volt e' spariran,
    e, ad onte dal to fast, prest finiran
la tó crudêl beltât e il miò torment.

Cheste è fatalitât di uman destin,
    che ogni biel à caiù curte durade,
e un pizzul pàs è dal principi al fin.
    Pietôse tu al miò amôr concêt l'entrade,
se no, crèdilu pur, pentîz sarìn
    tu di vêmi sprezzât, jo tant amade.

9.   Il presentin

Vò avès credût, mandanmi une rosade,
    di fammi lu fiat dut refreschiâ;
    ma propriamentri m'al vès fât brusâ
dai biei voj di cujè, cu l'ha puartade.
Ches tetis blanchis come une zanclade, *
    cu faressin un muart resuscitâ,
    cui mai varès credut, che d'impiâ
vessin fuarze, par dâi nome un' occhiade?

Copari! Se d'achiar vès l'avvocat,
    no imparait di grazie cheste squelle
di mandâmi a donâ fucch in tal lat.
    O pur se volès fâmint une bielle,
par vò tignîssi la rosade e 'l plat,
    e mandàimi a donâ la camarelle.

---

* curdled milk.

ERMES DI COLLOREDO
(1622-1892)

8.   The clock

Tick-tock, the never-varying beat of doom
    with which Time registers our every pace,
    converting months to years in headlong race,
with those same steps conducts us to the tomb.
Polymnia, think, to that same sound the bloom
    will vanish even from your lovely face,
    and soon, for all your pride, there'll be no trace
of your harsh beauty and my tortur'd gloom.

This is the fate to which mankind must bend,
    that beauty here below soon fades, and such
a little step it is from start to end.
    Accept my love and yield to pity's touch,
or else we'll both repent (you may depend):
    you, that you spurn'd; I, that I lov'd so much.

9.   The little present

In sending me a custard-pie you thought
    that you would thus refresh my weary head.
    In fact, I have a fever now instead,
thanks to the eyes of her by whom 'twas brought.
Those little milk-white breasts could well have wrought
    the resurrection even of the dead.
    Merely to glance at them - who would have said
it had the power to leave me so distraught?

Comrade! If you our friendship highly rate,
    you must give up these gestures, I'm afraid:
Send no more fire disguis'd in milky bait!
    The present I would like is this: to trade
with you the custard-pie and china plate.
    Keep these yourself, and let me have the maid.

10.   Ce ch' al vâl

'O ài tai uès tante malinconie
daspò ch'o soi vistût di cortesan
che ogni moment mi pâr lunc une mìe.

Jo 'o scomenzi a provâ ce cu è il malan,
a vivi di speranze, a mazzâ il vêr
- mistîr che in Cort si fâs simpri dut l'an.

. . . .

Jo che simpri in vite mê professai
di jessi in ogni cont e pûr e sclet,
'o ài di fâ chest mistîr? Nol sarà mai!

Il vivi di speranze al è un brudet
che in Cort si dà a dut past a chei mincjons
ch'a son stìtics d'inzen, dûrs d'intelet.

E jo ch'o vuèi dî clâr lis mês rasons,
che chel ch'o ài in bocje lu ài tal cûr,
no riès nuje in chestis tâls funzions.

Ma us zuri, al cospeto cjate-fûr,
che s'o puès tornâ il cul dentri in Gurìz,
'o vuèi ch'a stèntin a tirâmi fûr.

Al vâl plui cuet in pâs un pitiniz,
quatri cjastinis, doi muzzûi di most,
e cjaldâsi i zenoi cun quatri stiz;

. . . .

al vâl plui cu la pâs un toc di pan
e gjoldê la sô cjare libertât
e stâ dai granc' signôrs simpri lontan,

10.   True value

I have such melancholy in my bones
since I put on a courtier's livery,
that every moment on unending drones.

I learn at last what is that misery:
to feed on hope the while and murder truth -
a trade from which a Court is never free.

. . . . (1) . . . .

For me who have profess'd myself the foe
of all in life that is not frank and clean,
is this the trade for me? I answer, No.

To live off hope, this is the pudding lean
they give at Court to fools for every meal,
to costive brains and wits that aren't too keen.

I who prefer to utter what I feel
(and what I do not feel I cannot feign)
for such charades as these show little zeal.

I swear to you in language straight and plain,
when my Gorizzo welcomes back its host,
they'll have a job to get me out again.

Better by far a peaceful turnip-roast,
four chestnuts, two small goblets of new wine,
and four live coals with which my knees to toast;

. . . . (3) . . . .

Better by far a peaceful slice of bread -
to revel in one's own sweet liberty
and stay away from where the mighty tread,

cu no vâl e la Cort e la zitât
e i onôrs e i banchez e lis grandezzis,
l'àur e l'arint e ogni gran' dignitât.

. . . . '. . . . .

Pur che Cerere ogn'an mandi in ta l'àrie
san lu balzûl, e puessi, a l'ocorenze,
fâ la colazion in te panàrie;

pur che Baco mi fèi biele aparenze
di brentèi plens in tal miò foledôr,
e ch'o viodi a strizzâ la quintessenze,

rinunzi Franze, Spagne, e Imperatôr,
che si ròmpin lu cjâf tant diaul ch'a vuelin,
che no vuèi lâmi a fâ mazzâ par lôr!

than all your Courts and towns of high degree,
with honours, banquets, all that lordly grandeur,
the gold and silver and each dignity.

. . . . (1) . . . .

So long as Ceres every year piles in
my barn the hay and fails not to produce
the wherewithal for breakfast from my bin;

So long as Bacchus grants me the fair use
of brimful casks, and through the vat-room door
shows me the squeezing of the nectar-juice,

I'll do without France, Spain, the Emperor,
and they can go to hell for all I care:
I'm not their cannon-fodder any more.*

---

* Cf. the Romagnol proverb:

Viva la Franza, viva la Spagna!
Am n'infott, basta c'a magna.

(Long live France, long live Spain! I care not a fig
for them, so long as I can eat).

11.   Invît a Guriz

Jaroni, i rusignui dal miò boschet
    a i han biel petât man al sivilot,
e van provand un biel madrigalet,
    al to arrif di recitâ al prin bot.
Mene Ferrant, che lest all'è il fiaschet
    par sborfâ chel sò nas a bech frisot.
Ogni ucciel si sfadie di prest lâ in mude
par formâ un biel concert 'e tò vignude.

Un'oparete, cu farà fraccas
    ti preparin de selve i miei cantôrs,
la zore e la curnil faràn il bàs,
    la giaje e la badascule i tenors;
lu cuintr'alt la pojane e lu cagnàs,
    e ju soprans i tarabús sonors.
L'ultin sarà lu cuch, cul chiant divin,
che fra i altris par just Margaritin.

Sarà un'orchestre di grang virtuos,
    e lu grí sunarà lu chittarin;
la crazzule il liron, e 'l crot malòs
    la viol di giambe e lu violin;
la spinette lu farch, seben mendòs,
    ch'a nol viod senz'occhiaj nang da vicin;
e po une trombe cu passarà dut
sunarà d'Apulejo il nemalût.

Camerade, ven vie, ti fâs l'invît!
    Ma però, tu m'intinz? cu la parone;
che senze jè dut sarès dissavit,
    e lu vidiel mi pararès carbone.
Tu vedaràs lu miò Guriz florît
    d'ogni color cui plâs alla persone.
Ti spietti senze fal cun cuur costant,
ma mene anchie cun te lu bai Ferrant.

11.   <u>Invitation to Gorizzo</u>

O Jeremy,* the nightingales are all
    a-warbling in my little wooded close,
rehearsing such a pretty madrigal
    to greet you promptly when your carriage shows.
And bring Ferrante; there's a tankard tall,
    in which he can bedew his beaky nose.
Each bird is busy preening tail and breast,
to make a concert worthy of my guest.

They're putting on an operatic show,
    my singers of the wood, for you today.
The bass will be the hawfinch and the crow,
    the tenor be the magpie and the jay;
the hawks can be contralto, singing low,
    the bittern the soprano, I would say.
Last will the heavenly songster come, of June,
the cuckoo - and let's hope he'll be in tune.†

'Twill be an orchestra of virtuosi:
    the cricket will be playing his guitar;
the frog the lyre; the toad - well, I suppose he
    with viol or violin will be the star;
the mole will be the pianist, rather dozy
    because his sight does not reach very far;
and then the hero of that Apuleius
with trumpet's strident blaring will supply us.§

So come, my friend! This letter you empowers;
    but with your wife, remember: do not baulk
my hope of spending a few happy hours.
    Without her, veal would taste like salted pork.
You'll see Gorizzo gay with all its flowers,
    such hues as raise appreciative talk.
So, hopeful I await your wife and you;
    but bring my bailiff-friend, Ferrante, too.

* Count Gerolamo Savorgnan, brother-in-law of Ermes
and descendant of his namesake mentioned in the note on
No. 4.
† As the cuckoo's song is not generally considered divine,
Chiurlo supposes an ironical reference to an inferior
local singer.
§ The hero of Apuleius' <u>Metamorphosis</u> (3rd cent. A.D.)
is turned into a donkey. (For a similar orchestra compare Enzo Guerra's Romagnol poem, <u>E' cunzert dla sera.</u>)

12.   Deliri d'amôr

Jò mi declari, che varès a chiar
che mi fos scorteade ju la piel,
par che cun je fos fât un cussignel,
e dai miei uès giavât un guselar.

Ma che tu ju doperas, tu che lu prin
Affiet dal mond mi fàs sintí, vorès,
Che cussí tes tos mans simpri sarès,
E starès simpri stret in tal tò grin.

Jò mi contentarès anchie plui bass,
Che i miei budiei fossin daspaz par bon,
E intorteaz a foze di cordon,
Par che cun chesg tu ti lazzas lu cass.

Che cussí jò sarès content a plen,
Parcè senze suspiet senze fadie
Dal jevà dal soreli al tornà vie
Ti strenzarès ju flancs, e lu biel sen.

In summe al non è cruci, nè torment,
Nè pricipizi alcun, nè nissun risi,
Che par te nol patíss, anzi t'avisi,
Che par tò amor al si farès content.

. . . .

No brami robbe avè, nè pur un stich
Pensi di cresci dal miò poc terren,
Sei ueit il scring, se al no vul jessi plen,
Co soi in posses di te, soi vonde rich.

. . . .

Di sudâ sore i libris par avê
fame di leterât, no uei pensâi.
Se di te fâmi ben volê jo sai,
sai abastanze, e no uei plui savê.

12.   <u>Delirium of love</u>*

I hereby state that I would like to be
stript of my skin and well and truly flay'd,
so that a pin-cushion might thence be made
and from my bones a needle-case for thee.

For thy use, though, they must be, who dost please
me more than any lover understands.
Thus shall I be for ever in thy hands
and held for ever close upon thy knees.

I'd be content with a more humble part:
to have my entrails wound upon a reel
and twisted to a cord of silky steel,
to hold thy bodice tight beneath the heart.

Ah, this would be the pinnacle of grace;
for then so easily and seen by none,
from rising to the setting of the sun
thy body would be held in my embrace.

In short, there is no torture nor no pain,
no danger, hazard, crisis, lack, or need,
I would not undergo for thee; indeed,
my love of thee would make me glad again.

. . . .

I seek no property or other stuff,
and am content with my land's modest fare.
My chest may empty be, for all I care:
when I have you, then I am rich enough.

. . . .

And over dusty learned tomes to pore
in search of writer's fame, is not for me.
If I can make you love me, that will be
knowledge enough - I have no need for more.

---

* The complete poem consists of 85 verses.

Ce ocôr a là cerciant altre scriture
cun stente, cun sudôr, e cun impaz?
Quant che 'o ciali, ben miò, lu to mostaz,
jo léi sul plui biel libri de nature.

Jo sarès ben stimât un pampabeo,
se in cîl las cu l'ocial cerciant lis stelis,
se in tal to front in puès vedê dos bielis,
che al no vedè dos tals il Galileo.

. . . .

Che vegni pur la uerre, e cul moschet
Saltin pur fur ju brafs, e ju gajarz,
Saràn trombis par me ju tiei bussarz,
E chiamp de nestre uerre sarà il jet.

Ch'al regni pur siroch, che jò par me
No i peensi un bez, se vignîs simpri ploje,
Che simpri jò starai di buine voje,
Varrai simpri bon timp, se jò soi cun te.

De buere, e terremot, cu dà spavent
Al mond, in tant mi piarès impaz,
In quant, che mi staccassin dal to braz,
Ma essint in chel, jò murarès content.

Se mai puartàs un dí tant triste lus,
Che d'Udin ti vedès a fà partenze,
Jò di restà mai porès ve pazienze,
Ma larès come il chiar daur i bus.

E chí jò finís, ch'al mi s'ingroppe il cur,
Savind che un dí si vín po di lassà;
La Muart, che dug i grops fàs disleà,
Dislearà anchie il nestri di daur.

Ma nancie chest mi fàs avè timor,
Nè chest pinsiir al mi riès signestri,
Che crod ch'il nostri spirt il genio nestri
Anchie quand che sín muarz farà l'amor.

What need to go around and toiling look
for other writings difficult and drear,
when looking on thy face, my lovely dear,
I read at ease from Nature's fairest book?

I should be thought more foolish than I'd like,
if I went gazing at the stars up there,
when you have two down here so passing fair
that Galileo never saw the like.

. . . .

Let war come if it will, and overhead
let armies send their missiles' fiery hisses:
Bugle for me will be thy rousing kisses,
and our one battle-field will be a bed.

Let dry scirocco rule, 'twould be for me
a trifle merely, as would be the rain;
for I shall imperturbable remain,
and think it ever fine while I'm with thee.

Tempest or earthquake or such dread event
as frightens mortals, only so far harms
me as it can detach me from thy arms:
leave me in these, and I would die content.

Should ever dawn the day that could allow
my eyes to see you go from Udine,
I know I could not bring myself to stay,
but thou wouldst draw me as the ox the plough.

And here I end: the fearful verdict lowers
that we must part one day - I've not forgot.
For Death, that can untie the tightest knot,
will steal up from behind and untie ours.

And yet I'm not afraid of even this;
I look it in the face and do not quail.
For I believe our passion will not fail,
and after death our spirits still will kiss.

GIUSTO FONTANINI

(1666-1736)

13.   In muart dal Co. Ermes

Ciro, al è muart il Cigno dal Friûl,

e di zà l'è squindût in tal foran:

pensant che ué si vîf, si mûr doman,

duquant l'interno di spavent mi dûl.

La ribuele di Pindo in tal muzzûl[1]

a missar Febo è intorgolade in man,

e lis musis aflitis cumò stan

taponadis cun t'un neri fazzûl.[2]

La fulziche, la pive e il flaut, su l'ôr

dal monument leâz a une cimosse,

a' ricusin di rindi alcun tenor.

La godine sierade in t'une cosse

no à plui vôs; ma di chest grant cantôr

tu tu às ereditât la totorosse.[3]

---

1. goblet, from Latin modiolus.

2. On this kind of veil see the Bollettino della S. F. F.,
    1936 pp. 200-202.

3. Chiurlo and D'Aronco translate this word by "corna-
    musa" (bagpipes), but G. Perusini in an article in Ce
    fas-tu?, 1944 ("Strumenti musicali in Friuli") will
    not have this, and identifies it with the piva (piffero,
    a pipe of the oboe family) (pp. 255-6).

GIUSTO FONTANINI
(1666-1736)

13.   On the death of Count Ermes

So, Ciro, our Friuli's Swan is dead,

    and lies already underneath the soil.

    How suddenly we slough this mortal coil!

To be reminded, fills my heart with dread.

Lord Phoebus sees the Grecian wine once red

    grow turbid in his goblet like an oil;

    and now each stricken Muse wears, as a foil

for grief, a widow's veil around her head.

The bagpipes, whistle, and the flute denote

    a tomb-stone's decorated hem, denying

that they will ever sing another note.

    The little lute within a basket lying

is voiceless now; but of this mighty throat

    thou hast inherited the pastoral sighing.

GIORGIO COMINI

(1722-1812)

14.   La monacaziòn

. . . .

Ce te non è[1] si sint lontan lontan
    chiantà lis laude sante benedetis;
ce te non è si jot[2] di man in man
    in prucision le munie e le polzetis.
A fevin riverenzia a sior plevan
    e a sbassavin po i vuoi che povaretis.
La nuvizza devant el Crucifis
a slatinave che ere un paradis.

E la aveva i chiavei zu par le spale
    luncs e slis che parevin 'na palada,
vistuda come fos là ca si bale
    cun abiz che valevin una entrada.
Di flocs e flours, de viole rosse e zale
    la avea la piturina infrisotada.
In soma, a era, che bisuin in eis, [3]
dal chiaf una belezia insin ai peis.

E daspò che preât ha tant di cour
    in part in peis, in part in zenoglon,
chel vistit cussì biel a giavà four
    e zerin flocs e flours in t'un chianton;
una viesta ha vistît de un sol colour
    come chel verbigrazia del chiarbon,
e una goletta al cuol in su voltada,
che i 'e platava mieza la fazzada.

E una di chele munie che iodei
    co una fuorfe zentila e l'ha tosada,
parchiè là entra no vuàlin chiavei.
    A si tira daspuò dongia la grada
che fiona, serant i siò vuoi biei,
    e a se ha pognet là sot una sfilzada
par fâ jodi che al mont muorta liee era;
ma che muart finta a me pareva vera.

---

1. Eccoti (v. Grammar §36, Obs. i).
2. vede (v. Grammar §20, Obs. iii).
3. These four words are obscure, D'Aronco suggests
   bisogna for bisuin, but a noun would be more in place,
   with che as a Demonstrative Pronoun (ché).

GIORGIO COMINI

(1722-1812)

14.   The taking of the veil*

. . . .

A choir with litany of praises now
    can just be heard intoning in the distance.
The nuns and those about to take the vow
    with well-drill'd moves give mutual assistance.
They turn towards the priest and make a bow,
    then stand with lower'd eyes, without resistance.
The Latin of the novice sounds so nice,
one might have thought one was in Paradise.

And long and smooth her lovely tresses fall
    upon her shoulders like a silken screen.
She looks like one dress'd ready for a ball,
    with gown so rare it could have grac'd a queen.
Her bodice has its flowers and ribbons all
    mix'd with the red and yellow violet's sheen.
In short, that girl, the centre of the show,
was a real beauty right from top to toe.

And after praying with the fervour due,
    part standing up and partly kneeling down,
she doff'd her ribbons and her flowers, and threw
    into a corner the unwanted gown,
donning instead a dress of single hue,
    like coal (I will not qualify the noun),
with collar so turn'd up that not a trace
was visible of nearly half her face.

Then an attendant nun can shear her hair
    with gentle scissors right across the grain.
They want no lovely shining locks in there!
    Then nearer to her grated cell again
with downcast eyes she moves, that maiden fair,
    and lays her down beneath a counterpane.
Die to the world is what she's meant to do;
but that feign'd death to me seem'd all too true.

---

* Part of a Contrasto (v. p. 32) called Ulif e Madalena
written in the dialect of Cordenons (v. p. 62). The
speaker is the Magdalene, a figure who seems to Chiurlo
(Ant. p. 14) to typify "the religion of Friulan hearts,
calm, compassionate, human".

PIETRO ZORUTTI (1792-1867)

15.   Plovisine

Plovisine minudine,
lizerine,
tu vens jù cussi cidine
senze tons e senze lamps,
e tu dâs di bevi ai ciamps.
   Plovisine fine fine,
lizerine,
bagne bagne un freghenin
l'ort del pûar contadin:
senze te no mene nuie:
bagne bagne che' latuie,
bagne bagne chel radric
fin cumò tignûs a stic;
bagne l'ort del puar om,
bagne il ciamp del galantom.
   Plovisine minudine,
sta lontan da chel zardin
impastât cul mussilin.
Là i giacins e tulipans,
cun che' arie di sovrans,
son sborfâs sere e matine;
no àn bisugne del to umor,
za che ur baste il sborfadôr.
   Pes ciarandis, pe campagne,
plovisine, bagne bagne;
'e ti spiete la viole
che à patît un pôc di sut;
si rafres'ce, si console
a sintì chel umidut:
verginele de taviele,
senze il fum de l'ambizion,
jé modeste simpri e biele
là tra il ruscli e l'urtizzon.
   Plovisine lizerine,
ven cun me da un'altre bande;
une biele Tortorele
'e ti brame, 'e ti domande:
véle, véle ch' ninine benedete,
che saltuzze, che svolete,
fin che rive su la cime
di chel pòul par jessi prime
a vignîti a saludà:
plovisine, èccole cà...
. . . .

PIETRO ZORUTTI (1792-1867)

15.   Rain-shower

Little rain-drops pack'd so tightly,
falling lightly,
down you come resounding slightly
without thunder-clap or flash
on the thirsty fields to splash.
    Little rain-drops, drizzling brightly,
falling lightly,
water, water just a spot
the poor farmer's little plot:
you alone aid and abet us,
water, water here that lettuce,
water, water there that root,
freshen up the drooping shoot;
bathe the poor man's little plot,
bathe the good man's broader lot.
    Little rain-drops pack'd so tightly,
visit not the garden fat
with the dunghill's spreading mat.
Hyacinths and tulips there,
looking like some royal pair,
sprinkled daily they and nightly,
have no need of your soft dew:
let the sprinkler serve for you.
    Every hedge, each country-quarter,
little rain-drops, water, water;
there the violet is waiting
having suffer'd from the drought.
See, her strength she's recreating
underneath your water-spout:
virgin of the fields far sweeping,
at whose breast ambition stops,
she is fair and shyly peeping
'twixt the streamlet and the hops.
    Little rain-drops, falling lightly,
look what here I have to show you:
there's a little turtle-dove
longs and asks to stand below you.
See her, see the fledgling sprightly,
how the little bird is skipping,
oh so happy, leaping, dipping,
as to poplar's top she races
to be first with her embraces,
and our greeting bear:
little rain-drops, look! she's there.
. . . .

16.   Il lôf di Lunciamp

. . . .

"Chest al è pôc; ma provarìn di piês
      se ancimò s'intardìn a fâ vedete.
Il miò valôr jo prin farai palês,
      chè il murî par la patrie mi dilete;
e par punî cului il cîl cortês
      cheste robuste man l'à fuars elete.
Ah! se ognun vès coragio al par di me.
il mont a' nol sarès come che al è.

"Dodis musis p. . .✝sèin scielzudis
      fra duquanc' ju abitans di chest vilaz;
e jo, se permetês, farai da zudis
      se a sostignî l'atac saràn capaz.
Che sèin armâs di sclop e sablis nudis;
      Jo lôr capo sarai, lôr miei seguaz.
L'onôr de me' famèe al ûl cussì:
Ài decidût di vinci o di murî."

. . . .

Al prin ciantâ del gial ognun l'è pront
      la sable a meti indues, in spale il sclop.
Za duc' son preparâs ne l'istes pont,
      e dal gust di partî il cûr dà un sclop.
Vistût a curt e cun serene front
      il Capo al comparìs tel miez del trop;
ju met in file, po si dàn doi sbars;
lui si fâs indevant, e al ciule: mars!

Sùbit fûr di Lunciamp svelz come il lamp
      in restiel si distindin pe campagne;
si cîr par ogni sdrup, par ogni ciamp,
      e di cirì nissun 'e si sparagne:
ma alfin in tiare un viôt de zate il stamp,
      e cul voli e cul pît 'e la compagne;
al cuche in un cison alc che si môf,
e al sberle a plene vôs: - l'è il lôf! l'è il lôf!

* Thus Chiurlo prints without comment.

16.   The wolf of Campolungo

(A wolf comes down from the mountains and kills a
shepherd. Daniel undertakes to lead a band of 12 young
men in search of it. He makes a speech in the style of
one of Tasso's heroes)

"This is the least of it; there's worse to come,
    ev'n though it may take longer than expected.
I'll show my valour promptly more than some,
    and gladly die for you as I'm directed.
By heaven's decree, to castigate that scum
    these mighty arms of mine have been selected.
Would there were more like me! For in that case
The world would be a very different place.

"Choose twelve young bloods (this is my proposition),
    all in this village born and of this land.
I'll be the umpire (with your kind permission)
    as to their stomach for the fight we've plann'd;
their weapons - swords, with muskets in addition.
    I'll be their leader, they will be my band.
The honour of my line I'm bound to cherish;
'tis my resolve to conquer or to perish. "

(The men are chosen and the next day fixed for the hunt)

The cock had hardly crow'd when each was seen
    with sword girt on and gun on shoulder cast.
They're all prepar'd, all equally are keen:
    with eagerness to leave, their hearts beat fast.
In knee-length breeches and with brow serene
    before his troop their gallant Leader pass'd.
He bids 'Fall in', and from the double arch
Two shots ring out. Then comes the signal: March!

Straight from the village with the speed of light
    they all spread out to scour the countryside.
Up hill, down dale, o'er heavy soil or light,
    they seek him out wherever he may hide.
At last to one a paw-mark comes to sight,
    and for his eyes and feet becomes the guide.
He peers into the hedge, sees something stirring:
"The wolf! The wolf!" he shouts for others' hearing.

Al alze i vôi Denêl, e al dà un sospîr;
   ingusît dal plasé quasi al delire;
al comande ai campions di fa miez zîr
   e in ordin di bataie ju distire.
Palpière no si bat; ciolt l' è il respîr;
   si splànin ju arcabûs: da duc' si tire...
La pùare bestie è deventade un draz;
màncin i pols, e il sanc si spant a svuaz.

A la prede duc' côr; ma, oh, viste amare!
   ciàtin che il Lôf l' è trasformât in mus...
Oh vìtime inocent! anime rare!
   vivude in pùertât, nemìe del lus!
l' è chest il premi che furtune avare
   acorde 'e tó virtût? (crudel influs!)
di furôr, di vendete il cil rimbombe:
no vês mazzât un mùs, ma une colombe!

Onorât l'infeliz di sepolture,
   ogni valent al met la pive in sac.
Soturno il Capo cu la muse dure,
   avilît, pinsirôs a chest so smac,
si sint un cercli al ciâf, si disfigure,
   e al ciât in tiare sbarlufît e strac;
'i si romp la curdele dei bregôns,
e il coragio e il valôr van pai talôns.

. . . .

Par viodi la gran bestie 'e côr in fole
   la int curiose, e pùar Denêl glutis,
chè la vôs jé fermade in miez de gole.
   Si sfuarze infin, ma prime al arossìs,
po' al conte la fazende in ton bemole;
   devant che la finissi ognun capìs,
e fra i scivìi e il son des covertoriis
di chesc' tredis campions àn fin lis gloriis.

. . . .

Daniel looks up and sighs with much relief,
　　for joy delirious near to suffocation.
He orders a half-turn, and as their chief
　　appoints each champion to his battle-station.
With bated breath they stare a moment brief:
　　muskets are levell'd, triggers press'd: sensation!
The riddled beast falls down without a quiver,
and from the corpse the blood flows in a river.

They run towards it, see - O vision bitter!
　　The slaughter'd wolf turns out to be - a moke!
O innocence! O soul for man's love fitter,
　　stranger to luxury, to want bespoke,
is't thus ungenerous Fortune stoops to quit a
　　debt to your virtue? Let us then invoke
the ire and vengeance of outrag'd religion:
you would have better done to kill a pigeon.

They think it right the wretched beast to bury,
　　but in their pockets leave the victor's fife.
Their Leader's face is anything but merry
　　at this, the greatest failure of his life:
he feels a head-ache which is painful, very,
　　daz'd by a world with every torment rife.
Nor were his humour and morale improv'd
when braces snapp'd and breeches downward mov'd.

(They march back)

Of villagers, impatient all to see
　　the mighty beast, a crowd upon them rushes.
Poor Daniel gulps and finds his throat to be
　　block'd strangely, but at last with many blushes
he tells the tale in very minor key.
　　The listeners soon catch on to why he flushes,
and whistles and the clash of dustbin-lid
the Great Thirteen of all their glory rid.

(The wolf dies of laughing)

CARLO FAVETTI
(1819-1892)

17 .   Ai miei amís

Chel me país, che l'Alpe Giulia siara

e cul Lisunz va fin ne la marina,

quant viodarai? Quant bussarai ché tiara,

che nassi mi à viodût e là in ruina?

Lontan di te, o me Gurizza ciara,

una vita iò meni erànt, meschina;

quant finirà? E il len de la me bara

dulà sarà taiât? Cu lu induvina?

'L è ver, sòi esiliat nel paradis,

in patria mé, cui miei, e liber sòi,

e speri simpri in plui alegris dîs;

ma tantis voltis che pensànt io stoi

a chel che i'ài lassât nel me país,

mi ciati cu lis làgrimis nei voi.

CARLO FAVETTI

(1819-1892)

17.   To my friends

That land of mine the Julian Alps enclose,

which with Isonzo reaches to the sea,

when shall I view? when kiss the grass that grows

where I was born and found calamity?

O my Gorizia, dearest town, the woes

I suffer now, I suffer far from thee.

When will it end? My coffin's wood, who knows

what stranger's hand will cut, from what strange tree?

'Tis true I'm exil'd to a Paradise,

have family and friends, am not confin'd,

and not denied hope's soothing balm and spice.

But when I think of all I've left behind

in my own land, then more than once or twice

I find myself with scalding tears half-blind.

PIERI CORVAT
(1863-1933)

18.   Brindisi

Sèal benedet el sanc de vît, tan' bon

    quant c'al è bon! Sèal benedet, amîs,

pe buine companie c'al fâ, pal ton

    di bon umôr c'al svee tes companîs.

Sèal benedet e quant che une passion

    l'anime nus ingrispe, o lis fadîs

    nus macòlin i uès, o i ciavêi grîs

no consintin maiôr consolazion,

e quant c'al scôr a taule in ocasion

    di gnozzis o de nassite dai fis,

o di fiestis dai sanz e de nazion...

    Tra lis rosis de vite e lis urtîs,

sèal benedet el sanc de vît, tan bon

    quant c'al è bon! Ohilà! brindis, amîs!

PIERI CORVAT
(1863-1933)

18.   Toast

Blest be the vine's rich blood! When it is good,

how good it is! Blest be it, friends, I say,

for boon companionship, when, as we should,

we feel ourselves encourag'd to be gay.

Blest be it too when some quick passion would

ruffle our soul, or when the daily fray

has left us bruis'd and sore, or hair too grey

forbids the joys we'd welcome if we could.

Blest is the table where the wine-flask stood

to mark a wedding or a natal day

or holy feast or people's nationhood.

Let thorns or roses meet us on our way,

blest be the vine's rich blood! When it is good,

how good it is! A toast, my friends, I say!

19.   Robis bielis, robis brutis

Robis bielis, robis brutis
    che sucedin di lontan
i giornai che lis san dutis
    nus es còntin tal doman:

e si trate de Turchie,
    del Giapon, del...Kamtsciatcà,
ma si vîf cun culumie
    fra Padiâr e Cussignà.

. . . .

Vite stupide, leade,
    ogni di c'al passe un di:
come che' che jé passade
    sarà che' che à di vignì.

E ognidun l'à lis sôs voris,
    e ognidun il so paron...
Omenôns! ma come pioris
    o siaradis o a passon.

O mont grant, o mont di viodi,
    mont di gioldi... e no podé!
ocupâs simpri a proviodi
    el pagnut che si pò vé.

E nemîs e seciaduris
    e malans no màncin mai,
nè lis pizzulis brauris
    dei magnifics basoai...

Libertât che tant 'o ami!
    vite me' di presonîr!
Vie pal mont senze voltâmi
    'o larès tant vulintîr...

19.   <u>Weal and woe</u>

Weal and woe, disgrace or glory,
   dramas on some far-off stage:
read the whole exciting story
   on tomorrow's printed page.

Now of Turkey 'tis they're speaking,
   now Japan, now Kamchatkà,
while we merely go on eking
   out our lives in Cussignà.

. . . .

Stupid life, in chains unending,
   every dawn another day;
like the one that we've been spending
   is tomorrow on its way.

Each man has his daily battle,
   each one has a boss to bear.
Man alive! We live like cattle,
   lock'd up here and herded there.

O thou world that wakes our yearning,
   mighty world, see us instead
busy ever with the earning
   of our meagre daily bread.

Bores and enemies and troubles,
   these will plague us late or soon,
like the petty unprick'd bubbles
   of each highly plac'd buffoon.

Freedom that I love so madly!
   Freedom, my life's greatest lack!
O how through the world I'd gladly
   go, and never once look back!

ENRICO FRUCH
(1873-1932)

20.   Ti ài viodude

Ti ài viodude in automòbil
fûr di puarte di Praclûs.
Cun chel lusso che tu vevis,
cun chei lavris duc' tenzûs,

puare frute, e m'impensavi
co' tu levis a mulin,
e tant bon che tu parevis
cul vestît di regadin.

21.   Mandi, glesiute

Jè plantade tal cret che in alt la rêz
e scuindude tal bosc come in t'un nît,
fra la mont di San Roc che la protêz
e il Tiniment c'al côr alì da pît.

Mandi, glesiute dai miei vôns. Che cianti
la primevere o che l'autun si sfante
tai siei tramonz, simpri un segret confuart

mi ven di te, glesiute de me int,
e alore il cûr, chest vecio cûr, si sint
compagn del navigant c'al torne in puart.

ENRICO FRUCH

(1873-1932)

20.   I saw you

In a car I saw you riding
where the High Street northward dips,
dress'd to kill, a pamper'd missy,
with your bright-red painted lips.

And, poor girl, I fell to thinking
when you us'd to work in t' mill,
how you seem'd to me so pretty
in your dress of humble twill.

21.   Greetings, little church!

It stands as on a platform on the crest,
so nestling in the wood it hardly shows.
San Rocco's Mount protects it on the west,
and down below the Tagliamento flows.

Greetings, my grandsires' church. Let spring parade
her beauty or let autumn-sunsets fade
along the sky, to me you've always brought

a secret comfort, O my childhood's church,
and my old heart seems here to end its search,
like navigator coming back to port.

22.   <u>Il ciant del forment</u>

Quant che rît la primevere
de la Tôr al Tiniment,
ce tant biele
la taviele
dute verde di forment!

E d'istât, quant che il soreli
vie pal cîl di flame al pâr,
ce tant biele
la taviele
che vongòle come il mâr!

Dut chel mâr di spîs che lùsin
e fra miez il confenòn
che si drezze
e s'imborezze
par dai spice a la stagion;

dut chel mâr che si slontane
vie pal plan, di ca e di là,
ce belezze
ce ricezza
sul moment di seselâ!

Al è il pan de nestre tàule
c'al madrès cumo tal spi:
cui c'al are
la so tiare
al so premi al ciate lì.

Premi e glorie de fadìe
la taviele colôr d'àur;
cui c'al are
la so tiare
lu console chel tesaùr!

22.   The song of the corn

When the spring is gaily laughing
from the Tor to Tagliament;
how entrancing
is the glancing
green of cornfield's broad extent.

And when summer's sun is riding
through the sky in majesty,
O the breakers
of the acres
undulating like the sea.

All that sea of corn-ears shining
and the poppy lurking there,
haughty figure
drawn up bigger
to enhance the season's air.

All that sea on both sides spreading
through the valley, broad and deep.
O the pleasure,
O the treasure,
when the moment comes to reap!

'Tis the bread upon our table
ripening now within the ear.
All the toiling
and the moiling
finds its prize and guerdon here.

Prize and glory of the labour
are the spreading golden fields;
for the toiling
and the moiling
harvest consolation yields.

23.   <u>Aquilee</u>

E m'impensi di pizul, co tornavin

   i contadins del perdon di Barbane:

feminis, fruz, fantatis che ciantavin

   lis litaniis pe planure lontane.

E m'impensi di quant che mi contavin

   lis maraveis d'une citât romane,

dei patriarcis siei che comandavin

   su dute quante la tiare furlane:

de fie di Rome e mari di Vignesie,

di Aquilee, che à lassât nome une glesie

   in tai palûs e donge il ciampanîl.

   Citâs che son in pîs a mîl a mîl,

cui lis nomene? Al contrari, di cheste

muarte citât il non par simpri al resti.

23.   Aquileia

I mind me of my boyhood, when I saw

    the folk returning from Barbana's isle:*

women and boys and girls, whose voices bore

    their litanies abroad for mile on mile.

I mind me also of the fabled lore

    of some great Roman town which stood erstwhile,

and of its patriarchs, whose word was law

    where'er Friulan plain and mountain smile.

Daughter of Rome was she, of Venice mother,

that Aquileia, which has left no other

    trace than a marsh-girt church beside its tower.

A thousand cities stand in seeming power:

who speaks of them? With her they cannot vie:

of this dead town the name will never die.

---

* near Grado and site of a Sanctuary of the Madonna.
  It figures in Zaneto's amusing poem, I bragons di
  Zaneto.

24.   <u>Il ciant di Aquilee</u>

Contadin in che tu rompis la tiare
di Aquilee, ferme i bûs un moment:
sot il ciamp che la uàrzine 'e are,
sot la man che semene il forment,
tal soreli e ta l'ombre dal nûl,
jè une impronte di Rome e la storie
    e la glorie
     del nestri Friûl.

Barcarûl che tu vens di Barbane,
quant c'al sune l'antic ciampanîl,
no tu sintis un glon di ciampane
ma une vôs che ti rive dal cîl,
e l'eterne peraule ti dîs,
une vôs che traviarse la storie
    e la glorie
     del nestri paîs.

Pelegrine de ultime uere,
mari sante del nestri Soldât,
che bessole tu jentris la sere
a preâ sot i pins del Sagrât,
scolte, scolte lajù il rusignûl
che ti puarte cun tante dolcezze
    la ciarezze
     del nestri Friûl.

Tal seren di une clare matine,
eco, 'e rît la marine là in fonz:
alze i voi, o giarnazie latine,
su ché blancie corone di monz,
sul Friûl! E ten fede a l'idee
che no mûr: a la grande memorie
    e a la glorie
     de nestre Aquilee!

24.   The song of Aquileia

Ploughman, breaking fertile ground in furrows
here by Aquileia, halt and think:
'neath the field through which your ploughshare burrows,
'neath the soil in which the corn will sink,
sun or shade, in bright or misty hours,
lies the imprint of great Rome, the story
                    and the glory
                 of Friuli ours.

Boatman, from Barbana's island plying,
when the ancient belfry sudden tolls,
'tis no bell-note in the distance dying,
but the voice of Heaven across that rolls,
bearing word imperishably grand -
voice across the ages of the story
                    and the glory
                 of our fatherland.

Pilgrim of the wartime's anguish, mother,
giving up your son to die and slay,
who at even, separate each from other,
'neath the churchyard-pines come here to pray,
hark! the nightingale from secret bowers
sweetly singing thus on you impresses
                    the caresses
                 of Friuli ours.

Not a cloud disturbs the azure morning:
look! the sea smiles 'neath the southern sky.
Sons of Rome, upon that snow-white awning,
northern mountain-garland, cast your eye.
See Friuli! Keep faith with th' Idea
everlasting, with the mighty story
                    and the glory
                 of our Aquileia!

25.   <u>In biciclete</u>
                                         i

E vie corint. La biciclete 'e va
pe strade blance sot i boscs di pins.
Mùdin scene lis monz di ca e di là
e al ven dai prâs l'odôr dei ciclamins.

E vie corint. Passi Scluse e Resiute,
saludi Muez. ("Tu vâs cussì?" "Scuen lâ,
chè il viaz 'l è lunc e jò no puès stâ fêr. ").

Eco la Ciargne, eco al spalanche dute
la puarte il Tiniment. E salt al stà
come une lanze il tôr di Piluêr.

                                    ii

La biciclete 'e va. Lassi Venzon
siarât, che s'insumìe di un'atre ete,
cun t'une muinie dentri di un porton
e biei geranios su la balconete.

Soi fûr des muris e si slarge il cîl
denant di me. La biciclete 'e svole
tan che une plume e si viôt jù lontan.

Un caselant al svange l'ort, tranquil,
un stradarûl al mene la cariole,
un ciaradôr al va cul so dran dran.

25.   On my bicycle
                                    i

And off we go. The bicycle pell-mell
along the white road through the pine-wood speeds.
Mountain gives way to mountain, and I smell
the scent of cyclamen from flowery meads.

On, on I go, past Sclusa and Resiutta.
I wave to Muez. ("Not stopping?" "I must fly;
the way is long and I can only glance").

See Carnia there, see Tagliamento put a
wide open door before me. There nearby
Pioverno's tower stands upright like a lance.

                             ii

The bicycle speeds on. I pass through wall'd[1]
Venzone, of another epoch dreaming,
see nun in gateway, and above me, sprawl'd
upon the balconies, geraniums gleaming.

Outside the walls the sky begins to spread
more widely over me. Like feather'd arrow,
I skim the road that never seems to stop.

A road-man calmly digs his garden-bed,
a sweeper pushes on his little barrow,
a carter rides with rhythmic sound, clip-clop.

---

1. sc. the 14th century, from which many of its build-
    ings date. It is famous for its mysterious mummies:
    13 corpses found in 1637 to have resisted putrefaction
    in their tombs in the Duomo and now exhibited in the
    Cappella di San Michele nearby. Such auto-embalming
    is known also elsewhere (e.g. in the vaults of St.
    Michan's Church, Dublin); but the cause varies from
    place to place. Here it may be the fungus Hypha
    Bombyx, which (like Dublin's limestone) absorbs
    moisture from the body.

iii

Sot une cueste del San Simeon,
mitût in scrufujùt Bordan al tas,
la glesie d'Ospedâl cu' l'ultin glon
compagne qualchidun c'al mûr in pâs.

La biciclete 'e va viars la planure
tal s'ciafojàz. Di un nûl grisât 'e fui
l'ombre lunge sui biei ciamps di forment.

E di uàrdie al cianâl cun muse dure
Osôv 'l è là. Forsi al scolte ance lui
lis liendis che i conte il Tiniment.

26.   Al gnò figâr

Jò ti viôt ancimò parsore il mûr
del ort, vecio figâr,
s'ciavezzât, mal ridot e cussì dûr
di murî. Ven l'unviâr
(lu sentis-tu c'al ven?):
il vint ti puarte vie l'ultime fuee
e tu sês un puar len
e tu sunis di rot tan che une bree.
Ma te stagion plui buine,
quant che tornin lis violis tai fossai,
ancie tu, puar figâr, tu ti consolis,
ti passin duc' i mâi
e tu âs quasi braûre
cu la gnove montore verduline.
Po' ven l'istât, po' la sierade, e po'
sarà piês di cumò,
fin che une dì sunarâs di rot
par simpri e il to paron
capitarà lì sot cun t'un picon
a fâ lens di brusâ.

iii

On one of Simeone's verdant knolls
Bordano squats in silence. Further on
Ospedaletto's church forlornly tolls
the knell of one on his last journey gone.

The bicycle towards the plain descending
enters the heat, and o'er the golden ears
a cloud's dark shadow onward running swells.

Guarding the valley with its frown unbending
Osoppo stands. Perhaps it also hears
the legends which the Tagliamento tells.

26.   To my fig-tree

I see you still above the garden-wall
protruding, fig-tree old,
decrepit now and fragile, nor at all
ready to die. With winter's cold
(d'you feel it coming near?)
the wind will strip the last leaf from your flank,
and you will be a mere
old piece of wood and creaking like a plank.
The kinder season cures:
when in each ditch again the violet grows,
you too, poor fig-tree, will be comforted,
forgetting all your woes,
and feeling almost haughty
in that fine new green uniform of yours.
Then summer comes, the autumn, and I vow
it will be worse than now,
until one day you creak for the last time,
your trunk wide open cracks,
and then will come your master with an axe
and faggots make of you.

27.   <u>Par un mac di ciclamins</u>*

. . . .

E jò mi visi dal prin viaz in Guart,
    di une jevade fûr da l'ordenari.
    Jere gnot ancemò c'al ven gno pari:
"Su, durmionàt di frut, su c'al è tart!
Tu vas in Ciargne cun to agne File."
E mi consegne al ciaradôr di Vile.

Tacâs tal ciâr son doi di chei famòs
    ciavai di tîr di razze carintiane.
    Ciapìn, c'al criche il dì, la Tresemane
(vevin fât, prin di mòvisi, la crôs
par tiare) e intant che plui si avicinìn,
lis monz 'e piàrdin chel colôr turchìn.

Fasìn soste a Cuelalt, passìn Artigne,
    lassìn in bande Osôv cu la fortezze
    e adalt Glemone, che jè une belezze,
un quadri di pitôr. E jò - chel pigne
di bassarûl! - c'o imaginavi, prime,
lis monz in rie e cui paîs in cime!

Il ciaradôr fâs sclopetâ la scorie
    e trionfanz jentrìn a Ospedalet:
    'o salti abàs infurmiât, miez zuet.
Eco l'ustîr, eco la mangiadorie!
Ce ustere grasse e ce cusine grande
e ce odôr di mignestre pe locande!

---

* The complete poem consists of 15 stanzas.

27.   <u>For a bunch of cyclamen</u>

. . . .

I well remember (and will now relate)
   how I first went to Guart. It was a rather
   unusual wakening: in comes my father,
and "Up, you lazy-bones, " he said; "it's late!
You're off to Carnia to your Aunty Fila. "
So over to the waggoner from Villa.

Between the shafts stand two of those renown'd
   draught-horses of the kind Carinthia breeds.
   'Tis daybreak when we take the road that leads
straight to Tricesimo (upon the ground
first marking out a cross);* soon to our view
the nearing mountains lose their turquoise hue.

Collalto (where we stopp'd), Artegna past,
   we drive between Osoppo's solid fixture,
   and on the right, as pretty as a picture,
Gemona on the mountain-side. At last
the plainsman's fond idea I could drop,
that every mountain has a town on top!

To crack of whip we make triumphal entry
   into Ospedaletto: down I leap,
   and find I cannot walk - my leg's asleep.
Here is mine host, and round the tables, gentry.
His wife, how fat! Her kitchen, how immense!
And what a smell of dinner issues thence!

---

* Cf. the departure in G. Cencigh's <u>Aghe che passe</u> (1971),
p. 27: "Menot alore al à dât el segnâl de partenze...e
dopo fat un segno di crôs cul mani...tal pulvin de strade,
...i cjars 'e son partîs. " Similarly in Zaneto's poem,
<u>Gnozzis furlanis</u>, with the added details that the cross
is then broken up and thrown as far as possible.

Te locande si polse fin lis dôs,
    po in viaz da gnuv. Chei grèbanos, chei flancs
  des monz aduès! E il puint dai Riui blancs!
E il Tiniment c'al mande la so vôs!
Sint un sdrondenament di là di un ciamp:
al è il vapôr c'al passe come un lamp.

. . . .

Duc' chei pez che van su come colonis
    c'al pâr di sèi t'un domo! Sot i pins
  son sparnizâs a grums i ciclamins,
sui pericui si viòdin crôs e anconis,
su l'ôr de aghe 'e businin lis seis,
e su la strade 'e son tassis di breis.

E soresere, quan c'o rivi su,
    mi ven incuintri agne Filumene,
  grande come gno pari, cun che vene
sul cerneli ance jé. "Cemût lajù?
Duc' pulît?" Mi trabas'ce par ciargnel,
mi slapagne ciapât a brazacuel.

Tal doman di matine 'o viarz i scûrs
    e nome monz 'o viòt atôr atôr,
  e po tal bàs un mulinut c'al côr
a planc a planc, dut plen di muscli i mûrs.
Parsore i tez e i cocolârs 'e spiche
la glesie del païs s'un t'une piche.

. . . .

Ogni volte c'o ciati i ciclamins
    jò mi ricuardi di chest viaz in Guart.
  Son antigàis? E pur al è un cunfuart
tornâ indaûr cui agns, tornâ a chei prins
afiez: ta ches memorîs rinfres'ciâsi,
dei pinsîrs di cumò dismenteâsi.

We rested in the inn till two o'clock;
   then off again, past precipice and ridge,
   past towering mountain and the Rughi bridge,
while Tagliamento echoed from the rock.
Beyond a field I heard a sudden roar:
it was a train that flashing past us tore.

. . . .

The rows of firs, like pillars upward soaring,
   make a cathedral there, and scatter'd lines
   of cyclamen are growing 'neath the pines.
A cross, an image wait for their adoring;
the saw-mills purr upon the river's banks,
and on the road are stack'd up piles of planks.

When I arrive 'tis evening once again.
   Out comes to meet me Aunty Philomena,
   tall as my father, with the same big vein a
mark on her forehead too. "Well, how's the plain?
All well?" Much in the Carnic flow I miss,
being hugg'd the while with many a smacking kiss.

Next morn I throw the shutters open wide,
   and only mountains all around I see,
   and far below, a mill-wheel noiselessly
revolving by the mill's moss-cover'd side.
Above the limes and walnuts rising higher
upon a peak appears the church's spire.

. . . .

Whenever now I chance on cyclamen,
   this journey up to Guart comes back to me.
   Is't ancient history? But it can be
a comfort to retrace the years, to when
our dear ones liv'd: drink memory's quick'ning potion
and be releas'd from all today's emotion.

EMILIO NARDINI
(1862-1938)

28.   Lis stelis

A racuei ti vòi lis stelis

   tal gran prât dal firmament;

jempli il zei cu' lis plui bielis

   e po torni dal momènt.

Planc, planchìn, une par une,

   vie pe gnot vuei lâ cirint:

mi farai prestâ de lune

   la só sésule d'arint.

Cui sa l'Albe, simpri usade

   a ciatâlis, co ven fur,

cui sa mai se, invelegnade,

   no vora tornâ indaûr?

O, viodìnt che a ti lis dôi,

   dute in grinte ti dirà:

"No ti bàstino i tiei voi?

   lis mês stelis dami cà!"

EMILIO NARDINI
(1862-1938)

28.   The stars

Gathering stars for you I'm going

in the meadows of the sky.

A full basket I'll be showing

when I come back by-and-by.

One by one, in silence blindly,

down to pluck them I shall bend,

and her silver sickle kindly

I shall ask the moon to lend.

It may be that Daybreak, ever

wont to find them ere she burn,

will be so enrag'd that never,

nevermore she will return.

Or, when I with them present you,

she will ask you with a frown:

"Do your eyes then not content you?

Those are my stars; put them down!"

29.   <u>Lenghe e dialet</u>

1.

A chei Furlans che 'o viôt a stuarzi il nâs
    se qualchidùn al cîr di scrivi sclet
in tal nestri lengàz, che a lor no ur plâs;
    a chei Furlans che crodin che l'afiet
pe mari Itàlie impon in ogni câs
    di usâ la lenghe e fâ sparî il dialèt
fasint dî "babbo" ai fruz e nò "papà",
propri a lor in furlàn vuei ciacarâ.

3.

Scomenzi e us prei di tignîmi daûr.
    Un pinsîr, si capìs, sei brut o biel,
o legri o dolorôs, par saltâ fûr
    da la pizzule ciase dal cerviel,
o de ciase plui grande di un bon cûr,
    nol pò in public mostrâ nude la piel:
bisugne c'al si viesti di espressions
che son la so giachete e i siei bragóns.

7.

Tornìn al argumènt, vuei dî in ce mût
    che nus convèn vistî un pinsîr par fâ
c'al sedi ancimò lui dopo vistût;
    che tra la nestre înt al puedi lâ
cul stamp dal lûc dulà c'al è nassût,
    c'al vebi l'andè, l'estro, il fevelâ
sempliz dal popul che lu devi lei,
lombàrt, romàn, furlàn, sei ce c'al sei.

10.

Cialait lis contadinis quant che a vore,
    sparnizzadis pai ciamps in libertât,
van seselant sot il soreli in bore;
    cialailis ce tant bielis tal istât,
cu' la còtule curte, quasi sore
    i zenoi; e sul ciâf, ròs, inflamât
un fazzolèt; si drezzin un momènt,
come da un mar dut aur, sù dal formènt.

29.   <u>Language and dialect</u>

To those Friulans who turn up their noses
    whenever someone bravely tries to write
this tongue of ours, of which they are the foes;
    to those Friulans who do love aright
our mother Italy, but wrong suppose
    they must then wipe Friulan from our sight,
and make their sons say "babbo" for "papà":
to these I speak in their vernacular.

  . . . .

I am beginning, so attention please!
    All thoughts, 'tis clear, whether fine or lewd,
joyful or sad, if they would leap with ease
    from out the brain's small casket all subdued,
or from a kind heart's nobler mansion, these
    cannot appear in public in the nude.
They need the tropes the rhetorician teaches;
these constitute their jacket and their breeches.

  . . . .

Returning to the subject, hear how best
    a man may clothe a thought, that it may be
in truth itself what people call well-dress'd,
    and walk abroad among us fearlessly
bearing the hall-mark of its natal nest,
    with all the idiom and simplicity
of those who read the product of his quill,
Friulan, Lombard, Roman - what you will.

  . . . .

Look at the peasant-women when they're toiling
    among the fields all unconstrain'd and free;
they reap away beneath the hot sun boiling:
    how beautiful they are in summer! See
them there, with short skirt roll'd right up and coiling
    almost knee-high, while face glows ruddily
beneath the kerchief; then with back up-drawn
they stand above a golden sea of corn.

11.

Cialailis, mo, di fieste cu' lis mudis
 di messe grande, come che van vie
tignìnsi par un dêt, plui che vistudis
 imbredeadis di galanterie,
cui voi sbassâz, come che fossin nudis,
 plenis di pôre che lis ciolis vie...
Di fat qualunque, a viodilis, si acuarz
che, puaretis, fasin un gran sfuarz.

12.

Mudadis lis mudandis, jé cùssì
 ance par l'ûs de lenghe o dal dialèt,
e pari Dante tant 'a la capì
 che, ciatànt tal latin juste il difiet
d'un abit incolât, 'a la finì
 cul mètilu in casson par scrivi sclet
in volgàr, il lengàz ciolt sù de strade
discólz, senze golèt, senze velade.

14.

E, si capis, cun chel tantìn di pari,
 la lenghe, - la plui biele di chest mont -,
'e doventà di bot la lenghe mari.
 Ma, paraltri, bisugne tignî cont
che cun je si è fat l'abit leterari,
 chel abit che us disevi e che in confrònt
dai dialez, lizerins, al è un pivial
che in glesie al va benòn, ma in file mal.

15.

Tignìn, dunce, ben cont dai dialèz
 che dut e ben 's si pò dî cun lôr:
son fuarz te ràbie e dolz tai morosèz,
 san dî la gionde, san vaî il dolôr:
de la înt, lûc par lûc, mostrin i aspiez
 che miei nol podarès fâ un braf pitôr:
ogni nestri ricuart a lôr si lee,
tigninju cont, son quadris di famee.

But look at them on Sunday, when they don
   their clothes for church: they hold each other's hand,
and walk with all their ease of movement gone,
   encumber'd by that finery so grand,
and eyes downcast, as though with nothing on,
   afraid of being laugh'd at where they stand.
Poor girls! It needs no great debate,
that they are in a most unnatural state.

Mutatis now mutandis, this affair
   of dialect or language is the same;
and father Dante was so well aware
   of this, he saw where Latin was to blame,
a garb too starch'd for modern thoughts to wear.
   Laying it in the drawer whence it came,
he us'd instead the language of the street,
the vulgar tongue, in shirt-sleeves and bare feet.

. . . .

Now obviously, with such a great begetter,
   Italian, the fairest speech of all,
becomes at once a mother-tongue and better.
   But on the other hand we must recall,
its literary garb can be a fetter,
   and as I said, in terms of weight can fall
below the nimble dialect, as cope
suits ill at home, though well upon a pope.

So cherish dialects and hold aloft,
   for there is nothing they cannot express:
they're strong in anger, and in love are soft;
   they sing our joy and weep in our distress;
they show a nation's varied aspects, oft
   as well as finest painter could, no less.
To them our every memory is bound,
sweet album of the family in sound.

CELSO CESCUTTI (Argeo)
(1877-1966)

30.   <u>Gnot vagant</u>

Cimût chì ciatât
tel fìs de gnot scure,
zemût razirât?
L'è un luc bandonât,
l'è un sìt sconfinât,
bessôl, di paure:
    un gri spaventât,
    un nûl misteriôs,
    un mont mai spietât.
Tel spazi lontan
al rive dal plan
un zigo smuartît;
    un'altre zuite
    rispuint a l'invìt
    planc planc dal so sìt.
L'è un luc trapassât,
un timp cence vite,
un moment mai spietât.
    Il fin un rezìnt,
    un marmo, un blancôr,
    un' ombre, un lusôr.
    L'è un sìt mai sintût,
    l'è un mont mai vivût
restât cence int.
    Al vampe un lumìn;
    'ne ufierte 'smenteade
par sorte restade;
    e un zito di bant
    al sta compagnant
    chel nuie di prin.
    L'è un fin cence un vai,
    un sium scomparît,
    un cûr tramortît,
        un' eco di mai.

CELSO CESCUTTI (Argeo)
(1877-1966)

30.   Wandering night

But how hither brought
in the heart of darkness,
oh, how was I caught?
    'Tis a place unsought,
unbounded by aught:
all emptiness, starkness!
    a cricket distraught,
a mysterious cloud,
a world never thought.
    From the far inane,
from the distant plain,
comes a muffled hoot;
    then another owl
returns the salute
from its sheltering shoot.
    'Tis a place of nought,
where hours lifeless prowl,
a time never thought.
    A boundary-wall,
a marble all white,
a shadow, a light.
    'Tis a place never heard,
a world where none stirr'd,
unpeopled by all.
    The lamp-wicks fizz:
an offering unheeded
and no longer needed.
    And silence in vain
returns once again
where Nothingness is.
    'Tis a tearless close,
a dream lost too soon,
a heart in a swoon,
    an echo of woes.

SPARTACO MURATTI

(1875-1937)

31.   La massàrie di Pre Checo

A sintì chel discors il capelan
reste di clap, al si met a vaî,
e tra i sanglòz la ciape par la man
come par tratignîle di partì;
fin c'al sbroche il dolor: - O Mènie mê,
cemût vivi in chest mont cence di te?
Cui sarà bon di cuêi il jeur sul spêt,
e i fasûi cul musèt a la furlane,
e i foncs su la gridele a scote-dêt?
Cui di guciâmi i cialzetòns di lane?
Cui come te di sopressâ lis pletis
dai ciàmiz, di tignî cont des planetis?

. . . .

T'un colp di man va in ciàmare a mudâsi
e torne jù che no samee plui je:
lui nol fâs nacie ad-ore di sintâsi
che al si ciate denant pront il cafè,
la só pipe, il tabac e un bicerìn
di che' trape che 'i fâs vignì il morbin.
- O Marie, Sant' Antoni benedet!
No ài mai viodût un miracul compàgn.
Che il Signôr mi perdoni se 'o dîs sclet
che a piardi Mènie ài fat un gran guadàgn;
nome che chiste... cave occasionem,
ne nos inducat, Checo, in tentationem.

. . . .

SPARTACO MURATTI
(1875-1937)

31.   Father Checo's house-keeper

(Father Checo, a 30-year old priest in a Carnic village,
learns that his pearl of a house-keeper has to go into hospital)

> On hearing this, the priest could hardly stand,
> so thunderstruck he was: he starts to wail,
> and sobbing deeply takes her by the hand,
> as though sheer force to keep her could avail.
> At last his grief bursts out: "What shall I do,
> how shall I manage here depriv'd of you?
> Who's going to cook for me the spitted hare,
> the beans and sausage in Friulan style,
> or grill my mushrooms till their flesh will glare?
> Who's going to darn my woollen socks the while?
> Who'll press my shirts and leave so good a border
> as you, and keep my chasubles in order?"

(The housekeeper's remedy is to send her young niece,
Rosina, from the city)

> At once the niece goes to her room to change,
> and on descending seems a different girl.
> He's hardly time to take a seat when, strange,
> the coffee's vapours from the table curl,
> his pipe is ready for him, and a glass
> of wine invites to let all sad thoughts pass.
> "O Mary and Saint Antony the blest!
> I've never seen a miracle like this.
> The Lord forgive me, it must be confess'd
> this change has gain'd me more than I shall miss.
> Only, this girl.... cave occasionem,
> ne nos inducat in tentationem."

. . . .

in ogni câs
dopo di un mês che jere sù Rosine,
durave in che' canoniche une pâs,
un serèn tra il tinel e la cusine,
un lat e mîl cussì perfet che 'o dîs
che il compagn no si ciate in Paradîs.
　　Dome che il purgatori ere tal cûr
dal pùar predi, e al cresseve dì par dì;
ma lui no lu varès mai pandût fûr
se al ves crodût magari di murî.
Al diseve al Signôr: "Domine impetro
gratiam tuam", e a chel altri: "Vade retro!"

. . . .

　　E in che' glesiute blancie di montagne
cul so puarti denant tra i cistinârs,
che par che 'e svoli sore la campagne
che si piart jù pai ciamps e pai filârs,
denant a la Madone in zenoglon
al preave che 'i dès pâs e perdon.
　　Oh, si dabòn! Intant che cu la bocie
al dîs: - "Ave Marie", "Salve Regine" -
spaurît come un polèz che al cîr la clocie,
tal quadri de Madone al viôt Rosine,
e lui sot a vaî dut squintiât:
- Se no 'l ven un miràcul, soi danât...!
　　E il miràcul lu à fat la Madonute:
quanche, piardût il ciâf, une domènie
al stave par dî dut a di che frute,
jù tal sotpuarti al sint la vôs di Menie!
- Sestu cà? Isal za finît il mâl?
- Po 'i pàrin pôs doi mês in ospedâl?
　　L'indoman di matine 'e ven la vecie
cul solit cafè e lat in sagristie:
- Tu podevis polsâ, mandà to' gnece.
- Rosine? Lu salude; 'e lade vie.
Pre' Checo al mole un strît, al va par tiere,
e par vot dîs al sta in jet cu la fiere.
　　D'in che' dì, pôc al mangie e manco al bêf,
nol va a ciazze, nol zuie di tressiet;
ma che sei ploe, c'al sei soreli o nêf,
finide messe al ciape sù e al va dret
a preâ lassù in alt ogni matine
che' Madonute che somèe Rosine.

Be that as it may,
for that first month Rosina was his groom,
in that old vicarage such peace held sway
between the kitchen and the dining-room,
such milk and honey in a perfect splice,
that one would miss the like in Paradise.
    But Purgatory there was, within the heart
of that poor priest, and daily worse it grew;
but he had rather died, for his own part,
than that his secret any other knew.
He'd pray the Lord: "O Domine, impetro
gratiam tuam", and t'other: "Vade retro!"

(He loses his taste for hunting and begins to visit a little
church in the mountains)

    And in that little white-wash'd mountain-church
nestling up there amid the chestnut-trees,
which seems to launch itself as from a perch
above the fields and vineyards on the breeze,
he knelt before the Virgin and he pray'd
for peace, and pardon if in thought he stray'd.

    All very well! But while his lips are then
framing: "Ave Maria", "Salve Regina",
as frighten'd as a chick that's lost its hen,
behind the Virgin's face he sees Rosina.
Ah, then the bitter groan and beaten brow!
"Only a miracle can save me now."
    And Mary deigns that miracle to fashion:
one Sunday, when he could refrain no more,
when just about to tell the girl his passion,
he hears his old housekeeper at the door.
"What! Back already? Are you really well?"
"Is two months there not long enough a spell?"
    Next morning the old woman brings his piece
of bread and coffee, as she us'd to do.
"You could have stay'd in bed and sent your niece".
"Rosina? Gone, and says good-bye to you."
A cry bursts from his lips; he falls as dead,
and for a week lies feverish in bed.
    From then he has no appetite nor thirst,
he hunts no more, in cards no interest takes;
but rain or fine, let snow or tempest burst,
once Mass is over, off he goes and makes
a bee-line for that church, where he has seen a
Madonna with the features of Rosina.

BINDO CHIURLO
(1886-1943)

32.   'O ciantarài

O strade quietine sot i pôi,
   che tantis voltis tu mi menis vie,
savarestu menâmi ta chel trôi
   c'o levi a nolis cu la baronie?
'O cirivi cidin, cun furbarie,
   sui malics 'o slargiavi tant di vôi,
e ce sfladâ di glorie e di ligrie!
   e ce cori pe strade sot i pôi!

Cumò, stradute, mètimi in tal cûr
   chel gust, chel cîl seren, chel aiarìn
     c'o ciantarài di fâus restâ di plante:

'o ciantarài come lassù tal scûr
   chel rusignûl, che no 'l ciate padìn
     e s'ingusìs di gust, tan ben c'al ciante.

33.   Al Taiament

O Taiament, che tu vâs pal Friûl,
   cul to làvio di glerie, passonant,
   cumò che sglonf tu businis passant,
ti ricuàrdistu dai sais dal ciavrûl?
Lassù puar e cuiet come un riûl,
   lis puemis ti passavin fevelant,
    e tu tu ur levis vie ciacaruzzant
intôr i pîs, lizerìn come un tûl.

Ma, ciatât un roiuc' par ogni trôi,
   tu vegnis iú, tu ti sglonfis a plen,
    e tu ciapis possès de Furlanie.

Di là de grave, miec' scuindût tra i pôi,
   un ciampanîl al cuche, e a cui cu ven
   al bute, vie pe gnot, l'avemarie.

BINDO CHIURLO
(1886-1943)

32.   I'll sing

O silent road beneath the poplar-trees,
    whose beauty oft my wandering step decoys,
lead me, O lead me to that pathway, please,
    where once I gather'd nuts with other boys.
I'd look around with cunning, make no noise,
    and gape upon the bunch I could not seize.
What exultation swell'd my breast, what joys,
    as there I ran beneath the poplar-trees.

O little road, but let me feel them now:
    that joy, that gentle breeze, that sky serene,
    and with my song I'll make the world stand still.

I'll sing, as warbles on yon leafy bough
    that nightingale, which makes no pause between,
    and chokes for sheer delight at his own skill.

33.   To the Tagliamento

O Tagliament', who through Friuli go
    as though to pasture on your gravelly bed,
    now that you roar, with swollen waters fed,
do you recall the leaping of the roe?
Up there where like a brook you humbly flow,
    the girls would ford you with an easy tread,
    and round their feet upon your way you sped
with nimble waters babbling light and low.

But on your journey down, you draw your due
    from many little streams, and swoll'n with these,
    you take possession of Friuli there.

Beyond your bed, half-hidden to the view,
    a bell-tower peeps from out the poplar-trees,
    and through the darkness calls to evening-prayer.

34.   <u>Vilotis</u>

(i)   Passarute di nïade,
                odulute di prin svôl,
             s'al bastàs di fâ la ciase
                su la cruchigne di un pôl!

             S'al bastàs di fâ la ciase
                di patùs e di pantàn,
             e di vivi di rosade
                cence spindi un carantàn!

(ii)   Ce biel lâ cu la morose
                tal bearc' tra lûs e scûr,
             o poâsi insomp de braide
                co lis stelis sàltin fûr:

             sàltin fûr ad une ad une
                come frutis incorint;
             pâr che àlzin la velete
                sot la scopule dal vint.

(iii)   Dio mi mandi la mê ore
                clare e nete un dì d'unviâr,
             quan'che a l'alte ogni monte
                à dut blanc il so tabâr;

             quan'che pegre la taviele
                si dismole atôr, atôr,
             e cul puin su la manàrie,
                al sta in scolte il boscadôr.

34.   <u>Villotte</u>

(i)   Little sparrow, still a nestling,
               little lark on your first walk,
           would that all I need for housing
               were the poplar's branching fork!

           Would that all I need for housing
               were some twigs and muddy grease,
           and that I could live off dew-drops
               and not spend a penny-piece!

(ii)   Through the garden with a lov'd one
               sweet it is at dusk to go,
           or to lie upon the meadow
               when the stars begin to show:

           one by one they come out peeping,
               like a game of hide-and-seek;
           'tis as if they lift their kerchief
               as the breezes smack their cheek.

(iii)   May God send me my last hour
               crisp and clear, one winter's day,
           when the top of every mountain
               has its white cloak on display;

           when, all round, the spreading country
               slowly breaks its freezing bands,
           and with fist upon his hatchet,
               there the woodman listening stands.

GIOVANNI LORENZONI

(1884-1950)

35.   Ciampanis

Plôf. 'E sune une ciampane

    da lontan - cui sa dulà.

Jè di ziart 'ne vite umane

    che finìs di tribulâ.

Ze lancûr murî t'un'ore

    quanche il zîl al è inulât,

e la ploe 'e cole, 'e cole

    cun chel estro disperât.

Oh, une grazie, sì, domandi

    nome che' - pa l'ultin dì:

che 'l soreli un rai mi mandi

    sun chel pont c'o ài di murî.

GIOVANNI LORENZONI

(1884-1950)

35. <u>Bells</u>

Rain. There sounds a church-bell, tolling

in some village far away.

So another soul is rolling

off its load of tortur'd clay.

O the grief, to die expressly

when the sky is clouded o'er;

and the rain is pitilessly

settling down to pour and pour.

Ask of Heav'n one favour for me,

to console my dying breath:

that a sunbeam glisten o'er me

at the moment of my death.

FRANCESCA NIMIS-LOI

(1876-1959)

36.   A un olm

Olm antic e solitari,
    verd altâr drezzât al cil,
l'uragan nol ti spavente
    e dei niz tu sês asîl.

Jò di spes sole, pinsose,
    ti contemple cun rispièt;
d'un lontan passât mi conte
    la grandezze del to aspièt.

Dentri 'l tronc e vie pes ramis
    un misteri al pâr scuindût:
as-tu un'anime sdegnose
    che nissùn à cognossût?

E la èdare che simpri
    dute verde, cun amôr,
ti strenz fuart, ti lèe, t'inlazze,
    t'involuzze tôr a tôr:

ise, dimi, la compagne
    de to sorte, il to confuart;
ti s'ciafoje, o ti dà vite,
    ise il ben...o la to muart?

37.   La None

Tal tinèl guce la nòne;
    'e lavore daurman.
Al somèe che stèdi atente,
    ma il pinsir lu à tant lontan.

Si ricuarde d'une glesie
    d'un altâr e di un vel blanc,
une vere, un "sì", une firme,
    e po vie, cun lui al flanc.

Qualchi làgrime a la nòne
    sul lavor cole a planchin;
d'improvìs si rasserene,
    al è entrât un nevodìn!

FRANCESCA NIMIS-LOI
(1876-1959)

36.   To an elm

Ancient elm and solitary,
    altar green that seeks the sky,
to the birds you grant asylum
    and the tempest you defy.

Often will I, lonely, thoughtful,
    contemplate your form with awe;
and the grandeur of your aspect
    speaks of ages gone before.

In your trunk and through your branches
    some dark mystery seems to hide;
have you, all unknown, undream'd of,
    soul and spirit fill'd with pride?

And the ivy there that ever
    in its green and loving hold
clasps you, binds you, and so tightly
    twists around you fold on fold:

is it, tell me, the companion
    of your fate, your comfort still?
Does it strangle or revive you,
    does it save... or does it kill?

37.   The grandmother

In the parlour Granny's sewing -
    see the busy fingers' play.
You would think the work engrossing,
    but her thoughts are far away.

She is thinking of an altar,
    of the white veil of a bride,
of a ring, a "Yes", a signing,
    of who stood there at her side.

So while Granny works, the tears
    softly slide from cheek to chin.
Suddenly her features brighten,
    as a grandchild dances in.

PIETRO PASCOLI (Piero di Sandenêl)
                                    (1887-1955)

38.   Avemarie da matine

                 don, don, don...
         Sune, sune tu ciampane
              spant pa vile la tó vôs,
         entre dentri in ogni ciase
              svee la int dal so ripôs.

         Ciante il gial, al ciante il mierli,
              jeve l'odule dal prât,
         la taviele si risclare
              cul gnûf dì c'al à cricât.

         Armoniose une prejere
              va sù in alt viers il Signôr,
         il soreli il mont colore
              e ognun torne al so lavor.

PIETRO PASCOLI (Piero di Sandenêl)
(1887-1955)

38.   Morning bells

Ring out, bell, ring out and centre

on the town your music deep;

into every house now enter,

wake the people from their sleep.

Cock is crowing, blackbird singing,

o'er the meadow soars the lark;

dawn is once again beginning

from the fields to drive the dark.

Tuneful voices raise to Heaven

prayers for that for which we yearn;

sunbeams red the mountain leaven,

and to labour all return.

FRANCESCA MARINI BÀRNABA
(1877-

39.   Crepecûr

Zornade di ploe
senze salustri.
Colôr cinise
dentri e fûr di me.
Orès pièrdimi vie, cussì,
senza pensâ:
dismenteâ dut e no savê di vivi.
Ma ricuàrz trisc' e malâs
mi batin dentri il cûr
par fâsi vierzi.
Vegnît, za che tu olês,
memòriis di passion,
ricuàrz di bens pierdûz,
speranzis e siums
finîs tal nuie.
Vegnît. Il disgòt dai stringèis
'us compagne,
e lis lagrimis che colin
dai miei voi.
'I ài frêt.
No baste il fûg dal zoc
par s'cialdâ l'anime ingrisignide
né la vuestre presinze
dà calôr.
Ma vegnît istès
a fâmi compagnie,
ombris dal timp passât,
ma puartaimi cun vo
quant che vais vie.

FRANCESCA MARINI BÀRNABA
(1877-

39.   Heartbreak

A day of rain
without break in the clouds.
An ashen colour
inside and outside me.
I would just like to lose myself
without thinking:
forget everything, be unaware of living.
But sad, sick memories
beat within my heart
to make me open to them.
Come, since you wish it,
memories of my longing,
memories of lost joys
hopes and dreams
ending in nothing.
Come. The water dripping from the eaves
will accompany you,
and the tears stealing down
from my eyes.
I am cold.
The log-fire is not enough
to warm the frozen soul,
nor does your presence
give warmth.
But come all the same
to keep me company,
shadows of the past;
but take me with you
when you leave.

FRANCO DE GIRONCOLI
(1892-

40.   Elegie

Piàrdisi tal mâr dai siuns
come il scirocâl tai nui
ch'a si disgrope in ploe,

e la tiare si giolt
di tant vaiúm.

MARIA FORTE NICOLOSO
(1899-

41.   Novembar

Rositis frescjs
e dopo
zois flapidis.
A' son simpri contènz
i muarz cidins.
Il pizzighet sbaldît
al bruse in grum
mazzés disvuidâs.
Il fum latisìn
al fâs plui miesti
il simiteri.
Ce dolz
cialâsi ancimò.
I muarz sot tiere
no àn plui
flusumie.

FRANCO DE GIRONCOLI
(1892-

40.   Elegy

To lose oneself in a sea of dreams
as the scirocco does in the clouds,
whose denoûment is rain,

and the earth revels
in such a weeping.

MARIA FORTE NICOLOSO
(1899-

41.   November

Fresh little roses
and later
wither'd wreaths.
They are always content,
the quiet dead.
The grave-digger, thoughts elsewhere,
burns a heap
of scatter'd bunches.
The milky smoke
saddens still more
the cemetery.
How sweet
to gaze on each other still.
The dead underground
no longer have a
physiognomy.

ENRICA CRAGNOLINI
                              (1904-

42.   <u>Lune gnove di iugn</u>

Lune gnove di iugn

sèsule fine

pal formènt madûr;

lune dal ricòlt spetât,

lune di un bramât,

a lunc, amôr.

Lune gnove,

sul blanc tremôr di agacis,

sul blanc profum

che al incioche la sere.

Lune in scolte,

sul prât,

lune.

ENRICA CRAGNOLINI
(1904-

42.   New moon in June

New moon of June,

slender sickle

for the ripe corn;

moon of the awaited harvest,

moon of a lov'd one

long yearn'd for.

New moon,

over the white quivering of the acacias,

over the white perfume

which intoxicates the evening.

Listening moon,

over the meadow,

moon.

ANTONIO DELUISA

(1906-

43.   Mandi

Iò ti saludarai simpri cussì
   co vignarai sot sere, a fâ l'amôr
   in ciase to, o quant ch'al miò lavor
larai ogni matine, apene dì;

iò ti saludarai simpri cussì,
   sei un sflandôr il cîl, o sei nulât;
   e s'o sarai content o disperât,
dal miò salût tu podarâs capî;

Iò ti saludarai simpri cussì,
   se vie pal mont mi tociarà di là;
   ma il cûr miò, di lontan, al tornarà,
sot gnot, cidìn, dongie di te, culì...

iò ti saludarai simpri cussì,
   une bussade e "mandi", ciar miò ben:
   chest, dal miò afièt par te al sarà il pen,
e "mandi" ti dirai prin di murî.

ANTONIO DELUISA
(1906-

43.   Mandi*

Thus shall I always greet you, sweet, thus say,
   whene'er at eventide I come to woo
   you in your home, or each day, as I do,
pass on my way to work, at break of day.

Thus shall I always greet you, sweet, thus say,
   whate'er the weather, cloudy or set fair,
   and whether I am glad or in despair
(and which I am, my greeting will convey).

Thus shall I always greet you, sweet, thus say,
   if I must wander off across the sea;
   my heart will still return by night, and be
beside you here, however long the way.

Thus shall I always greet you, sweet, thus say;
   a kiss, and "Mandi", - this, my sweetheart true,
   shall be the earnest of my love for you,
this be my last word when I pass away.

---

* Like Italian Ciao and Spanish Adios, Friulan Mandi
  is both a greeting and a farewell (cf. No. 21 and
  App. 1, Nos. 8 and 11, xx).

ADELGISO FIOR
(1916-

44. <u>Inscindalasci</u>

O ce biel inscindalasci
    di chest mont, cencie sunsûr;
e savei che domo l'aria
    si è 'ndacuarta ch'a si mûr.

E murî di gnot, tun stâli,
    con' ch'a si à ciapât il sum,
e no vê rancors di sorta
    e no fâ sufrî nissun.

45. <u>Al è muart un pianista</u>

Al è muart un pianista
e al duâr
cu las mans in crous.
Las gotas da cera
'a lu sclipignin.
La lûs dal sorêli
'a passa la lûs das ciandelas.
In tinel
il piano al tâs.
Ma un tarli
'a lu rosea.
Al iempla la ciasa
cul so sunsûr.
Al par ch'al mangi la cassa.

ADELGISO FIOR
(1916-

44.   To go away

O how fine if our departure
    from this world were without fuss,
and we knew the air the only
    witness we were dying thus.

Die at night in mountain-shelter,
    while we sleep without reprieve,
with no anger or resentment,
    knowing none is left to grieve.

45.   A pianist has died

A pianist has died
and he sleeps
with cross'd hands.
The drops of wax
splash him.
The light of the sun
overwhelms the light of the candles.
In the parlour
the piano is silent.
But a worm
is gnawing it.
It fills the house
with its whisper.
It is as though it were eating the coffin.

NOVELLA AURORA CANTARUTTI

(1920-

46.   Planchinìn

Voa da vai planchinìn
come li' vîs,
di vierta
co 'a li'cùncin,
e la cjera in gjonda
'a na sa di ce doul
ch'a vàin li' vîs.

RENZA SNAIDERO

(1920-

47.   L'ore dolze

Butâsi sul prât
tal soreli dal dopomisdì
cu la muse in te jarbe,
cu la bocje in te tiare...

La mê ore dolze...

E sintîsi a sfantâ
tal odôr vîf dal nembri;
sintîsi a lâ in nie tal celest
e deventâ prât, cîl, Signôr.

AURELIO CANTONI

(1922-

48.   Ploe

Une ploe fine 'e cole
sui cops duc' grîs di cheste zitât viere
ch'e à la siere di un puar frut malât
che nissun console.

Dopomisdì lis stradis a' son cussì strachis
che il cinglinâ dal tram al pâr un sun
di campanel sclapât.
Partiare sot i pis qualchi fuèe
si cuvjarz di aghe e di pantan,
e dut si plèe tun dûl di sjum lontan
glotût come un clap tun flum.

NOVELLA AURORA CANTARUTTI

(1920-

46.   Softly

Desire to weep softly
like the vines,
in spring
when they are prun'd
and the exultant earth
knows nothing of this pain
that makes the vines weep.

RENZA SNAIDERO

(1920-

47.   Sweet hour

To throw oneself on the sward
in the midday-sun
with one's face in the grass
with one's mouth in the earth...

My sweet hour...

And feel oneself dissolve
in the living scent of the turf;
feel oneself go into nothingness in the blue,
and become sward, sky, Lord.

AURELIO CANTONI

(1922-

48.   Rain

A fine rain is descending
on the grey tiles of this old town
with its look of a poor sick child
no-one is tending.

After midday the streets are so tired
that the clanking of the tram seems the sound
of a crack'd bell.
On the ground beneath our feet mass'd leaves
are cover'd with water and mud,
and everything is bow'd in the grief of a distant dream,
gulp'd down like a stone in the river.

DINO VIRGILI
(1925-

49.   La vegle

Serenade:
    Serenade di rosis e di grîs
    par chê mê fantazzute indurmidide.
    Lis stelis sul balcon in sfese a' cùchin
    jenfri un ramaz di spiarsolâr in rose:
    al sdrindùle tun nizzul di durmî...
    'O orès platâmi achì sot la palade,
    butâti un clap tal scûr, tacâ a cjantâ...
    Balcon adalt...e tù tun jet di rosis
    (chê dì, tal prât, lis rosis tôr la muse).
    Ninâ, cuessutis clipis di favìt...

Gnotolade:
    Canzion di biele vôs tal miez de strade
    cul sivilòt di scuarz, la lune insomp
    e i grîs imò te braide, e jê durmî...
    Ninâ, che i lens tal ort a' butin fûr:
    domàn ti zimiaràn i butui creis...
    E jo 'o orès jêssi in chel revoc di lune
    ch'e ti cjarine il cuarp indurmidît
    e mai nol cricàs dì come ogni dì...
    Canzion tal miez de strade di un ch'al passe...
    Ninâ, bucjute tìnare di sup...

Madins:
    Sisilis svearinis sul pujûl:
    a' crìzzin...Fantazzine, za al sclaris!...
    e tù tu pûs cjantâ cul cûr siarât.
    La bielestele 'e je jevade adore:
    tu viarz la balcugnele indarindade,
    dàj un basìn a pìz, torne a durmî!...
    Lajù chel cjâr ch'al cloche sul stradon
    al mene vie cun sè il lancûr de gnot,
    e al lasse un clâr seren ienfri i ramaz.
    Ninâ, vugluz 'studâz di latisûl...

DINO VIRGILI
(1925-

49.   The vigil

Serenade:
    A serenade of roses and of crickets
    for that sweet girl of mine up there asleep.
    The stars peep through the window's half-clos'd shutters
    from 'midst the branches of a peach-tree's bloom;
    it's swaying in the see-saw of a sleep...
    I'd like to hide here 'neath the palisade,
    throw stone up at your shutter, start to sing...
    Balcony there... and you in bed of roses
    (that day upon the grass, your rose-ring'd face)
    Nina, little warm thighs of a wren...

Night:
    A fine voice finely singing in the street,
    with wooden pipe and overhead the moon,
    and in the field the crickets, while she sleeps.
    Nina, the orchard-trees begin to bloom:
    tomorrow new-born buds will sway for you...
    I'd like to be in that moon's tremulous beam
    caressing now your sleeping body there,
    that day just for this once might never dawn.
    A street-song sung by someone passing by...
    Nina, soft little mouth of deadnettle...

Matins:
    Hark, early rising swallows on the hill:
    they chatter... Look, my girl, it is the dawn!...
    and you can sing with that clos'd heart of yours.
    The morning-star is risen, up betimes:
    open your casement with its silver sheen,
    blow down a kiss, and then go back to sleep....
    That waggon rattling on the road down there
    is bearing off the languor of the night,
    and leaves serenity within the boughs.
    Nina, quench'd little eyes of sow-thistle...

Dismote:
    'E à viarz i vôi: soreli sul balcon,
    la viarte vive tal balcon in rose...
    Orès cjapâti, vuîte, chi tal braz...
    Ma di ce sajal il to sen? di viole?
    Nè di zì nè di viole: al sa di frute...
    Cumò 'e jè in cjamesin dongje l'antîl
    cui vôi inceâz, si met in comedon.
    E la mê vôs dilunc il troi de braide
    cu la rosade a gotis tai ramàz...
    Jo 'o soi dome une vôs ch'e cjante, imò.

DOMENICO NALDINI
(1929-

50.   Primavera

    Lizeris li' sisilis
    'a svualin su li' stradis
    e tai cops 'a sighin.

    Primavera 'a si dirès,
    in tal país, odorous,
    clipit antic
    al bat il prin soreli.

    La glisia rosa,
    la beorcia
    di colours si inumidissin.

    In ta un barcon
    content un frut al siga
    a li' sisilis novis
    che atôr 'a svualin.

Awakening:
    Her eyes are open; sun on balcony,
    spring lives upon the balcony in bloom...
    I'd like to seize you, pipit, in my arms...
    Your bosom's fragrance - is it violets?
    Not violets nor lilies, just a girl's...
    And now she's in her night-dress by the sill;
    with dazzled eyes she leans upon her elbows.
    My voice along the pathway through the field
    and dewdrops dripping, dripping from the branches...
    And I am but a voice that's singing, still.

DOMENICO NALDINI
(1929-

50.   Spring

    Nimbly the swallows
    fly above the roads
    and cry on the roof-tops.

    Spring one would say,
    in the village, scented;
    warm, ancient,
    the first sunbeams strike.

    The pink church,
    the waste land
    grow damp with colours.

    Upon a balcony
    a boy contented calls
    to the new swallows
    flying around.

ALAN BRUSINI
(1923-

51.   Mans vueidis

Uê mi scjampe dut:
i pinsirs, i vôi des feminis,
l'ombre e la lûs dal dî
che mi smalite tes mans
come un jeur ferît.
Uê mi scjampe dut
come s'o vès lassât
lis mans sul zoc.
Tant vâl spietâ la gnot:
lis ceis ch'a invuluzzin tal scûr
dutis lis robis.

NADIA PAULUZZO
(1931-

52.   'Ne piciule tombe

A mi dami, Diu, 'ne piciule
tombe di glerie
niciade da li' bugadis di vint.
'Ne tombe blancie in somp di un cuel.
Dongie 'l cîl.
E qualchi margarite nassude di me,
zale e lustre
come une flame trimule.
Lasse ch'o sinti, Diu, il ciant di rosade
de òdule
e la rane che grache
basse, tai rivai.
Iò ti darai, Signôr, il miò tasê.

ALAN BRUSINI
(1923-

51.   Empty hands

Today everything escapes me:
thoughts, the eyes of women,
the shadow and light of day,
which moves restlessly in my hands
like a wounded hare.
Today everything escapes me
as if I had left
my hands on the block.
I might as well wait for night:
the eyelashes which wrap in darkness
everything.

NADIA PAULUZZO
(1931-

52.   A little grave

As for me, give me, God, a little
grave of gravel,
rock'd by gusts of wind.
A white grave on top of a hill.
Near the sky.
And let some daisies born of me,
yellow and shining,
quiver like a flame.
Let me hear, God, the dewy song
of the lark
and the frog croaking
deep-ton'd, on the banks.
I will give you, Lord, my silence.

PIER PAOLO PASOLINI
(1922-

53.   'A planzin li' vis...

'A planzin li' vis;
e in quanciu di lour
ch'a li' vevin sarpidis pulit!
E vuei nuia:
muart, sanc, dolour,
e il soreli tai nis.

Crist, fa passâ chisti' oris
di dolour massa alt,
ch'a no rivin i cours a puartâlu.

'A planzin li' vis, e tu, Crist,
dani* coragiu di vivi enciamò.

                    * ni is Casarsese for nus.

ENOS COSTANTINI
(1950-

54.   Gnot di Nadâl

Frêt ch'al imbramiva
mâglas di sanc sul asfalt
e un muart.

Dulà éristu Bambin Gjesù?

55.   Monumento ai caduti

A nô nus àn dit:
"E' bello morire per la patria".
'O vin crodût,
ma nol è stât biel.

PIER PAOLO PASOLINI
(1922-

53.   The vines are weeping...

The vines are weeping;
and how many of those
who prun'd them well, weep too!
And today nothing:
death, blood, pain's throes,
and the sun in the nests.

Christ, let these hours pass,
hours of pain too deep
for hearts to endure.

The vines weep, and do thou, Christ,
give us courage to go on living.

ENOS COSTANTINI
(1950-

54.   Christmas night

A numbing cold.
stains of blood on the tarmac
and one dead.

Where were you, Baby Jesus?

55.   Monument to the fallen

They told us:
"It is beautiful to die for one's country".
We believed,
but it wasn't beautiful.

APPENDIX 1

POESIA   POPOLARE

(a) Nine-nane

1.
Ninâ, pipin di scuñe,
to mari che ti à fat a si consume;
ninâ, pipin di conce,
to mari che ti à fat a ti sta donge;
ninâ, pipin colone,
to mari che ti à fat no ti bandone.

(b) Filastroche

2.
. . . .
"E ce strade veso fate, missêr Lavoreben?".
"Le ài ciatade fate, che Dio us dedi dal ben."
"La vês ciatade fate?".
"Vevio di fale iò po'?".

"Fin dulà seso rivât, missêr Lavoreben?".
"Fin là dai miei cusins, che (ecc.)".
"Fin là dai vuestris cusins?".
"Vevio di stâ te strade po'?".

"E dula us àno menât a durmî, missêr Lavoreben?".
"In te stalute cu' la vaciute, che (ecc.)".
"In te stalute cu' la vaciute?".
"In tun iet di plumis, po'?".

"E ce us àno dât di fâ, missêr Lavoreben?".
"'O sòi lât a passòn cu' la vaciute, che (ecc.)".
"A passòn cu' la vaciute?".
"Vevio di stâ in poltrone po'?".

"E cun ce paràviso indevànt la vaciute, missêr Lavoreben"
"Cun tune bachetute, che (ecc.)".
"Cun tune bachetute?".
"Vévio di tirale pe code po'?".
. . . .

APPENDIX 1

FOLK - POETRY

(a) <u>Lullaby</u>

1.   Rock-a-bye baby, in cradle so fair,
        your mother who made you is worn out with care.
        Rock-a-bye baby, in chair so dear,
        your mother who made you is by you here.
        Rock-a-bye baby, the house's hope,
        your mother who made you will never elope.

(b) <u>Nonsense-poetry</u>*

2.   . . . .
        "And what road did you make (take), Mr. Workwell?"
        "I found it made, God bless you."
        "You found it made?"
        "Was I to make it myself?"

        "How far did you go, Mr. Workwell?"
        "As far as my cousin's house."
        "As far as your cousin's house?"
        "Was I to stay on the road?"

        "And where did they let you sleep, Mr. Workwell?"
        "In the stall with the cow."
        "In the stall with the cow?"
        "In a feather-bed, I suppose?"

        "And what did they give you to do, Mr. Workwell?"
        "I went to pasture the cow."
        "You went to pasture the cow?"
        "Was I to stay in an arm-chair?"

        "And with what did you drive the cow, Mr. Workwell?"
        "With a stick."
        "With a stick?"
        "Was I to pull it by the tail?"

        . . . .
        *For children's games and their various rigma-
        roles see <u>Ce fas-tu?</u>, 1944, pp. 308-315 ("Giochi
        e conte di fanciulli nel Cividalese").

(c) <u>Prejere</u> (Orazion)

3.   Maria Vergina das montutas e das montiselas
          filava lin e stuarzeva seda.
          Biel stuarzint e biel drezzansi
          s'incuarzè c'a era gravidela.
          "Po' Joisus jo! cun cui sòio gravidela,
          che no ai partit peraula
          nè cun om nè cun femina batiada,
          nòme norsera cun san Jusèf da Padua?
          Se jo vès achì il gno curtelìn
          vorès tiràmel entre il cûr e l'anima. "

          Ma risponde chel Bambin del corpo fora:
          "Vo, ciare Mari, no steit a fà cussì;
          se vo fais cussì, dutes las santes maris
          'a varessin da fà cussì.

          Vo vîs da fà un Bambin tant bon,
          un Bambin tant ciar,
          che di clap al savarà fà pan
          e di aghe al savarà fà vin.

          Al fasarà trentetrè agn il pelegrin,
          al sarà un piciul scolarût,
          ch'al larà a ciantâ
          la 'pistule par dut. "

(c) Prayer

3.   Mary the Virgin of mountains and hills
        was spinning flax and unravelling silk.
        While she unwound and was straightening up,
        she sudden perceiv'd that she was with child.
        "Jesus! By whom am I made with child,
        who have spoken with fewer
        than a single Christian, be it man or woman,
        except last night with St. Joseph of Padua?
        If I had here my own little knife,
        I'd stab myself 'twixt my heart and my soul."

        But from her body then replies the Babe:
        "Do not thus, dear Mother;
        if you do thus, all holy mothers too
        would have to do the same.

        You are to bear a Babe so good,
        a Babe so dear,
        that of a stone he will make bread,
        and out of water he'll make wine.

        Thirty-three years he'll be a pilgrim, and
        he'll be a little scholar too,
        who'll go out to sing
        the gospel everywhere."

(d) Scongiuro

4.
Santa Bàrbula e sant Simon,
che nus uardin dal fug e dal ton,
dal ton e da la saeta,
Santa Bàrbula benedeta!

(e) Parodia

5.
Pater noster quit quit,
'a è tre dîs ch'i noi ài dit;
se gno pari 'a no mi dà pan,
no lu dîs nencia doman;
se me mari 'a no mi dà mignestra,
no lu dîs nencia a la fiesta.

(f) Danze

6.
La puarte siarade,
lis clâs 'e son sú:
al passe chel zovin,
al viarz e al va sú.

La mari in cusine:
"Ce fastu lassú?"
"L'è il giat su pe s'cialis,
ch'al cor sú e iú."

Al giave lis scarpis:
guai fâsi sintî!
La ciape, la busse,
la met a durmî.

"Po cagne di fie,
ce fastu lassú?"
"Lis coltris coladis!
Cumò lis ciol sú."

(d) Conjuration

4.

Saint Barbula, Saint Simon, pray,
fire and thunder keep away.
Ward off thunder-bolt and -clap,
Saint Barbula, save from mishap.

(e) Parody

5.

Paternoster, quit quit,
for three days I have not said it.
If I get no bread from father,
I'll not say 't tomorrow either;
if from mother no minestra,
I'll not say it ev'n at festa.

(f) Dance-song

6.

Clos'd is the entrance,
the keys are upstairs.
Along comes a young man:
a creak on the stairs.

The mother in kitchen:
"What's happening up there?"
"'Tis pussy a-scampering
up-'n-down on the stair."

He takes off his boots - to
be caught is his dread.
He hugs her and kisses,
and puts her to bed.

"You bitch of a daughter,
what's happening up there?"
"The bed-clothes have slipp'd off;
I'm putting all square."

(g) <u>Coroz</u>

7.

Tite gno benedet,

dulà veso poiât lu vuesti falcet?

Tite gno ciar,

dulà veso poiât il vuesti codâr?

Tite gno di cûr,

ch'a è oro di seâ chel artigôl!

Oh ievait sú, Tite,

no stait a fâ portâ!

'O seis pûr tant zoven, Tite,

no podeso ciaminâ?

(g) <u>Laments for the dead</u>

7.   O my Tite, once so blithe,

              where have you laid away your little scythe?

              O my Tite, O my own,

              where have you laid the holster of your hone?*

              For, dear Tite, you must know

              'tis time to start that aftermath to mow!

              O get up, Tite!

              At being carried you should baulk,

              young, so young, my Tite, still:

              can you not walk?

---

* Cf. p. 54 and the peasant Bepo in G. Cencigh's
  <u>Aghe che passe</u> (1971), "Water that passes", p. 33:
  <u>Bepo al steve tornant a cjase dal cjamp...cul falcet</u>
  <u>su la spale, e 'l codar daur el cul,...</u> ("Beppo was
  returning home from the field with sickle on his
  shoulder and whet-stone at his hip").

8.   . . . .

Pieri, pas cinc plaes dal Redentôr,
chi prei, perdònimi
s'a no sei stade adeguade cun te!
Oh Signôr, Pieri,
quarantesîs agns 'a vin stâ' a durmî insieme
duci doi sun t'un plumàc',
e no si vin nancie mai det "miarde", no, Pieri!
Cûr gno, Pieri, cimû' sestu sparî' in t'un moment!
'Ai fat di dut, pue', ài fat ogni strabalz,
debiz di une bande e di chê ate,
e mi ài fint impegnâs i linzui,
i linzui mi ài vindut, Pieri,
par socòrichi, Pieri,
in ta to malatiate, muse me, cûr gno!
Signôr benedet,
mi vendevi ancie la me persone iò
par iudâchi, sastu, Pieri!

. . . .

'a vin fat di dut par tirâ su la famee;
'a vin tanc' pups, Pieri,
e un di une bande e un di chê ate,
come ch'a ian vulû', Pieri!
Oh Pieri, Pieri,
cetant ben ch'a chi ài vulû'!
'Ai simpri fate la part dal gno dovè
cun te iò, Pieri, in dut e pardut,
e viou'ch'a chi sei stade une femine fedêl!
Va mo', Pieri, va, omenòn gno, va, cûr gno!
Mandi, Pieri!
Pree pa me, muse me! Mandi, mandi, Pieri!

---

1. ch represents hard Carnic prepalatal c for t of the
    pronoun ti.

2. For "vious", 2nd sg. pres. of vedê. The same form
    occurs in the comic "De Profundis" of the Carnic
    writer, G. Rupil (1858-1931) (D'Aronco, Antologia,
    p. 439).

8. . . . .(4 lines)

Peter, by the five wounds of the Redeemer,
I beg you, pardon me
if I have ever disappointed you!
O Lord, Peter,
forty-six years we have slept together,
the two of us on one mattress,
and we never said a bad word to each other, no, Peter!
O my heart, Peter, how you vanish'd in a moment!
I did everything, too, made every effort,
debts here, there, and everywhere,
even pawn'd the sheets,
have sold the sheets, Peter,
to help you, Peter,
in your illness, my dear one, my heart!
Blessed Lord,
I would have sold even my body, I would,
to help you, do you realize, Peter!

. . . .(6 lines)

We did everything to bring up the family;
we have so many children, Peter,
here, there, and everywhere,
just as they wish'd, Peter!
O Peter, Peter,
how I lov'd you!
I have always done my duty
by you, Peter, in everything and everywhere,
and you see, I have always been a faithful wife to you!
Go now, Peter, go, my big man, go, my heart!
Farewell, Peter!
Pray for me! Farewell, farewell, Peter!*

---

* The most interesting point about this Lament is that it
was collected (in Carnia) in 1959, long after the custom
of thus lamenting a death was believed to be extinct
(Il Tesaur, 1960, p. 10).

(h) Racconto agiografico

9.   Sant Alessio inlubià
                fasè consei e si maridà:
                come vué la ciolè,
                come doman la lassà.
                "Ai fat vôt di castitàt
                di fà siet ain di virginitàt
                e 'l me librút tal lassarai. "
                "Ài abandonat miò pari,
                ài abandonat mia mari
                l'aur e l'arínt
                e ancemò mi orès lassà. "
                E 'l ciapa sú el so librút
                e al là a fâ pinitinza;
                quan' ch'al è un tantín indenànt
                al ven el so inemí
                par intentalu
                e 'i disè:
                "Lessio, Belessio,
                tu às el to ben a ciasa
                e tu vas a zirí mal:
                iè la to muier e dama
                sui barcóns
                che va a spas cui compagnons!"
                "O no no, no podis cròdilu,
                'o ài lassàt la me muier e dama
                cusínt e vaínt
                sun chel barcon di prima. "
                E 'l ciapa sú el so librút
                e 'l torna indaúr.
                Quan' che la so muier e dama lu viodè,
                duta quanta si ralegrè.
                "O no no, dona sovrane,
                sòi vignút a puartàus un avís
                che io ieri dismenteàt. "
                E 'l ciapa sú el so librút
                e 'l torna indaúr.
                . . . .

(h) <u>Hagiographical narrative</u>*

9.   Saint Alessio, in love, just tarried
to ask his friends, and then got married:
one day he took her,
next day he forsook her.
"I've made a vow of chastity,
to keep seven years' virginity;
my little book I'll leave to you. "
"I left my father,
I left my mother,
gold and silver,
and still you want to leave me. "
Then up he takes his little book,
and off he goes, a contrite sinner.
Far he has not gone,
when the enemy appears
to tempt him,
saying:
"Lessio, Belessio,
your weal is at home,
and you go seeking woe:
your lady-wife appears
on balconies
and keeps men company!"
"No, no; I cannot believe it.
I left my lady-wife
sewing and wailing
on that balcony of ours. "
And up he takes his little book
-and goes back home.
His lady-wife at sight of him
rejoic'd exceedingly.
"No, no my queen,
I have but come to tell you something
which I had forgotten. "
And up he takes his little book
and off he goes again. . . .

---

* An even more "popular" Veneto-Emilian version of
this legend is given and discussed in <u>Il Tesaur</u>, 1959,
p. 8 and 1960, p. 2.

(i) Strambotto

10.   E tu, ninine, sestu benedete,
               tìriti in nà e dami un pôc di plete.
               No sta a fâtal dî plui di une volte,
               tìriti in na e dami un pôc di coltre.

(j) <u>Vilotis</u>

11.   i.   Ai bussât la me morose,
                       e l'ai dit al siôr plevan;
                       a mi à dat par pinitince
                       che la bussi ance doman.

         ii.   Jé ben biele la frutate,
                       ma tociâle no si pò;
                       se tociâle si podeve,
                       la varès tociade jo.

         iii.   Maridaisi, fantacinis,
                       maridaisis al prin c' al ven:
                       viodis ben c' ance la jerbe
                       quan ch' è sece al va in fen.

(i) Strambotto*

10.   Forgive me, sweetheart, if I must complain:
               move nearer; let me have a bit of sheet.
           And mind I do not have to ask again:
               move nearer - now the blanket's off my feet!

(j) Villotte†

11. i.   When I kiss'd my sweetheart, duly
               to the priest I told it, who
           straight absolv'd me on condition
               that I kiss tomorrow too.

     ii.   Yes, the girl is very pretty,
               but she's not for touching, no.
           Were it possible to touch her,
               I myself had had a go.

     iii. Find a husband quickly, maidens;
               take the first who comes your way.
           Look upon the grass, how quickly
               once it's dry, it ends up hay.

---

* A hendecasyllabic strophe of four to ten or more lines
with "feminine" ending, satirical in tone, and introduced into Italy from Provence in the 13th century.
Examples in Friulan are few and mostly derived from
Venetian. The genre and its name have been derived
from the Provençal (often satiric) estribot (from estrif
"quarrel"; cf. "strife") and the other genre called
Contrasto, on which see Intr. p. 32 and Poem No. 1.

† See Introduction, p. 34.

iv.   Montagnutis, ribassaisi,
fait un fregul di splendôr,
tant ch'o viodi ancie une volte
là ch'o levi a fâ l'amôr.

v.   Domandade une rosute,
ié mi à dit che no son sôs;
domandade par morose,
mes à dadis dutis dôs.

vi.   Joi, ce peraulis dolcis
che mi dîs il miò morôs!
A lis disin ancie i altris,
ma no son come lis sôs.

vii.   Se ti doi une bussade,
'i al dirastu al to morôs?
Parce ustu che 'i al disi,
se ancie lui al è golôs?

viii.   Oh, cialait ce biel garoful,
ce garoful ben metût!
In tal sen di ché bambine
al somèe c'al sei nassût.

ix.   Al vaiva lu soreli
al viodélu a partî.
Iò ch'i soi la so murosa
no lu àio di vaî?

x.   Se Salamòn tornàs in tiere,
lui ch'al ere professôr,
nol varès tante maniere
come vo di fâ l'amôr.

xi.   Aga, aga e simpri aga,
mai 'na gota di bon vin;
sola, sola e simpri sola,
mai podê gambiâ distìn!

xii.   Duc' mi disin: "Cia', ce biela,
cia', ce butul di sclopòn!",
ma nissun fra tanc' batecui
di sposâmi nol è bon.

iv.   Little mountains, sink your summits,
             let a little sunshine through,
       just enough for me to gaze on
           where I us'd to go and woo.

v.   When I begg'd one of her roses,
           she to give was rather loth;
      when I woo'd her as my sweetheart,
          then she straightway gave me both.

vi.   O the words my lover whispers!
           Hearing them, how sweet it is!
      Others say them too, but somehow
          they have not the sound of his.

vii.   Would you tell your lover, if a
           kiss upon your lips I plac'd?
      Why on earth should I so tell him,
          if he also likes the taste?

viii.   Look upon that sweet carnation,
           how that place it doth adorn!
      In the bosom of that girl, it
          looks as if it had been born.

ix.   Ev'n the sun itself was crying
           when it saw him say good-bye;
      how much more must I, his sweetheart,
          be allow'd for him to cry!

x.   Not King Solomon returning,
           though in wisdom all above,
      could compete with you in learning,
          when it comes to making love.

xi.   Water, water, always water,
           never of good wine a tot!
      Lonely girl, for ever lonely,
          would that I could change my lot!

xii.   They all say to me: "You're lovely;
           you're a sweet carnation-bud":
      and yet, when it comes to marriage,
          every flatt'rer is a dud.

xiii.   Catinute generose,
tu tu 'i plasis a ognidun!
Tu di duc' tu sês morose
e la spose di nissun.

xiv.   Sclopecûrs, passions penosis
stan tai cûrs inamorâz;
e vaî no zove nuie,
nè murî da disperâz.

xv.   La rosade da la sere
bagne il flôr dal sentiment;
la rosade da matine
bagne il flôr dal pentiment.

xvi.   Volìn gioldi l'alegrie
come zovins che nó sìn;
sunarà l'avemarie
dopo muarz che nó sarìn.

xvii.   A murî, murî, pazienze!
in chest mont no vìn di stâ;
ma jé dure la sentenze,
no savê dulà si va!

xviii.   Benedez chei di une volte,
ma son mêi chei di cumò:
une volte jo no eri,
e cumò soi ance jò.

xix.   Se lis stelis fossin bassis
che podessin fevelâ,
contaressin robis bielis
che ancimò nissun lis sa.

xx.   Al è lât a mont soreli,
al è lât par duc' i doi,
une strente di manine...
mandi, mandi, che jo voi.

xiii.   O my generous little Shirley,
             you're the joy of everyone;
         you are everybody's girlie,
             and will be the wife of none.

xiv.   Heartbreak and an anguish'd longing
             lovers' hearts have always tried;
         weeping will avail you nothing,
             nor committing suicide.

xv.   Ah, the dew that falls at even
             bathes the flower of love intense;
         but the dewdrops of the morning
             bathe the flower of penitence.

xvi.   All we ask is to be care-free
             like the youngsters that we are;
         calling still will be the belfry
             after we are dead and far.

xvii.   Dying's one thing - that we lastly
             have to cut this worldly bond;
         but it makes the sentence ghastly,
             not to know what lies beyond.

xviii.   Men of former times were happy;
             happier still the present age.
         Once the world went on without me;
             now I too am on the stage.

xix.   If the stars could stoop from heaven
             and could utter human word,
         they would tell of marvels such as
             human ear has never heard.

xx.   See, the sun has set already,
             set for both of us; and so
         let me hold your hand a moment...
             mandi, mandi, off I go.

(k)   Canzonete

12.   La biele Sompladine

. . . .

(iv)   'E sunin lis ciampanis, dis ié,
          lassìn di ris'cielâ.
     Lis processions 'e passin;
          aninlis a cialâ.

. . . .

(xv)   Se i Tumiezzins no vegnin, dis ié,
          io no stupis di lôr:
     ai Sanz ben pôc 'e crodin,
          e pôc ancie al Signôr.

(xvii)   Oh ciale ce meracul, dis ié,
          iu Glemonàs, daûr.
     Oh, ce biel trop di pioris!
          un vert, un neri, un scûr.

(xviii)   Son blancs, son ros, son moros, dis ié,
          son d'ogni fate siet;
     ma pâr che sepin meti
          ben la nuvizze in iet!

(xxii)   E chel vielút ch'al cimie, dis ié,
          e che al pedee cul flât,
     al pâr ch'al sedi un furbo
          ben plui che no malât.

(xxiv)   Lassín, lassín che passin, dis ié,
          tornín a ris'cielâ;
     val plui lu miò Iaroni,
          che dut il lôr passà.

(xxv)   La biele Sompladine, oh ié,
          cun tante presunzion,
     'e à ciolt un vieli, un gobo, oh ié!
          che al iere un pôc di bon.

(k) Song (Scolding)

12.   Comely Sompladina

(She is haymaking when she hears the church-bells)

(iv)   I hear the church-bells ring, says she;
                it's time a rest we took.
            There'll be processions passing;
                let's go and have a look.

(She makes unflattering comments on the various
    village-contingents)

(xv)   If none come from Tolmezzo, says she,
                I do not find it odd.
            They have small faith in sainthood,
                and little more in God.

(xvii)   O look at that great wonder, says she,
                Gemona at the back.
            O what a flock of sheep it is,
                one green, one dark, one black!

(xviii)   They're white, they're pink, they're dark, says she,
                seven different kinds of head.
            I bet they're good at putting
                their little brides to bed.

(xxii)   And that old man there winking, says she,
                and also breaking wind,
            I bet he's not so ailing,
                to judge by how he grinn'd.

(xxiv)   But let them go on marching, says she;
                the hay must still be made.
            I rate my own dear Johnny
                above their whole parade.

(xxv)   The comely Sompladina, oh jé!
                so difficult to suit,
            has married an old hunchback,
                and ne'er-do-well to boot.

(1) Narrative songs

13.   La biela Bruneta*

La biela Bruneta 'a è in presòn,
                    'a no si sa par ce resòn.
Manda a dî a chel sió pari,
                    ch'al la vadi a giavâ di presòn.

Chel sió pari al manda a dî:
                    "S'a è in presòn, ch'a stessi uvì,
che in presòn possa murî!"

. . . .

Chel sió giovon manda a dî:
                    "Da la presòn la fas iscî!
'I metarai giupa e giupòn,
                    la fasarai iscî di presòn!"

"Biela Bruneta, ies fôr di bal
                    che ció pari al vôl murî!"

"Si gno pari al vôl murî,
                    geit, portailu a sepelî;
rossa e vert mi vuèi vistî
                    e di bal no vuèi iscî."

. . . .

"Si il gno giovon al vôl murî,
                    duta da negri mi vuèi vistî,
e su la so tomba vuèi gî a vaî."

_____

* First published in 1942.

(1) <u>Narrative songs</u>

13.   <u>Fair Bruneta</u>

The lovely Bruneta lies in gaol,
                    and o'er the reason hangs a veil.
Go find her father and bid him go,
                    and spring his daughter out of gaol.

Her father bids the answer bear:
                    "If she's in gaol, she may stay there,
and die there too, for all I care."

(To the same message her mother, brother, and sister
make the same reply; but when they tell her sweetheart,)

Her sweetheart sends the message back:
                    "Those prison-walls I soon shall crack.
Let me but dress, and do not doubt,
                    in no time I shall have her out."

"Lovely Bruneta, leave the ball.
                    Your father's ailing and hears death's call!"

"If my father must pass away,
                    take him and in the churchyard lay.
Red and green I'm wearing today,
                    and in the ball I intend to stay."

(To the same news about her relations she makes the
same reply, varying only the colours of her dress; but
when it is her sweetheart who is dying,)

"If my sweetheart must fall on sleep,
                    my black dress I shall wear and keep,
and over his grave I shall go and weep."

14.   Catine biele

"Indulà vastu, Catine biele?"
"O voi a moris di baràz, o missâr pari."

"Mostrimi lis moris di baràz, Catine biele."
"La ciavra lis à mangiadis, o missâr pari."

"Mostrimi la ciavra, Catine biele."
"Il beciâr la à copade, o missâr pari."

"Mostrimi il beciâr, Catine biele."
"Il beciâr al è sotiara, o missâr pari."

"Mostrimi la tiara, Catine biele."
"La nêf la à taponada, o missâr pari."

"Mostrimi la nêf, Catine biele."
"Il soreli la à disfada, o missâr pari."

"Mostrimi il soreli, Catine biele."
"Il soreli 'l è lât a mont, o missâr pari."

"Mostrimi la mont, Catine biele."
"La mont 'a iè sun doi pai, o missâr pari."

"Mostrimi i pai, Catine biele."
"I pai son brusâz, o missâr pari."

"Iò me ne voi, Catine biele,
Iò me ne voi, Catarinele."

14.   Fair Katharine

"Where are you going, my fair Katie?"
"I'm going a-blackberrying, father."

"Show me the blackberries, my fair Katie."
"The goat has eaten them, father."

"Show me the goat, my fair Katie."
"The butcher has slaughter'd it, father."

"Show me the butcher, my fair Katie."
"He is under the ground, father."

"Show me the ground, my fair Katie."
"The snow has cover'd it, father."

"Show me the snow, my fair Katie."
"The sun has melted it, father."

"Show me the sun, my fair Katie."
"The sun is behind the hill, father."

"Show me the hill, my fair Katie."
"The hill is on two poles, father."

"Show me the poles, my fair Katie."
"The poles are burnt, father."

"I'm off, my fair Katie,
I'm off, my little Katharine."

(m) <u>Indovinelli</u>*

15.   (i)   Cui che la fâs, la fâs par vendi;
            cui che la compre, no la dopre;
            cui che la dopre, no la viôt.

                              (La casse di muart)

      (ii)   'I ài une s'ciatule di pierutinis
             dutis rossis, dutis finis,
             dutis bielis e d'un colôr:
             cui ch'al induvine al è un dotôr.

                              (Il miluz ingranât)

      (iii)   Ciamp blanc,
                   semenze nere,
                   doi che cialin,
                   cinc che arin.

                              (La man ch'a scrîf)

---

*Cf. G. Tassoni, <u>Proverbi e indovinelli</u>, - <u>Folklore</u>
<u>mantovano</u> (Olschki, 1955) and Michele di Filippis,
<u>The literary riddle in the 17th century</u> (which includes
some by Michelangelo).

(m) <u>Riddles</u>

15. (i) He who makes it, makes it to sell.
    He who buys it, does not use it.
    He who uses it, does not see it.
                              (A coffin)

    (ii) I have a box with many a little stone,
    each delicate and red, and all my own;
    all beautiful, their colour is the same:
    if you guess this, add "Doctor" to your name.
                              (A pomegranate)

    (iii)   White field,
                         black seed,
                         two looking,
                         five ploughing.
                              (A writing hand)*

---

*This is none other than the <u>Indovinello Veronese</u>, fam-
ous as the earliest document in Italian (Dionisotti and
Grayson, <u>Early Italian Texts</u>, p. 1). This Friulan version, like the other dialectal ones quoted by E. C. Bondi
in the Romagnol magazine <u>La Pie</u> of March-April 1951,
p. 72, substitutes for the pen as plough the two eyes.
This is strange, because the <u>vomer di penna</u> (Petrarch
cxxviii. 5) is the germ of the simile; cf. the etymology
of <u>write</u> (cut, engrave, as on Runic stones; German
<u>reissen</u>, <u>ritzen</u>), <u>scrivere</u>, <u>graphein</u>, all originally
meaning <u>scratch</u>. Perhaps it was felt that the oxen had
already implied the plough. The significance of the eyes,
however, varies: in Romagnol they <u>arbega</u>, sc. <u>erpicano</u>,
i. e. rake over the ground, i. e. re-read the text; in
Parmigiano <u>non fanno niente</u> and in Marchigiano <u>stanno a
vedere</u>, i. e. are idle spectators; while the <u>guarda</u> of
Ticinese and Trevigiano agrees with Friulan's <u>cialin</u> presumably in meaning that both pen and plough have to be
guided, or possibly, as another Parmigiano version im-
plies (<u>due vigili pel campo</u>), that the field must be guar-
ded. On the question of the meaning of <u>pareba</u>, it is worth
noting that <u>parâ</u> is the normal Friulan word for "driving
forward" (cf. poem App. 1 No. 2). Bondi points out that
the simile is found in Paulus Diaconus (<u>ca.</u> 725-797),
Eusebius (260-340), and the comic poet T. Quinctius
Atta (d. 77 B.C.). Cf. <u>Corriere del Friuli</u>, Jan. 1974.

(n) Mûz di dî *

16. (1) La buine dote la dà il pari, la buine femine
il Signor.

(2) L'ore di gustâ pai siôrs 'e jè quan' che àn
fan, pai pitocs quan' che and' àn.

(3) L'è stât un sôl galantom in chest mont, e
ance chel lu àn piciât.

(4) Lari pizzul, no stâ robâ, che il lari grant
ti piciarà.

(5) L'ultin tabar l'è fat senze sachetis.

(6) Se al plûf il dì d'Ascense,
quarante dìs no si sta cenze.

(7)   Farai
'l è fradi di no fâ mai.

(8) Miôr un no su tun plat di buine ziere
che un sì tun podìn di brute maniere.

(9) Cui che ten cont pal spinèl, spant pal
cocòn.

(10) I litigànz 'e fasin il past, iu avocàz lu
mangin.

(11) La fan 'e mude la fave in màndulis.

(12) Ogni len 'l à il so carûl.

(13) 'L è miei dî "Puar me" che "puars nó".

(14) Miei un iustament magri che une sentenze
grasse.

(15) Dôs feminis e un'ocie fasin un marciât.

---

* For a list of proverbs written down in the 16th century
see D'Aronco's <u>Antologia</u>, p. 84.

(n) Proverbs

16. (1)   The father gives the good dowry, the Lord
          gives the good woman.

    (2)   Dinner-time for gentlemen is when they are hun-
          gry, for beggars when they have something to eat.

    (3)   There has been only one good man in this world,
          and even him they hanged.

    (4)   Little thief, do not steal, or the big thief will
          hang you.

    (5)   One's last coat is made without pockets.

    (6)   If it rains Ascension Day,
          forty days 'twill be that way.

    (7)   "I shall do" is ever
          brother of doing never.

    (8)   Better a "No" on plate of cheerful jowl
          than "Yes" in bucket of a sullen scowl.

    (9)   He who is thrifty with the tap is wasteful with
          the bung.

    (10) The litigants prepare the meal, the lawyers
          eat it.

    (11) Hunger changes beans into almonds.

    (12) Every wood has its worm.

    (13) Better to say "Poor me" than "Poor us".

    (14) Better a lean conciliation than a fat court-
          order.

    (15) Two women and a goose make a market.

BIOGRAPHICAL NOTES ON THE PROSE-WRITERS *

Prose

RENATO APPI (b. 1923), clerk, writes for the stage in

both Italian and Friulan.   His L'ultin perdon (ca. 1960)

is accounted by some "the most serious" play in the

whole Friulan repertory, doubtless on account of its

complete break with tradition and use of the technique

associated with modern Irish and American drama.

D'Aronco, the first to notice this quality, prefers

however Appi's "impressionist" poetry. He uses a

western dialect.

CARLO MICHELE d'ATTEMS (1711-1774), first arch-

bishop of Gorizia (after the suppression of the Patri-

archate of Aquileia in 1751) did not disdain as such

to preach in Friulan as well as in Italian and Slovene.

This indication of the prestige of the language is in

accord with the compilation of a Commentary on the

Gospels in Friulan by a 4th-century Bishop of Aquileia

(Introd. pp. 25 and 31).

Discors ne la visita pastoral   10

* See note on p. 139.

ANTONIO BELLONI (d.1554), notary, is remembered

only for two letters which happen to be of more than

merely philological interest.

A M. Zuantoni di Cortone 8

AURELIO CANTONI (v. p. 156)

Une peraule 21

RICCARDO CASTELLANI (b.1910), schoolmaster,

having discovered from his own reading the linguistic

affinity of Friulan and French, decided there was no

reason why the lesser Romance tongue should not

resemble its great sister in the aesthetic sphere also.

Hence the abandonment of parochial themes and a

meticulous attention to purity of diction and accuracy

of syntax. In his poetry this expressed itself in the

precedence given to form over substance.

GINO CENCIGH (b.1928), civil servant, has revealed

his poetic and narrative talent in "Aghe che passe"

(1971).

Lant a molin 26

LUZIO DI CJANDIT (Lucio Peressi)

A writer of short stories

COUNT ERMES DI COLLOREDO (v. p. 146)

Proteste dal autôr   9(a)

Dialogo d'une citine cul confessôr   9(b)

FEDERIGO COMELLI (1826-1892), engineer (he wrote

a "Plan for a water-supply to Gorizia" in 1887), had to

spend much of his time outside Friuli as a result of his

patriotic activities in favour of an Italian Gorizia. His

prose is in a deliberately elevated style, as though to

prove that Friulan is fit for something more than folk-

tales and jocose narrative. Two poems, rescued by

Chiurlo from misattribution to others, deservedly

figure in Friulan anthologies.

GIOVANNI BATTISTA CORGNALI (1887-1956), lawyer

and man of letters (he was Chief Librarian of Udine's

magnificent Biblioteca Comunale from 1922 to 1954),

is ranked next to Ascoli in terms of Friulan scholar-

ship. No-one laboured with greater devotion than he

over the buried literary patrimony of Friuli. Co-

founder of the S. F. F., in his own writings he

vindicates Friulan's claims to cultural parity with
its sister-tongues.

Sui marciepîs di Rive Bartuline   14

RANIERI MARIO COSSAR (1884-1963), teacher, has
published several studies of folklore and collections
of Friulan legends.

Storia dai tre naranz   18

LEA D'ORLANDI (d.1965), though important in the history
of Friulan poetry (p. 49), deserves mention here for
her comedy, "Al è mior ce che Dio mande", published
in Ce fas-tu? of 31 Dec. 1944.

CHINO ERMACORA (1894-1957), journalist, worked as
a kind of Public Relations Officer for Friuli, writing
numerous works on aspects of its life, including a
Guide to Udine, and founding a Society, "Friuli nel
mondo", whose magazine he edited.

Par Ercole Carletti   15

ANNA FABRIS (1872-1959), schoolmistress, is remembered less for her occasional verses than for her
comedies and her Friulan patriotism.

Ambulatori in vile   16

ARTURO FERUGLIO (1859-1967), accountant, was

a prolific writer of comic works, both theatrical

and literary. (Introd. p. 59). His humour, self-

confessedly inspired by Jerome K. Jerome, is often

satirical. His story-telling instinct led him also to

translate some of the Gospel parables (App. 2, Nos.

3-4).

Cul timp si mendarà   19

GIOVANNI GORTANI (1830-1912), lawyer, garibaldino,

and printer, settled finally in Carnia on the unification

of Italy in 1866. Like his cousin Luigi, he set himself

to collect legends, stories, documents, and <u>vilotis</u>

(p. 34) of his region, stimulated to it by regret for

a world crumbling before his eyes. This mixture of

sadness and humour confers its special note on his

story-telling, making it at once popular and personal.

Lant jú pe Tresimane   13

LUIGI GORTANI (1850-1908), engineer (he built roads,

aqueducts, dams, bridges, schools in Friuli and rail-

ways in Spain), fortunately extended his collecting of

Friuli's flora to that of her folktales, which he had the

sense and skill to reproduce with the minimum of

conscious elaboration.

PIER SILVERIO LEICHT (1874-1956), historian, pro-

fessor in the Universities of Bologna and Rome, sen-

ator, was "the most authoritative personality in the

field of Friulan culture in the first half of the century"

(D'Aronco) (Introd. p. 59). Among his works is a

Breve Stori del Friuli and Parlamento friulano.

GIUSEPPE MARCHETTI (b. 1902), priest, teacher of

history and Latin, and author of a Grammatica friu-

lana (1953), followed Corgnali in using Friulan for

the treatment of scientific and other serious themes.

Much of his work appeared in Patrie dal Friûl, a

periodical founded in 1946 and openly "nationalist" in

tone. As befitted a philologist, he paid particular

attention to vocabulary, purging and enriching the

language according to need.

Amôr pes peraulis   20

SOMEDA DE MARCO (v. p. 151).

Vilie di Nadâl   17

GIUSEPPE MARIONI (1880-1957), lawyer, is assured of

remembrance less as the historian of his native Civi-

dale than as the author of several comedies.

PIETRO MENIS (b. 1892), author of stories and legends

notable for their authentic Friulan language, would

have been Friuli's first novelist (cf. D. Virgili, p.

58), if only his novel Il cipres sul cuc ("The cypress

on the peak"), finished in 1940, had been published.

A shorter novel Sul agâr ("On the furrow") appeared

in 1970.

Gno nono   24

ALVIERO NEGRO (b. 1920) has stimulated other members

of Risultive to write for the theatre. His own plays

have broken with the comic tradition in favour of top-

ical themes such as the demolition of houses in the

path of a motor-way (La cjase, 1966). A later play,

however, taps Friulan folklore and reintroduces us to

the mother of St. Peter (cf. No. 20).

VALENTINO OSTERMANN (1841-1904), teacher of

Ital. Lit., collected folktales as part of his study

of popular traditions.

UGO PELLIS (1882-1943), famous for his writings on

linguistic themes in Italian and German (he was Editor

of the <u>Atlante linguistico italiano</u>), found in Friulano

a field ideally suited to his enthusiasm and badly need-

ing his ability. (He was a co-founder of the S. F. F.)

The scepticism and pessimism of his poetry appear

also in his prose-poem, <u>Al rusignul svuarbât</u>, which

D'Aronco has called "one of the first gems of a reviv-

ing Friulan poetry". Pellis was one of the first to feel

the need for this renovation (Introd. pp. 59-60), but

his anticipation of the movement took the form of

experiments in the classical metres.

CATERINA PERCOTO (1812-1887) was first encouraged

to write (in Italian) by the poet Dall'Ongaro, and with

such justification that her <u>Racconti</u> were presented to

the public by no less a person than the formidable critic,

N. Tommaseo (1858). She was fortunately not misled

by this success into neglecting the language of the

people amongst whom, as a "contessa contadina" in

the village of San Lorenzo (near Bolzano), she spent

most of her life. And with that language she acquired

also the legends and traditions of the region, and it

was in that language that they cried out to be narrated.

Stories conceived in the collective Friulan conscious-

ness and expressing the essential Friulan character as

much and as characteristically as their <u>vilotis</u> (p. 34)

required to be told in the Friulan language; and it is

this perfect wedding of form to thought which makes

Percoto's <u>Scritti friulani</u> such an artistic achievement.

They are untranslatable, as Percoto's own attempts

prove. One of them, <u>Lis striis di Germanie</u>, has the

double distinction of being called "a gem" by Dall'

Ongaro and of inspiring Carducci's poem <u>In Carnia</u>.

Il voli di chest mont   12

LUCIO PERESSI: see LUZIO DI CJANDIT

PRE CHECO PLACEREAN (b. 1923) is taking an active

part in the restoration of Friulan to the Church. He

has translated the <u>Gospels</u> and the <u>Acts</u> and, in collab-

oration with Pieri Londar, the <u>Epistles</u> and <u>Apocalypse</u>.

With his recent collection of sermons on the unity of

the Church in Friuli he has thoroughly vindicated the

claim of Friulan to be the language of the pulpit.

La letare di Pauli a chei di Rome, 1, 8-12. App. 3, 1

The Lord's Prayer   App. 3, 3

Il Vanseli seont San Luche, xv, 11-32   App. 3, 2

RIEDO PUPPO (b.1921), schoolmaster, is the author of

tales based on local tradition and village-life. The

collection Par un pel (1960) went through six editions

in eleven years and possesses a subtle humour rare in

Friulan writing.

Il Crist di Quilin   25

GIUSEPPE FERNANDO DEL TORRE (1815-1894), chem-

ist, is another proof of the fact that artistic endowment

"will out", whatever the circumstances may be. Thus

his annual "Calendar" (Il Contadinel), devoted to the

severely practical life of the countryside, has occa-

sional flashes of inspiration, when the language rises

to its theme. Hence it is not so odd that his Dialogue,

La gran comete dal 1865, bears more than a superfi-

cial resemblance to Leopardi's Dialogo di un venditore

d'almanacchi e di un passeggere (D'Aronco, pp.

280-1).

RINALDO VIDONI (b. 1904), clerk, can boast "the first

attempt in prose to free Friulan from a certain 'local

colour'" (D'Aronco). In fact, his tale, <u>I pins di San</u>
<u>Ciandit</u>, was at first criticized for lack of regional
content.

DOMENICO ZANNIER (b. 1930), priest, has shown his
devotion to Friuli not only in poems, sermons, and
tales, but also in founding the first "Scuele libare
furlane" in his native village.

El palut   23

DOLFO ZORZUT (1894-1960), schoolmaster, published
his first <u>fable</u> in Friulan at the age of 16. (It had been
preceded by a collection of <u>vilotis</u> two years earlier).
Indefatigable in his search for stories, he was scholar
enough to state his sources, and so much the born
artist that the unmistakable imprint of his own personality left their original simplicity intact. In 1960 he
was the sole surviving co-founder of the S. F. F.

PROSE

1. Entries from various account-books (1345-1396):

   (a) R den.xx che fo venduda la peverada che romans*
       de la charitat. (1349)
       *"remained" (Italian rimase, from the verb
       rimanere replaced in modern Friulan by restâ).

   (b) Spendey per legnis chu furin comperadis per lavar
       li bleons de li poveri den.12. (1357)

   (c) Par doi ceris pizuliz devant la Virgin. (1357)
       (Confraternita dei Battuti di Udine)

   (d) Spendei per una seredura di zep* che fo mesa su
       lu usso del chanpanili den.24. (1360)
       *Zep (stump, stock) is used for len (wood) because
       such artefacts required the harder part of the
       tree. An illustrated article on these locks by
       G.B. Corgnali in the Boll.della S.F.F. of 1936
       (pp. 203-5) points out that similar locks in metal
       have been found in Pompeii.

2. Sentences for translation into Latin, with Key, based
   on A Latin Grammar for Friulans by "Petrus de civitate
   Austrie", called elsewhere "famosus Grammaticae
   professor", which was used by the School of Notaries
   at Cividale in the second half of the 14th century:

   > O domlans, quals son byelis, uno naturalmentri,
   > l'altro per fuarco di freandis, a myo pare, si
   > sforcas pluy di conplase ad alt(ri) ch'a vestris
   > maric, chosa per la qual vos arinpintires davu
   > la mu(art).

   > Acustuy, lu qual, abandonâ lu studi de la gnot,
   > sta a udi flabis di feminis dongo lu fug, uay a luy!
   > quant el sara grant.

   > La me madreso, molt pluy byelo di quantis dun-
   > celis chu tu vedes ue, m'arecres cegna doy covins,
   > gli quagl un e l'atri ven fat passa duto 'l di pe lo so
   > contrado.

PROSE

1. (a) Received 20d. from the sale of the sauce left over
from charity.

  (b) For logs bought to wash the sheets of the poor I
  spent 12d.

  (c) For two little candles before the Virgin.

  (d) For a wooden lock put on the belfry-door I spent
  24d.

2.   O ladies, who are beautiful, some naturally, others
by dint of cosmetics, you are, in my opinion, trying
to please others more than your husbands, a thing
you will repent of after your death.

He who, forsaking study by night, listens to women's
tales by the fire-side, woe to him when he is grown
up!

It annoys me that my beloved, the fairest of all
girls you have seen today, exchanges glances with
two young men who happen to be in her neighbour-
hood throughout the day.

                                   (ca. 1360)

3. Letter to Cividale Town Council (ca. 1400):

Ali savi e dischreç provedors e al chonsegl di Cividat
signors mei charisims.

...el è ver signors mei chi io ai tolet di lo det
ciudio duchati xl ad inprest e si ai fat chi me moglier
si a inpromitut par ichon* me per questi midiesimi
dinari del det çudio e questi midiesimi dinari io li
invisti in vin e diei achest midiesim vin a Francesch
Sunich...lo det Francesch no mi a posut dar li deti
dinari e chusi io soi romagnut in debida....

> Bartolomio Tronbeta vostri   dadi adi xxij di april
>   minim servidor   in Plec

* con (cf. Spanish para con)

4. An administrative instruction (1416):

Se notori e manifest a zaschidun della fradaglio di
Sento Mario chom Margiaretto moglier chu fo de Zuan
di Ruvignaz saynt in buino malmuerio e in bon intellet
per la Diogratia vuglint per remission delg sie pec-
chiaz e per l'animo delg sie passaz, lassà davur la so
muart allo detto fradaglio un star di forment e miez e
un quinz di vin, lu qual forment e vin si debo vigní
pagiat soro lo braydo del Mestron, lo qual braydo si
è puesto in gliu confins di Luinis, con chest chu lo
fradaglio debo fa in pan lu det star di forment e lu
det pan si si debo partí in lu dí chu lo detto fradaglio
ven di Sento Mario del Zorn e quest ello vols chu fos
fat ogni an imperpetualmentri* com appar instrument
per man di Ser Nichula del Filitin nodar...

(From the Confraternita dei Battuti in Cividale)

> * Probably influenced by the Latin in perpetuum,
> though such confusion of negative and positive
> is not infrequent in dialect (cf. Romagnol
> amparsibul (possible) in Pulon Matt 2, 22,4).
> But cf. Introd. p. 30, note 15.

3. To the wise and prudent Superintendents and Council
of Cividale, my very dear sirs.

...it is true, gentlemen, that I borrowed 40
ducats from the said Jew and made my wife guaran-
trix for this same sum belonging to the Jew, and that
I invested this same money in wine and gave this same
wine to Francesco Sunich... The said Francesco has
not been able to give me the said money and so I have
remained in debt.

Bartholomew Trombeta your   22 April
most humble servant   Plezzo

(<u>ca</u>. 1400)

4. Be it known and manifest to each one of the Confraternity of St. Mary that Margaret, former wife of John of
Ruvignaz, being in full possession of her memory and
intellect through the grace of God, wishing, for the
remission of her sins and the soul of her departed, to
leave to the said Confraternity after her death a bushel
and a half of corn and a 32-litre tub of wine, which
corn and wine must be paid for out of the farm of
Mestron, which farm is situated in the territory of
Luinis, on condition that the Confraternity must make
bread from the said bushel of corn, and the said bread
must be distributed on the day that the said Confraternity comes from St. Mary of Zorn, and this she
desires to be done every year in perpetuity, as by
this instrument from the hand of Mr. Nicola del
Filitin, notary...

(1419)

5. <u>Extract from a schoolboy's exercise-book</u> of translations from Friulan and Venetian into Latin (1440):*

In ce timp, e in ce pericul no sin, tu lu pus vedi: in
lu qual, benche assai voltis jo ti ebe avisat di chiossis
inusitadis, nuglediment chest, lu qual al presint ti
scriv, è si fatt, che mai denant dririo non fo uldit,
ni cognossut.

(From the Archivio notarile, Udine)

   * D'Aronco corrects Bianchi's dating (1330), but
     has himself inadvertently printed almost the same
     text under that date and as a private letter. (He
     prints "oris" for "voltis" and "vedê" for "vedi".)

6. <u>A denunciation, from a notary's file</u> (1460):

.... io domandai al Chargnel soldi 40. Mestri Mis si
è li e rispuint e si disé: Chulau,* ven lá di casa me
che io ta li darai. Io li rispondei, lasín a doman ch'a
l'è massa tart. Lui rispondé: se tu no vens, io no ta
li darai doman che io voi fora de casa e cussi io zei
davur de lui e si lu clamai circha tre horis o veramen-
tri quattro e dis: Mestri Mis, io soi chí, daimi li
denari. Lui non fas altri ch'al mi sburtá la puarta
par miz e fasmi chi chiadé in terre.

   * The name of the plaintiff (cf. D'Aronco, <u>Ant.</u> 136,
     line 10).

5. In what times, and in what danger we are, you can
   see; in which, though I have informed you of unusual
   matters on many occasions, nevertheless what I am
   now writing to you is such that it has never been
   heard of or known up to now.

   (1440)

6. I asked the man from Carnia for 40 sous. Master
   Mis is there and replied saying: "You come to my
   house and I will give them to you." I replied: "Let
   us leave it till tomorrow, as it is very late." He
   answered: "If you do not come, I shall not give
   them to you tomorrow, because I am going away
   from home"; and so I went after him and called to
   him for about three hours or really it was four, and
   said: "I am here; give me the money." All he did
   was to slam the door in my face and make me fall
   to the ground.

   (1460)

7. Evidence in a civil case involving a schoolmaster
   and a parent (1473):

   Maestro Bertulo: Metît a menc, mestri Rainalt,
      ch'io viot vuestri figl yessi un disviat e grossolan
      e quant che fos in chiaf dal an, si per so grossese
      o disviament al non aves imparat, a vus displas-
      ares a payâ cinc ducac si chu paya gli altris amiis
      mituus, che ducgh gli altris si han ben la ment di
      payâ e imparin vulintir, e parzò vuardat il vuestri
      fat.
   Rainaldo: Par cinc ducac ch'io spinde in un an, pur
      ch'al impari pur tant ch'al sepe attindi a la stazon,
      al mi baste assai.

8. Antonio Belloni writes to a friend dissuading him
   from writing a Geography of Friuli (1542):

   Vo mi domandas cun grande instantie, chu fazint vo
   un dissegn di tutte cheste Patrie di Friul, io vuegli
   daus in note gliu Chystielg duch hierin dentro agl
   timps dagl Patriarchys et non si ciatin vuedi se no
   ruinaz..... Io havevi aggrumat d' Instrumenz antichs
   qualchi bielle memorie des chiosis de Patrie chun
   fantasie di fâ un Chudisut, ma io mi tollei iu dell'
   imprese, astret d'altro impaz et dubitant di piardi lu
   timp sì chun piart plui chu sta a petenâ chianuz di
   domans fine a di seris. Vuardasi vuò, chu lis vuestris lunghis fadijs intor lu dissegn senze stil, no
   fazij vaij la vuestre briaduze chu vul alg di metti iu
   pe gole; ch'io non stimi, ch'al se ben fatt che l'hom
   s'affadij d'honorâ la Patrie chun sos scritturis o
   dipinturis e lassi in chest miez la so briade di ciase
   murî di fan, chu nissune rason dal mont patiss che
   par un puchitine di glorie vane nus lassin vignî sul
   nestri sangh tante ruine. Massime quant chu servint
   a commun, si serviss nissun, che chun timp si porà
   ben ciatâ qualchi persone, chu senze alcun so signestri farà tal uffici par so aplasê et cum galantarie; et
   la Patrie, si vuedi vul iessi servide, ha ben lu mut.
   Stait san.

7. <u>Bertolo</u> (the teacher): Remember, Mr. Rainalt, that
    I see your son as an undisciplined lout, and that
    when it is New Year's Day, if he had learnt nothing
    as a result of his gross behaviour and lack of dis-
    cipline, you would dislike paying five ducats as all
    the other pupils* pay, for all the others remember
    that they have to pay and they learn willingly; and
    so, watch it.
    <u>Rainaldo</u>: As for the five ducats which I spend in a
    year, provided he learns enough to be able to
    attend to the shop, I am well content.
                                                        (1473)
    * taking "amiis mituus" to mean "friends put
    (in the school)".

8. You ask me with great insistence whether, as you are
    making a plan of the whole of Friuli, I will give you
    some notes on all the castles that were in it at the
    time of the Patriarchs and which today are nothing
    but ruins... I had accumulated from old documents
    some fine records of Friulan affairs with the idea of
    writing a little history, but I abandoned the under-
    taking, being busy with other matters and suspecting
    that I would be losing more time than those who comb
    their lap-dogs from morning to eve. Take care then
    that your long toil over the rough draft do not inflict
    suffering on your family, which wants something to
    put in its belly; for I do not reckon it a good thing,
    that a man should strive to honour his Country with
    his writings or paintings and thereby let his family
    die of hunger; for no reason in the world allows us to
    let such ruin come upon our flesh and blood for the
    sake of a little empty glory. Especially when, in ser-
    ving the common weal, one serves no-one in particu-
    lar, and with time some person will certainly be found
    who will perform such a service for his own pleasure
    and with elegance, without any disaster to himself;
    and the Country, if it wants to be served today, knows
    how to be so. Farewell.
                                                        (1542)

9.   (a) <u>Ermes di Colloredo's Preface to a satirical</u>
         <u>Dialogue</u> (No. 14b) (<u>ca.</u> 1670):

La Comedie, par che disin diviars Autors, no fo inventade

solamentri par ricrea i circostanz, ma di plui anchie e

principalmentri par che podessin approfitassi e correzi ju

costums, parcè che al dî di Ciceron la Comedie e jè une

imitazion de nestre vite, un spieli de consuetudine e un'

imagine de veretat, e second un altri autor e jè une spezie

di favole, de qual s'impare a cognossi ce cu sei util in te

vite umane e ce cu sei in te vite umane d'aburî com'

impropri, disonest e vizios. Anzi par chest i Romans,

al dî di Scaligero, e permetterin ai siei Poez di schiadenâ

la so maldicenze e di schernî a so beneplacit i vizis,

acciochè ju Popui sul timor d'un ciatif concet voltassin

de buine bande i siei anims dissipaz e scorrez, che erin

traviaz de virtuz. Onde par tant anchie io in tal formâ

chest Intermiez, no hai intindut solamentri d'esponi un

divertiment, ma ancie insieme cul metti in burle il con-

tegno familiar des Chittinis, di dâ mutif di ravediment a

ches che usin ste indiscretezze.....

9.   (a)

Comedy, as various authors say, was not invented only to
amuse the public, but even more and principally so that
they could profit by it and correct manners, because
according to Cicero Comedy is an imitation of our life,
a mirror of custom and an image of truth, and according
to another author it is a kind of fable, from which one
learns to know what is useful in human life and what in
human life is to be eschewed as improper, dishonest and
vicious. Indeed, it was for this reason that the Romans,
according to Scaliger, allowed their Poets to give full
rein to their slander and to mock at vice to their heart's
content, in order that Peoples, through fear of a bad
reputation, might turn their dissipated, licentious minds,
which had wandered from the path of virtue, towards the
good. Wherefore I too, in composing this Intermezzo,
have intended, not only to provide amusement, but also
at the same time, by making fun of the familiar behaviour
of a hypocrite, to enable those who are guilty of this
indiscretion to mend their ways. . . .

(ca. 1670)

(b) Dialogo di une citine cul Confessor (1670)

Citine: Deo gratias, bon Siôr Padre.

Padre: Bondì, fie.

Citine: E ce miracul, siôr padre, co lu ciati sôl:
             sei laudât il Signôr, jo varai par un poc
             di timp di dîi quatri peraulis, c'al è tant
             timp co lu brami.

Padre: Vês fortune dal ciârt par cheste volte,
             ma sbrigaisi biel prest.

Citine: Po caspite, siôr padre, Dio vuardi a
             tignîlu plui dal necessari, jo varès di
             rindi cont; sai ben c'al è il dové c'al
             consoli ancie ju altris che la spiètin.

Padre: Juste, fie! Dît sù vo: no piardit
             timp........

Citine: Siôr sì, siôr sì, siôr padre. Ah, Signor,
             jo orès jessi sorde e vuarbe, plui prest
             che no vedê e sintî chel cu viôt a cu sint!

Padre: Po no ve', ciare fie, anzi ringraziait
             Idio c'us lasse i sentimenz par podêlu
             servî.

Citine: Eh, siôr padre, s'al savès! quant ch'io passi
             devant a chei doi lucs dal Ridut e de Rachete
             e cu si viódin simpri cierz fraris e cierz
             religiôs, mi sint propri a passâ il cûr dal mal
             esempli che dàn a la citât; e s'al sintìs ce che
             dìsin! Ahimè! mi dàn pene nome a revuardâmi....

(b) Dialogue between a hypocrite and her Confessor

Hypocrite: Thanks be to God, my good Father.

Father: Good-day, daughter.

Hyp.:   And what a miracle, Father, that I find you
            alone: the Lord be praised, I shall have to
            have a few words with you for a little time; I
            have been longing for the chance for so long.

F.:   You are certainly lucky this time, but
            hurry up.

Hyp.:   Heaven forbid, Father, that I should keep you
            longer than necessary; I should feel guilty. I
            know well that you have to console the others
            also who are waiting.

F.:   Just so, daughter! Come on then, tell me;
            don't waste time.......

Hyp.:   Yes, yes, Father. Ah, Good Lord, I would
            rather be deaf and blind than see and hear what
            I see and hear!

F.:   Don't say so, dear daughter, but rather thank
            God that he leaves you your senses so that you
            can serve him.

Hyp.:   But Father, if you only knew! when I pass in
            front of those two places, Ridut and Rachetta,
            and there are always certain friars and certain
            nuns to be seen, I feel my heart really miss a
            beat for the bad example which they give to the
            town; and if you heard what they say! Alas! it
            hurts me even to think of it....

10. A sermon by Carlo Michele d'Attems, first bishop
     of Gorizia (1760):

Fidei miei ciars, dutis lis visitis che si fazin in chist
mond, per il plui a puartin qualchi util, qualchi consolazion, qualchi vantaz. I paris vadin a ciatâ i lor fîs. I
amîs, i visins si vísitin di spes cul fin di zovassi un cul
altri, di domandâ qualchi ajut, socors e consèi. I prin-
cips, i res vadin a visitâ lis citâz, lis fortezis, lis fron-
tieris per meti in sicurezza lis provincijs e per liberâ i
siei sudiz da lis ueris e opressions dei nimîs. I miedis,
i ciroics vadin spes dai malaz e pazienz par prescrivi i
rimiedis e procurâ cun dug i miez di fai ricuperâ la salut.

11. Extracts from two sermons*

(a) Onoraz e chiars Borghesans, avin la complasenze
    finalmentri che dut dentre cheste singolar Basiliche
    Parrochial si è rinnovat, dut soddisfe al voli e alla
    devozion. Sblianciade la Glesie, restave il pulpit;
    riformat il pulpit, restave l'organo; eccolo finalmen-
    tri anchie chel ridot in biele forme...Possidenz,
    merciedanz, artistsc, jo mi rivolz a voaltris...onde
    il mercenari gioldi il frut dellis sos fadiis.

                        Pagani Valentino (ca. 1820)

(b) ....la smanie di diffondi l'instruzion del Popul è tal,
    cussi grande...che no si sint altri che a inculcâ cun
    igni...cheste massime...Che il ben jessi tant indi-
    vidual che social al derive da une ben regolade istru-
    zion all'è imaginabil: e quant plui istrutt all'è un
    popul, tant maiormentri al sa corrispuindi ai doves
    che lu lein alla societat fra cui al vif.

                                       (ca. 1850)

    *From two of the thousand MSS-sermons to be
    found in the Biblioteca Comunale of Udine (cf.
    Bollettino della S.F.F., 1). Sermons in
    Friulan were the norm down to 1915, when
    Italian was adopted for the sake of the numerous
    soldiers from other parts of Italy.

10.

My dear faithful, every kind of visit that one makes in
this world affords for the most part some profit, some
consolation, some advantage. Parents call on their children. Friends and neighbours visit each other for the
purpose of mutual benefit, to ask for help, succour, and
advice. Princes and kings visit cities, fortresses, fron-
tiers to secure their provinces and to free their subjects
from wars and the oppression of enemies. Doctors and
surgeons often visit the sick and their patients to prescribe
remedies and try by every means to restore their health.

(1760)

11.

(a) Honoured and dear Citizens, at last we have the pleas-
    ure of knowing that everything in this remarkable
    Parish Church has been restored, everything satisfies
    the eye and the needs of the worshipper. The Church
    once white-washed, there remained the pulpit; the
    pulpit repaired, there remained the organ; and now
    finally here is that too restored to its beauty... Land-
    owners, merchants, artists, I turn to you... so that
    the hired servant may enjoy the fruits of his toil.

(ca. 1820)

(b) ...the passion for the spread of education among the
    people is such and so great...that there is no talk but
    of inculcating into everyone...this maxim...That well-
    being, both individual and social, derives from an effi-
    cient educational system - this is a thoroughly reason-
    able proposition; and the better educated a nation is,
    the better it is able to fulfil the obligations which bind
    it to the society among which it lives.

(ca. 1850)

12.   Il vôli di chest mont

Quant che il Signor insieme cun San Pieri al léve pal
mont, une matine in sul cricà dal dì e' passavin su di
un puint. Un cercandul, vieli e pezzotôs, cui vôs bas
e cun tante di corone in man al steve lì impostât, e
plen di devozion al tirave ju paternostris e avemarîs.
'I dè di vôli San Pieri e plen di rispiet al giavà il
ciapel; ma il Signor vie pe sô strade senze contalu,
cialant d'un' altre bande. Quant che forin in te' vile
e' s'intoparin in t'une sdrume di fantaz che ciantavin
vilotis sot di une fignestre. Cui veve in bocie lu
sivilot di scusse, cui ucave, cui saltave. San Pieri
cialant di brut al procurave di sghindâsi e di passà vie
cidin par no vé da fa cun che' baronìe. Il Signor invece
ur dè il bon dì, e fermât a ciacarà, plen di amor la
faze divine e ingropât la vos, ju benedive. - Passadis
lis ciasis e za fur dei pîs, internâz in t'une stradele
di campagne, San Pieri al rompè il silenzio.

    "Saveso, Signor, che vô mi pares curiôs plui
d'un pôc? E'incontrìn sun chel puint un puor diaul che
al preave cun t'une devozionone di fa compunzion ai
clàs, e vô sês passât vie senze saludalu, senze dài
nancie une cialade, anzi cun t'une muse dure che parevis invelegnât e cumò po che si sin intivâs insomp
la vile in che' nae di galopins che varan fat Dio sa ce
gnotolade, e che, massepassuz e plens di vin, in pit di
là a ciase a durmì e' stevin lì a sburì fur il morbin
ciantazzant a qualchi polzete, sior sì cun chei s'impos-
tais a fa complimenz, ju benediis e ju ciarezzais."

12.   The eye of this world

At dawn one morning when our Lord and St. Peter were
going about the world, they crossed a bridge. A ragged
old beggar was standing there with lowered eyes and a
great rosary in his hand, and piously pouring out Paternosters and Avemarias. St. Peter looked at him and
respectfully took off his hat; but our Lord continued on
his way without heeding him and looking the other way.
When they reached the village, they met a crowd of young
people who were singing villotte beneath a window. One
was playing on a wooden pipe, another was shouting, another leaping up and down. St. Peter scowled and tried to
avoid them and to pass by quietly so as to have nothing to
do with those young revellers. Our Lord, however,
greeted them, and stopping to talk, his divine face full of
love and his voice deep with emotion, gave them his blessing. When they had passed the last house and were alone
on a country-road, St. Peter broke his silence.

"Do you know, Lord, you seem to me more than a
little strange? On that bridge we meet a poor devil praying with such devotion as would have melted a stone, and
you passed him without greeting him, without even looking
at him, indeed with a frown as though you were angry;
and just now when we met those young rowdies in the village, who must have spent the night in God knows what
sort of revelry and who, instead of going home to sleep
off their orgy of food and wine, stayed up to let off steam
by serenading some girl, them you stop to compliment,
you give them your blessing, and show them affection."

"Puor Pieri, " i disè il Signor, "tu tu cialis cul voli di
chest mont, ma jo 'o ài un altri vôli e 'o viôt plui indentri.
Sastu chel cercandul quantis che an di à fatis in te' sô vite?
e cumò vignût vieli senze pentîsi al crôt di justâle cun chei
quatri paternostris che al sta lì smurmuiant. Chei zovins
invece sot di che' fignestre 'e àn l'anime nete e la lor
alegrie 'e ven da un cûr bon. Ir e' son stadis gnozzis, e
in che' ciamarute 'e duâr la nuvizze che jé de lor vile.
'E jé jessude de sô ciase, 'e à bandonât pari e mari, fradis e sûrs. Son stâz sù dute la gnot a tignì legris i puors
viei che le an piardude, e' an balât, e' àn bevût, e vuè di
matine, invece di lâ a polsâ, e' son vignûz a fa un ciant
sot il balcon de nuvizze par saludale e ralegrale, par
consolâ il cûr di chel che le à ciolete. Pieri: benedez
chei fantaz, benedetis lis lor vilotis e la lor cortesie:
al e un mazzet di rosis fres'cis che a mî mi san bon mil
voltis miêi che duc' i rosaris a sec del galantomp dal
puint. "

Caterina Percoto, 1812-1887

13.   Lant iú pe Tresemane*

Al è propri di ché bande ancie il famôs puint dal Moraràt,
che ai ciaradôrs di Ciargne 'ur faseve vignî i sudôrs frêz
nome a sintilu a nomenâ. Cetanc' di lôr, e cetantis voltis,
viazànt bessoi, e massime di gnot, no si erino avicinâz
cul cûr in man al pas terribil, tanche se vessin di lâ a la
muart, savínt che ogn' altre dì si discoreve di un o del
altri che vevin petât dentri in tei sassíns, che vevin
pierdût dut, e va e no va lassade ancie la piel!

Al è ben vêr che la iustizie, ogni volte che 'n gafave
qualchidun, no 'ur 'e sparagnave, ma iu faseve piciâ sul
puint stes, par che servis di esempli, e po' 'iu lassave
lì a pendolòn pa cene dai corvàs.

Giovanni Gortani, 1830-1912

* The road linking Udine and Tricesimo.
  Cf. Poem No. 27, verse 2.

"Poor Peter," said our Lord, "you look with the eye
of this world, but I have another eye and I see deeper
inside. Do you know how much evil that beggar did in the
course of his life? and now, having reached an unrepen-
tant old age, he thinks to put matters right with a few
muttered paternosters. But those young men under that
window have an unspoiled soul and their gaiety comes
from a kind heart. Yesterday there was a wedding, and
in that little room there sleeps the bride, a girl from
their own village. She has left her home, left mother
and father, brothers and sisters. They have been up all
night keeping in good heart the poor old folks who have
lost her, they have danced, they have drunk, and this
morning, instead of going to bed, they have come to sing
beneath the bride's balcony, to greet her and cheer her
up, to gladden the heart of the man who has taken her.
Peter: blest are those young people, blessed their villotte
and their kindness. It is a bunch of fresh roses which
to me smell a thousand times sweeter than all the dry
rosaries of your good man on the bridge."

Caterina Percoto, 1812-1887

13.   On the road to Tricesimo*

It is just here that there is also the famous Morarat bridge,
the mere name of which makes Carnic waggoners break out
into a cold sweat. How many of them, and how often, as
they travelled alone, and particularly at night, had not
approached the terrible pass with their hearts in their
mouths, as if they were going to their death, knowing that
every other day there was talk of someone or other who
had fallen in with murderers and lost everything, and as
likely as not been killed as well!

It is true that, when they caught any of them, the
authorities showed no mercy, but had them hanged on the
bridge itself, so that they might serve as an example, and
then left them hanging there for the crows to feed on.

Giovanni Gortani, 1830-1912

*   11 km. N.E. of Udine, and so called from
    being on the thirtieth milestone from Aquileia
    to Zuglio (Introd. p. 10).

14.   Sui marciepîs di Rive Bartuline

A Udin, su pe Rive Bartuline, 'e passin ogni dí miârs e
miârs di personis, ma une vore pocis 'e àn timp di cialâ
indulà che metin i pîs....Duncie, 'o vês di savê che
diluncvie, da disot i puartis di Minisín fin a la glesie di
San Cristoful, i marciapîs 'e son semenâz di cais granc'
come salàmps. Une vere cucagne!
'O ài cirût di savê d'indulà che vignivin chesc' cais o
caessis, e mi rispuinderin che si tratave di produzion
ciargnele (Fôr di Sore); ma sul cont di scuviarzi di ce
gienar che fossin, nissun iere capàz d'inluminâmi. Dome
in chesc' ultins dîs, in grazie dal dotôr Bruno Martinis,
appassionât une vore di storie naturâl, 'o ài podût savê
un dret.
    Duncie, lis pieris neris, che siarvin di marciapît in
Rive Bartuline e in qualchi altri lûc, culì a Udin, 'e par-
tegnin a la formazion raibliane (Carnic), Trias superior.
'E vegnin iú de alte Val dal Tilimènt, indulà che cheste
formazion 'e iè svilupade... Chest plan al è stât ben
studiât des bandis di Dogne, dulà che al è une vore potent
e ch'al è plen di fòssii.

                              Giovanni B. Corgnali, 1887-1956

15.   Par Ercole Carletti

...Nus à lassâz ancie lui, come tanc' atris, come nó 'i
lassarín tanc' atris; nus à lassâz biel planc, squasi in
ponte di pîs, il ciâf in bande, la pipute in bocie, la borse
sot il braz, come quant ch'al rivave ai nestris congres,
a lis nestris bielis sagris...
    Lu saludavin, e lui al rispuindeve simpri par furlan;
se si scrivevi in lenghe, la so rispuiste 'a iere - nol ocôr
dilu - in furlan. Al è par chest che usgnot...'o volin
mandai 'l nestri salut, e in furlan, pardit! par che nus
sinti miôr e che nus rispuindi subit, come in vite, il ciâf
in bande, une lûs di nobiltât tal voli clâr, sot il cerneli
pinsirôs...
    Come lui pôs 'e àn amât chist biel Friûl...Imparín
di lui...a amalu...a volessi duc' un pôc di ben. Chiste
'e iè la vôs dai muarz, la vôs del poete ch'al è tornât
usgnot fra nó.

                              Chino Ermacora, 1894-1957

14.   On the pavements of Rive Bartuline

Every day thousands and thousands of people walk along
the Rive Bartuline in Udine, but very few have the time
to look where they are putting their feet....Well, you must
know that as far as the Church of St. Christopher the pavements are sown with snails as big as sausages! A real
feast!
    I haye tried to find out from where these snails came,
and the answer was that they were produced in Carnia;
but as for discovering of what kind they were, no-one
could illuminate me. Only recently, thanks to Dr. Bruno
Martinis, a keen student of Natural History, have I been
able to learn something.
    So, the black stones which serve as pavement in the
Rive Bartuline and elsewhere in Udine belong to the Carnic
variety of the Upper Triassic age. They come down from
the upper valley of the Tagliamento, where this formation
evolved... It has been thoroughly studied in the region of
Dogne, where it is very potent and full of fossils.

                              Giovanni B. Corgnali, 1887-1956

15.   For Ercole Carletti

He too has left us, like so many others, as we shall leave
so many others; he has left us softly, almost on tip-toe,
his head on one side, pipe in mouth, case under his arm,
just as when he used to arrive at our meetings, at our
lovely festivals...
    We would greet him, and he would always reply in
Friulan; if anyone wrote to him in Italian, his reply -
needless to say - was in Friulan. It is for this reason that
tonight...we want to send him our greeting, and in Friulan
of course, so that he may the better hear us and reply to us
at once, as he did in life, with his head on one side, the light
of nobility in the clear eyes beneath the thoughtful brow.
    Few have loved this beautiful Friuli as he did...Let
us learn from him...to love it...to love each other just
a little. This is the voice of the dead, the voice of the
poet who tonight has returned to be among us.

                              Chino Ermacora, 1894-1957

16.   Ambulatori in vile

Scene quarte: Il dotôr, un lavoradôr e Giovanin.

Giov. (Al torne): Sior dotôr viodiè? (I mostre un pacùt.)
      Al è tornât chel lavoradôr. Lu fâs entrà.

      (Il lavoradôr al entre.)

Dot. : Ce volevistu?

Lav. : Si ricuarde pur si, di me? Soi sot Casse. Lui
       mi à fat il certificât di sta quindis dîs a ciase.
       E jò soi vignût a viodi s'al fâs un plasè di
       sprolungiâmal. No mi sint ben, anciemò.

Dot. : Cemût? No tu ti sintis ben, cun che scusse chi
       tu âs lì? A ti comude di sta a ciase, e jò i ài di
       prestâmi a l'ingian? Oh! cussì si met lis ciartis
       a puest, e l'Italie ancie.

Lav. : Eh! lui s'al sà alc, c'al tasi; la casse no treme
       par qualchi dì.

Dot. : Ma no tu capissis chi tu mi fâs fa l'impostôr, tu
       mi fâs dì ce ca no l'è?

Lav. : E sior dotôr, e lui la capissie, dome cumò, che
       il mond al sta su dome a fuarce di bausîs?

Dot. : E tu chi tu sês om cristian, un om catolic, tu
       iudis a fâ la malte par fa stà sù cussì il mond?
       E ancie jò, i ài di iudà? (Al ciape il certificât
       e al scrîf.) Ciape, ciape: ma ca sei l'ultime
       volte che tu vens par fâmi fâ chel ca nol larès
       fat.

      (Il lavoradôr al salude e al va.)

                                        Anute Fabris, 1872-1959

16.   Surgery in town

    Scene iv: the doctor, a workman, and Johnny.

John (returns): Doctor, look! (He shows a packet.) That
    workman has come back. I'll show him in.

    (The workman comes in.)

Doct.: What did you want?

Work.: You remember me, don't you? I'm under Casse.
    You gave me a certificate to stay a fortnight at
    home, and I've come to see if you'll do me the fav-
    our of extending it for me. I still don't feel well.

Doct.: How? You don't feel well, with that tough hide of
    yours? It suits you to stay at home, and I have to
    aid and abet your deceit? Oh, that's the way to
    make one's business prosper, and Italy too.

Work.: If you know something, keep quiet about it, eh?
    The firm won't collapse on account of a day or two.

Doct.: But don't you understand that you are making me
    a trickster, making me say what isn't true?

Work.: Doctor, surely you realize now that the world
    keeps going only thanks to lies?

Doct.: And you who are a Christian and a Catholic help
    to make the cement to keep the world in that way?
    And I have to help too? (He takes the certificate
    and writes.) Take it, take it, but let it be the
    last time that you come to make me do what had
    better not be done.

    (The workman says good-bye and leaves.)

                       Anute Fabris, 1872-1959

17.   Vilie di Nadâl

                            Scene ii

Toni (entrant): Doman matine tu tacarâs la ciavale
                 grise e tu larâs a Udin a cambiâ la semenze
                 dal forment là dal Consorzio. (Al si sente
                 dongie il banc di lavôr e al si met a tirâ
                 un mani di falciâr.)

Pieri: Baste che no nus sucedi come che jè capitât
                 al Moro dal Blanc, e sarès ben biele.

Toni: Che isal sucedût?

Pieri: No lu sâl? La contin par dut, ma è vere,
                 sâl, ostro se è vere, cun tantis nainis vué di
                 amassos, di calmîrs, di ufucis, decrès e ce
                 sao jò, fâs a pueste par mantignî la înt di
                 bant a russâsi pai uficis dulà che al salte
                 fûr l'imbroi par dut.....

Toni: Ma contimi su la storie dal Moro...tu sês
                 un tabajòt.

Pieri: Alore se soi un tabajòt, no i conti nuie.

Toni: Po ben fâs di mancul.

Pieri: No, nuie, anzi la conti distès.....Il Moro
                 dal Blanc une dì ben insacant il forment al
                 à piardut la so curtisse e no son stâs sans,
                 nol à podût ciatâle. T'al indomàn al è lât
                 a puartâ al Consorzio un sac di forment par
                 sgambiâlu cun chel selezionât par semenze...

Toni: Ma ce jentrial il forment cu la curtisse?

Pieri: Po corpo dal sciròc che al entre, c'al spieti!
                 Là i disin che al torni fra qualchi dì, parzé che
                 il forment di semenze al doveve rivâ da la
                 Toscane. Dopo tre dîs al va, al pae la difer-
                 enze di presit, al ritire il sac di forment ben
                 sigilât cun tant di timbro e di tabele, al ven a
                 ciase, al svuede il sac sul solâr parzé che nol
                 patissi e...par entri no ciatial la so curtisse!

Toni: Che il folc ju trai! Alore al ere il so forment.

Pieri: Sigûr, cu la curtisse che al veve piardût, e se
                 no ere ché, cui si inacuarzeve? Ao mo rason
                 di tabajâ cumò?

                            Pieri Someda de Marco, 1891-1970

17.   Christmas Eve

                        Scene ii

Tony (coming in): Tomorrow morning you will harness
    the grey horse and go to Udine to exchange the
    corn-seed at the Consortium. (He sits down
    at his work-bench and starts to polish a scythe-
    handle.)
Peter: So long as there does not happen to us what hap-
    pened to Moro dal Blanc, it will be all right.
Tony: What happened?
Peter: Don't you know? It's all over the town, but it's
    true, you know, I'll say it is, with all this ever-
    lasting stockpiling, controlled price-lists, offices,
    decrees and what have you, all set up just to cre-
    ate useless jobs for the boys so that they can snore
    away in their offices, which are just nests of
    fiddling.
Tony: Tell me what happened... you're a chatterbox.
Peter: If I'm a chatterbox, I won't tell you anything.
Tony: All right, don't.
Peter: No, nothing; or rather I'll tell it all the same...
    One day while packing his corn, Moro lost his
    knife, and for all his invocations of saints he
    could not find it. The next day he took a sack of
    corn to the Consortium to exchange it for one
    selected for sowing...
Tony: But what has the corn to do with the knife?
Peter: It has plenty to do with it; just you wait! There
    he is told to come back in a few days, because
    the seed-corn has to arrive from Tuscany. After
    three days he returns, pays the difference in
    price, receives the sack of corn well sealed and
    stamped and labelled, comes home, empties the
    sack in the barn so that the seed shall not spoil,
    and... what does he find inside but his knife!
Tony: Well, I'm damned! So it was his own corn.
Peter: Sure it was, with the knife which he had lost, and
    but for that no-one would have noticed! Now am
    I a chatterbox?

            Pieri Someda de Marco, 1891-1970

18.   <u>Storia dai tre neranz</u>

Iara una volta un contadin, che lant in sercia di doi com-
paris par batiâ la fia si veva piardût di strada. Cul tant
zirâ di ca e di là si veva in fin ciatât in tun bosc e, plen
di set e plen di fan che iara, si veva butât sintâ sora un
tronc di arbul e si veva tacât a vaî.

   Si veva cumpena butât iú che veva viodût passâ par
chel troi una bruta femina, cun tuna cossa su la schena,
che 'i gi veva diti: "Iò capissi che tu ses plen di set, ma
se tu ús fàtila passà, va là in chel palaz in somp dal bosc,
sun chel rivàl, e co ti viodaràn vigní, ti aviarzaràn subit
il puartòn.

   Ti avisi parò, pal to ben, di compuartati zemút che
ti disarai iò.

   Dovaràs in prin di dut onzi il puartòn cul savòn, dopo
cialà di scovà ben li s'cialis; fàs chisc' lavórs, laràs in
cusina e là viodaràs un grun di giatis, un pocis che lavaràn
i creps, altris che iu suiaràn e altris antimò che scovaràn
il paviment; tu spessea indevànt e rivaràs in tuna ciàmara.

   Là ciataràs plen di cians, un pos sbataràn i tapès, un
pos netaràn il polvar, altris lavaràn li' lastris e un doi
scovaràn par tiara; tu passa indevànt e va in tuna altra
ciàmara.

   In chista ti si presentarà un mazzèl di int, atòr pai
murs saràn rimpíns di fiar, comi chei che son ta beciariis,
e sun chei saràn impiciàs cuarps di parsonis, che poc timp
prima iarin ancimò in vita; tu tira indevànt e va ta ultima
ciàmara.

   Là ciataràs una siora sintada sora un canapè, che
ciaressarà un ciaf di mus sui soi zenoi. Co ié ti viodarà,
ti farà un grun di domandis par savè ze che ias viodút
prima di rivà sin ca di ié. Sul armàr viodaràs tre biei
neranz, tu cioiu sú e metiu ta sacheta, che saran la to
fortuna. . . . "

                              <u>Ranieri Mario Cossar</u>, 1884-1963

18.   The story of the three oranges*

Once upon a time there was a peasant who while going in
search of two friends to baptize his daughter, lost his way.
After wandering around he had finally found himself in a
wood, and being extremely hungry and thirsty, he had thrown
himself down on a tree-trunk and had begun to weep.

He had hardly sat down when he saw an ugly woman
coming along the path, carrying something on her back,
who said to him: "I realize that you are very thirsty, but
if you wish to slake your thirst, go to that palace at the end
of the wood, on that bank over there, and when they see
you coming, they will at once open the door.

I warn you, however, for your own good, to behave
as I shall tell you.

First of all you will have to smear the door with soap,
then see to sweeping the stairs properly; these tasks done,
you will go into the kitchen and there you will see a crowd
of cats, some washing crockery, others drying it, and yet
others sweeping the floor; hasten on and you will come to
a bedroom.

You will find it full of dogs, some beating the carpets,
some dusting, others cleaning the windows, and one or two
sweeping the floor; pass on and go into another room.

In this you will see a swarm of people, and around the
walls there will be iron hooks of the kind used by butchers,
and on those there will be hanging human bodies - people
who not long before were still alive; proceed on your way
and go into the last room.

There you will find a lady seated on a sofa caressing a
donkey's head on her knees. When she sees you, she will
ask you a deal of questions to find out what you saw before
you reached her. On the sideboard you will see three fine
oranges; pick them up and put them in your pocket. They
will be your fortune...."

Ranieri Mario Cossar, 1884-1963

*No. 408 in the Aarne-Thompson classification of Folk-tales.

19.   Cul timp si mendarà

Il Pari Eterno e San Pieri e' jerin vignûz une biele zornade
a cirì la caritât in Furlanie; e la nestre int, simpri plene
di bon cûr cui tribulâz, 'e implenive di ogni ben di Dio il
sac che i doi vecios e' puartavin su lis spalis; tant che il
Pari Eterno, un dopo gustâ, al dis a San Pieri:

"Ciò, Pieri, i furlans no son po che gran brute giarnàz-
zie che tu mi pituravis timp indaûr in Paradìs: in dutis lis
puartis c'o vin batût, nus àn simpri contentâz, tant c'o
dovarin nomenâ un segretari par c'al tegni cont de robe
c'o puartìn a ciase e nus prepari di mangiâ. Noaltris,
Pieri, no vin timp di piardi cu lis pignatis!"

Al rispuint San Pieri: "Si clame jù un agnul dal
Paradìs e dut si cumbine!"

"Ma ce Paradìs!" al zonte il Pari Eterno, "se chel
c'al ven cun noaltris no'l à pratiche dal Friul, tant vâl
c'al valeva. I furlans e' doprin un lengaz cussì osteôs
tal fevelâ che i agnui no capissin une malandrete e nus
fasaran lâ simpri in bestie. Po ve' lì c'al è un furlan!
Miôr di lui." E al segne a San Pieri un contadin pezzotôs
c'al ciapave su cu la pale lis buiazzis de strade e lis poi-
ave in t'une zèe c'al tignive donge. San Pieri, spaventât,
si met lis mans tai ciavei: "Signorut benedet! Seso
deventât mat?" al dis. "Puar tant che lu viodês, se vês
bisugne di lui par un lavôr, al scomenze a molâ fur sen-
tenzis e a blestemâ piês di un turc."....Se no'l ves vût
chel brut vizi di blestemâ..., il Pari Eterno e San Pieri
no si sintivin mâl in companie dal furlan; massimamentri
tal fâ da mangiâ se giavave pulît, lui!

19.   He'll improve with time

The Eternal Father and St. Peter had come one fine day to
seek alms in Friuli; and our people, always full of compassion for the unfortunate, filled the sack which the two old
men were carrying on their shoulders with all manner of
good things; so much so that the Eternal Father said one
afternoon to St. Peter:

"Well, Peter, the Friulans are not after all the nasty
lot you described to me some time ago in Paradise: at
every door where we have knocked, we have received
something, so that we shall have to engage a secretary
to keep account of the stuff that we are taking home and
to prepare our meals. As for us, Peter, we haven't time
to waste over cooking-pots!"

St. Peter replies: "One just calls an angel down from
Paradise, and everything is in order!"

"What Paradise?", goes on the Eternal Father, "if the
one who will accompany us is not familiar with Friuli, he
might as well stay at home. The Friulans use a language
which is such a tongue-twister that the angels can't make
head or tail of it, and they will make us get very angry.
But look, there's a Friulan over there! Just in time!"
And he points out to St. Peter a ragged peasant who was
picking up with a spade the dung on the road and putting it
in a basket he had nearby. St. Peter, terrified, put his
hands in his hair: "Good Lord! Have you gone mad?" he
said. "Poor as you see he is, if you needed him for a
job, he starts grumbling and cursing worse than a Turk."
.... If he had not had that beastly vice of cursing..., the
Eternal Father and St. Peter would have felt quite at their
ease in the Friulan's company; especially as a cook he
gave a good account of himself!

Une sabide matine il Pari Eterno al puarte a ciase un biel cavret e al pree il furlan di cueilu e cuinzâlu pulidût pulidût. Il cogo si met a l'opare e al prepare in ordin lis pitanzis par ore di cene; ma viars lis quatri, forsi pal masse lavorâ, i capite une slisse malandrete e par cuietâla un fregul al met a frizi cu la sponge i interiôrs de bestie e cussì al ti fâs fûr une biele mirindute.

La sere, gran complimenz dal Pari Eterno pe grande sapienze. "Dut ben, dut ben cuet; ma...ma i mance une robe," al dîs San Pieri. "E ce i mancial, sior sproto, c'al vûl meti simpri la lenghe indulà che no'l covente?" al rispuint rôs in muse il furlan. "E' mancin in taule i interiôrs de bestie, po!" "E jè vere!" al zonte il Pari Eterno, "e cui iu àl mangiâz?" Il furlan s'infote ancimò di plui e al peste i pîs. "'O scomenzi a vênt fin parsore i voi di voaltris pezzotôs!" al dis. "Ce crodêso che iu vedi mangiâz propri jo chesc' benedez interiôrs? Po no saveso che i cavrez neris e' son senze e chel c'o vês puartât voaltris al jere propri un cavret neri?" Al mole fûr un mocul grant come une ciase e al s'ciampe disore a durmî.

"Veso sintût?" al dîs San Pieri; "veso sintût, benedet omp! No'l è nome blestemadôr, ma ance bausâr! Us vevi visât, jo!" "Lassìn cori, Pieri, lassìn cori. Cul timp si mendarà!"

Arturo Feruglio, 1895-1967

One Saturday morning the Eternal Father brings home
a fine kid and asks the Friulan to cook and prepare it
properly for the table. The cook sets to work and pre-
pares the helpings for supper-time; but towards four
o'clock, perhaps as a result of so much work, he feels
the pangs of hunger, and to soothe them a little he fries
the giblets in butter and makes a nice little snack.

That evening he was greatly complimented by the
Father Eternal on his skill. "Very well cooked; but
...something is lacking," said St. Peter. "And what
is lacking, Mr. Grumbler who always wants to stick
his nose in where it doesn't belong?" replies the Friulan,
red in the face. "The giblets are not on the table, are
they?" "That's true," adds the Eternal Father, "and
who has eaten them?" The Friulan gets still angrier
and stamps his feet. "I'm beginning to get fed-up with
you tramps!" he said. "Do you think it was I who ate
these blessed giblets? Don't you know that black kids
haven't any and that what you brought home was in fact
a black kid?" Then with a mighty oath he dashed
upstairs to sleep.

"Did you hear that?" said St. Peter; "did you hear
that, my good friend? He is not only a blasphemer, but
also a liar! I warned you!" "Never mind, Peter, never
mind. He'll improve with time!"

Arturo Feruglio, 1895-1967

20.   Amôr pes peraulis

A' son putropis lis manieris di amâ la peraule: une
maniere 'e je chê dal poete, ch'al misure, ch'al
scolte, ch'al palpe, e ch'al volte e al rivolte la
peraule par sintî ce forme, ce risistenze, ce sun
e ce colôr ch'e à, e cemût che si pò insedâle tal
zûc e tal spirt musicâl dal discors poètic; ma se
no j plâs, la bute vie o che la sfuarze e la modifiche
a so mût. Un'altre maniere 'e je chê dal gram-
àtic, che j cîr lis cumissuris, par stuarzile e
pleâle in mût ch'e jentri juste te urdidure de
proposizion. Un'altre 'e je chê dal glotòlic,
ch'al ûl savê di ce pari e di ce mari ch'e ven,
e ce fradis e ce sûrs ch'e à, e a ce famèe di
lenghis antighis ch'e parten. Un'altre maniere
'e je ancje chê dal tabajòt, che la dopre a orêle,
par dret e par traviars, a proposit e a sproposit,
e la maltrate cence savê e cence domandâ ni ce
ch'e je, ni dontri ch'e ven, ni ce ch'e val, ni
cemût ch'e sta in chel sît dulà che lui la met.
Siôr Tite Cuargnâl al jere in pôc di dut, furche
un tabajòt (che, di chê bande, nol jere pericul
ch'al strassàs une sole peraule di masse); ma
plui di dut al jere un "lessicografo" e, duncje,
un "filologo" pûr: e il "filologo" al è chel tâl,
ch'al tire fûr une peraule di un serit antîc o gnûf
e sui lavris di un ch'al fevele, e la cjape cun tun
pâr di tanaiutis d'aur, cun dute la grazie e la
dilicatezze di chest mont e cun dut il rispiet,
come che al fasarés un orésim cun tun brilant
o cun tune pierute di grant valôr; il "filologo" la
scrutine come ch'e je, cence fâi ombre di violenze
ni par drezzâle, ni par iustâle, ni par doprâle;
cence lâ a cjalâ s'e je 'ristocratiche o popolane,
s'e je nete o s'e je sporcje, ni ce utilitât che si
pò rigiavâ di jê: content di savê ch'e je, e ce
valôr precîs ch'e à, e cui che l'à doprade e quant
e indulà; e dibot temerôs di fâj mâl se je covente
ancje a lui di metile in vore.

                                   Giuseppe Marchetti, 1902-1966

20.   <u>The love of words</u>

There are several ways of loving words: one
way is that of the poet, who measures, listens,
feels, and who turns the word this way and that
to see what shape, what resistance, what sound,
and what colour it has, and how it can be inserted
into the musical play and spirit of poetic discourse;
but if he does not like it, he throws it away or forces
and modifies it to suit his purpose. Another way is
that of the grammarian, who looks for its components,
to twist and bend it so that it may enter correctly into
the structure of the sentence. Another is that of the
etymologist, who wants to know from what father and
mother it comes, and what brothers and sisters it
has, and to what family of ancient tongues it belongs.
Another manner is that of the chatterbox, who plays
it by ear, rightly and wrongly, in context and out of
it, and who maltreats it without knowing and without
asking either what it is or whence it comes or what
it is worth or how it fits in where he puts it. Signor
Corgnali was a little of all these except the chatterbox (for on that side there was no danger of his
wasting a single word); but above all he was a "lexi-
cographer" and so a pure "philologist"; and the philologist is one who extracts a word from an old or
a new document or takes it from the lips of a
speaker, and picks it up with a pair of golden
pincers, with all the delicate grace in the world,
as a goldsmith would do with a diamond or a precious stone; the "philologist" scrutinizes it as it
is, without using the slightest violence either to
straighten it out or to adjust it or to use it; without looking to see whether it is aristocratic or popular, clean or dirty, or what use one can get out of
it: content to know what it is, and what its exact
value is, and who has used it, and when and where;
and almost fearful of hurting it if he himself also
has to put it to work.

                          <u>Giuseppe Marchetti</u>, 1902-1966

21. Une peraule!

Linde... 'e jere la femine dal ustir Martin. Linde 'e
jere squasi biele, e quan' che 'e faseve bocje da ridi 'e
jere propri biele; ma no faseve mai bocje da ridi. Dongje
di chel omp che nol diseve nancje "Bondì" e ch'al viarzeve
la bocje sì e no tre voltis in tune zornade, Linde 'e viveve
par so cont, lavorant plui che podeve par dismenteâsi di
jessi in chest mont. Lu veve cjolt di pôc, cussì po', par
no restâ vedrane: 'e veve squasi trentecinc agn e di
zovine si jere fate ciacarâ.

Martin al jere un biel omp: jê 'e scrupulave che il
so temperament siarât al dipendès di qualchi displasê
sepulît dentri, e cul timp a lâ 'e pensave di ciatâ la fate
di disgropâlu.

...A' jerin tre quatri dîs che Linde 'e veve alc. A
no vê mai nuje, alc al è alc! Linde 'e jere contente...
"J al disarai usgnot," 'e pensà dut il dì. Siarade l'ostarie
- a' siaravin tôr dîs - a' cenàrin come simpri, lôr doi di
bessoi, disore.... 'E lavà la massarie, la mete sul dis-
goteplàz... Lui al jere cuiet e al sbisiave plancut daprûf
di un campanel eletric.

"Martin! Martin! Martin, 'o ài un frut!"
Lui alzà i voi, la cjalà un moment e al tornà a remenâ
plancut intôr dal so argagn; e al pareve che nol ves sintût
nuje di nuje.

Jê 'e zigà a fuart: " 'O ài un frut!"
Lui tornà a cjalale un tic plui a lunc; ma dopo al
disbassà un' altre volte il ciâf su chel imprestut.

" 'O ài un frut, Martin, 'o ài un frut!"
...Si butà par tiare vaint: "Une peraule!" 'e
scunzurave vaint, "une peraule!"
"Ce astu?" al domandà Martin.
Un lusôr al rivave su pal stradon sdrondenant: la
fasse di lûs che no finive in nissun sît 'e passà sul sofit
come une scove e si dislontanà imburide.

Aurelio Cantoni, 1922-

21.   One word!

Linda...was the wife of the publican Martin. Linda was
almost beautiful, and when she smiled she was really
beautiful; but she never smiled. In the company of that
man who would not say even "Good day" and who opened
his mouth perhaps three times a day, Linda lived her own
life, working as hard as she could so as to forget that she
was in this world. She had accepted him not long before,
just so as not to remain a spinster: she was nearly thirty-
five and in her younger days had got herself talked about.
   Martin was a handsome man. She suspected that his
closed character was the result of some unpleasant exper-
ience buried inside him, and she thought that as time went
on she would find the means to untie the knot.....
   For three or four days Linda had felt something the
matter with her. When one never feels anything, something really is something. Linda was glad..."I'll tell
him this evening, " she thought all through the day. After
closing time - around ten o'clock - they had supper as
always, the two of them alone, upstairs...She washed the
dishes, put them on the drying-board. He was silent and
quietly tinkering with an electric bell.
   "Martin! Martin! Martin! I'm going to have a baby!"
   He raised his eyes, looked at her for a moment, and
resumed his tinkering. He seemed to have heard absolutely nothing.
   She shouted out loud: "I'm going to have a baby!"
   He looked at her again a shade longer; but then he
lowered his head again over that gadget.
   "I'm going to have a baby, Martin, I'm going to
have a baby!"
   ...She threw herself to the ground, weeping. "One
word, " she begged him, weeping, "one word!"
   "What's the matter with you?" asked Martin.
   A gleam of light came up from the noisy street. The
restless beam passed over the ceiling like a broom and
sped away.

                                    Aurelio Cantoni, 1922-

22. Patrie dal Friûl (Ugn-Lui, 1964)

Cumò 'o sin sui paradôrs

Il Friûl al à cognussudis cetantis invasions e no si rive a
savê ce meracul che lu veti salvât soredut te prime metât
di chest secul co centenârs di soldâz di ogni gjarnazie,
par agn, 'e meterin ledrîs tal nestri e nus sledrisarin
cjase, cjamps e stale...

'O sin d'acordo che il Friûl al è deventât sotan di doi
parons: Rome e Triest; che 'o vin cumò un comissari di
guviâr, sessanteun deputâz regjonal, doi prefez, tre depu-
tazions provinciâls, insieme cun dut il rest ch'e lavoraran
soredut a pro dal stât che par so cont nus ten peâz a curte
cjadene ancje cul statût speciâl....

Il gjenocidi al seguitarà la sô vore, la nestre int 'e
abandonarà saldo lis cjasis, la tiare, la nestre lenghe dis-
vidrignide insieme cun dut ce ch'al sa di furlan 'e vegnarà
in curt a cjatâsi sui paradôrs.

Chei che nus àn judât a sostegnî chest sfuei ch'al fo il
prin a domandâ une autonomie pe minorance etniche ladine
e di scuasi 20 agn al scombat par une regjon furlane, no
podaran dî che "Patrie" 'e veti acetât chel tradiment che
nus àn cumbinât te ilusion di bonâ la situazion, intant che
si pronte il colp di gracie legalizât.

23.   El palût

I palûs si pierdin dulin-iú viers el Tiliment, ch'al ciante
in tal iet di graves cence cunfin. 'I fasin di cinturie el
cuel di Susàns e les Clautanes, les primes che s'inrosin
in ta l'aurore: cretes nudes, mons pàlides, infarinades di
nêf. Une poesie strane e maluseriose 'e ientre tal cûr.
'O mi visi les contes dai viei: "..E vignivin les aganes..."
Par lôr ancie cheste ciere false e plene di mos'cins 'e
veve l'inciant smarît des robes vieles di famee.

Domenico Zannier, 1930-

22. Patrie dal Friûl (June-July, 1964)

Now we have our backs to the wall

Friuli has known so many invasions, and it is only a miracle that has saved it, especially in the first half of this
century, when hundreds of soldiers of every race took root
in our soil and uprooted us from house and fields and stable...

We agree that Friuli has become the subject of two masters: Rome and Triest; that we now have a government-
commissioner, 61 regional deputies, two prefects, three
provincial deputations; together with all the rest, who will
work above all in the interest of the state, which for its part
keeps us on a tight rein even with the special statute....

Genocide will carry on its work, our people will con-
tinue to abandon houses and land, and our language, extir-
pated together with everything that smacks of Friulan,
will soon find itself in extremis.

Those who have helped us to maintain this sheet, which
was the first to ask for independence for the Ladin ethnic
minority and which for nearly 20 years has been fighting
for a Friulan region, will not be able to say that the "Patrie"
has accepted the betrayal deliberately perpetrated upon us
under the pretence of improving the situation while prepar-
ing the legalized coup de grâce.

23.   The marsh

The marshes lose themselves down there towards the
Tagliamento, which is singing in its limitless gravelly
bed. It is girdled by the neck of Susans and the Clautanes,
the first peaks to redden in the dawn: bare ridges, pale
mountains, besprinkled with snow. A strange disturbing
poetry enters the heart. I remember the old folks' tales:
"..And the spirits came..." For them even this false gnat-
ridden scene had the strange enchantment of old domestic
things.

                    Domenico Zannier, 1930-

24.   Gno nono

... Une volte gno nono al doveve ciapâ la strade di Vendoi,
jú pe rive de Cente, siché al scugnive passâ denant dal
Simitieri de glesie vecie, là che polsave la so femine.

No veve sunât l'Ave Marie ancimò nò, e vualtris 'o
saves che, fintremai che no sune une campane a buinore
lis animis dai muars 'e zirin te gnot.

El nono al veve un pocie di pore, al è ver, ma al va
indenant istes.

Come che us ài dite, al leve jú pe rive, siché dopo di
vê scierât el ciar, par jessi plui sigùr di no viodi nuje, ti
veve metude la man su la schene dal nemâl de só bande.
('O saves - nomo si? - che a meti la man su la schene di
un bò o di un mus no si viôt ne striis ne muars, parvie che
chestis bestiis 'e son stadis compagnis dal Signor te stale
di Betlem?) Ma a un cert moment la scierae no ten plui e
i nemai 'comencin a cori denant dal ciar ciamât. Ce vevial
di fâ, biât omp? Al capis che te curve lì disòt al sarès
deventât un disastro. Dutis lis risorsis par podê dâ pol-
ente a lis sôs creaturis 'e saressin ladis in fum.

Nono si met in zenoglòn su la strade glazzade e lì, cu'
la scorie tra lis mans tignudis sù, al pree la so femine
muarte che lu judi par amôr dai soi fruz.

No voles crodi? Denant dal ciar si à viodût, dit e fat,
un sflandôr e lis bestiis fermâsi lì come se, nò un, ma
quatri zocs 'e vessin metuz tes ruedis.

Lu ài sintût ancie jo a contâ chest fat di vecio, e
bisugnave viodi cemût che al deventave fevelant de so
pore femine.

Pieri Menis, 1892-

24.* <u>My grandfather</u>

My grandfather once had to take the road to Vendoi, down
the incline near Cente, which meant he had to pass by the
cemetery of the old church, where his wife was buried.

<u>Ave Maria</u> had not yet sounded, and you know that
until a bell sounds in the early morning the spirits of
the dead wander in the night.

My grandfather was a little afraid, it's true, but he
went on all the same.

As I said, he was going down the slope, so that after
having braked the cart, he put his hand on the back of the
nearer animal so as to be more sure of not seeing anything. (You know of course that if you put your hand on
the back of an ox or a donkey you will not see either
witches or ghosts, because these animals were the com-
panions of our Lord in the cattle-shed at Bethlehem.) But
at a certain moment the brake no longer holds and the animals begin to run on with the laden cart. What was he to do,
poor man? He realizes that there would be a catastrophe at
the curve at the bottom. All he possessed that enabled him
to feed his children would have gone up in smoke.

Grandfather knelt down on the frozen road and there,
with the whip in his upraised hands, he prayed his dead
wife that she would help him for the sake of his children.

Believe it or not, a blaze of light immediately appeared
in front of the cart, and the animals stopped as though not
one, but four pieces of wood had been thrust into the wheels.

I myself heard him tell this story as an old man, and
you should have seen his face when he spoke of his poor
wife.

<u>Pieri Menis</u>, 1892-

---

* From <u>Ce fas-tu?</u>, Dec. 1944.

25.   Il Crist di Quilin

De Cjuje la strade 'e va jù a plomp...Sul volt al è un
Crist e lì, dongje dal Crist, 'e jere la cjase di Quilin....

    Lu veve fat lui, chel Crist, Quilin, di len stagjonât
sun tune crôs di zàmar e po murât, lì, sul volt, tun
clapon plui grant di un fogolâr. E sot-vie al tignive
svuangjât un stroput pes rosis e a ret dai pîs dal Crist,
sul clap, al veve metût un bòssul di granate, simpri cun
tune rose dentri o cun tune rame di vert.

    Quilin nol lave in glesie parvie che lui al voleve vê
dafâ cul paron, no cui fatôrs - al diseve. E il paron, il
Crist, lui lu veve lì, fûr de puarte de cjase. Cussì al
tratave diretamentri cun Lui, a tu par tu; ma al tignive
Quilin la contabilitât: dâ e vê-di-vê. Une rose al Crist
e tantis blestemis perdonadis, un Gloria Patri e tantis
fiestis di podê lavorâ, un inchin e tantis cjochis smentea-
dis. E daûr la so contabilitât al fo un galantomp. Nol
fasè mal a nissun; juste il plevan al cjatà ce dî che
Quilin, aplicant il so criteri contàbil, al crodé simpri
di podê sparagnâ il quartês cun tun salût di cjapiel al
Crist....

    S'inmalà une volte sole, juste par murî.....Il plevan
al domandà di viòdilu e j lè dongje planchin planchin.
Quilin al zavariave, ma quant ch'al vignì a sè e al cog-
nossè il predi, no lu parà vie e nancje no lu clamà il
"fatôr".

    "Siôr plevan, " j disè, "che j puarti une rose al Crist;
'o ài sbaliât i conz: 'o ài lassade fûr une zornade di
blestemis. "

    Il plevan al molà dut, al cjapà-su un mazet di rosis,
di corse, e lis puartà tal bossul di granate, sot i pîs dal
Crist, sul clap. Po al tornà-su tun salt e al cjatà Quilin
che si segnave, e al rivà juste a benedîlu.

                                    Riedo Puppo, 1920-

25.   Quilin's Christ

From Cjuje the road descends steeply...At the turning
there is a Christ, and there, near the Christ, there was
Quilin's house...

He, Quilin, had made that Christ, with seasoned wood
on a hornbeam cross, and there at the turning he had ce-
mented it onto a huge stone bigger than a fire-place. And
underneath he had dug a little flower-bed for some roses,
and on the stone beside Christ's feet he had put a little
red metal vase, always containing a rose or a piece of
greenery in it.

Quilin never went to church because he wanted to deal
direct with the boss, not with his agents - as he used to put
it. And he had the boss, Christ, just there, outside his
front-door. So he would deal directly with Him, on familiar terms; but Quilin kept his own accounts, and on a
strictly quid-pro-quo basis. One rose to Christ, and so
many curses forgiven; one Gloria Patri and so much work
allowed on holy days; one reverent bow and so many drunken
bouts forgotten. And behind this accountancy he was a good
man. He never harmed anyone. Only the vicar could complain that in applying his theory of bookkeeping, Quilin thought
he could save a tithe by taking off his hat to that Christ...

He only once fell ill, and then it was to die... The vicar
asked to see him and approached him on tip-toe. Quilin
was delirious, but when he came to himself and recognized
the priest, he did not chase him away and did not even call
him the "agent".

"Vicar, " he said, "will you take a rose to the Christ?
I made a mistake in my accounts: I left out one day of
cursing. "

The vicar dropped everything, hurriedly picked a bunch
of roses, and put them in the metal vase at the feet of
Christ, on the stone. Then he dashed back upstairs and
found Quilin crossing himself, and he was just in time to
give him a blessing.

                                    Riedo Puppo, 1920-

26.   <u>Lant a molin</u>*

...Viars lis undis, finît el molinâr di faj el lavor..., cjariât sul cjaruz el sac de farine e chel de semula, al è partît par tornâ a cjase. Però tornant indaûr, la strade no ere pui in rive jù, ma 'dut al incontrâri....A miege rive al ere cussì strac, sfinît e sudât, che al à scugnût fermâsi un moment a tirâ flât. No lu véssial fât.

El cjaruz, cul pês al à comenzât a tornâ indaûr e Carlin, cun duc' i sôi sfuars par fermâlu, sbrissant te glerie, nol à podut fâ altri che tornâ indaûr cun lui fin dapît de rive.

In chel par furtune al passe el plevan e 'j dîs: "Ce fâtu chi, Carlin, polsistu?" "Sì, siôr plevan. 'O tiri flât, parcéche 'o sei scanât e no puès pui lâ indenant. 'O ài cirût di lâ sù pe ribe, ma no rivi a fâle. 'O jeri lât sù fin a miez, ma par fermâmi a tirâ flât, el cjaruz al è tornât indaûr."

"Ma no îse nissune buine anime che ti dà une man?"

"Magari! Ma fin cumò nol è passât mai nissun."

"Spete alore che ti judi jo," repliche el plevan, e dopo tirât sù la gabane cun tune man, cun chê altre si met a sburtâ par daûr el cjaruz....

Finalmentri 'e rivin insomp e dopo la cjase de Pio Fire, di front de glesie si fermin, stracs, sfinîs, e sudâs a tirâ flât.

"Orpo, Carlin," al dîs el plevan sflanchinant, "tu vevis reson di dîsi che no tu rivavis a fâle. Al è masse pês par te. No sai tò mari jo, ce sentiment che à vût di mandâti a molin cun tun sac cussì grant. No podevistu dî a tò mari che ti vês dâs mancul chilos?" "Ma sì che lu ài dite!"

E 'l plevan curiôs: "E ce ti a'e rispuindût?"

"Mi à dite di no preocuparmi parcéche par strade 'o varès cjatât di sigûr qualchi dordul che mi varès dade une man. Meno mal che à induvinât."

                              Gino Cencigh
                    (from <u>Aghe che passe</u>, 1971)

---

* The same story is told in the first person by Stecchetti in his Romagnol sonnet, <u>Buon Cuore</u>.

26.   <u>Going to the mill</u>

Towards eleven o'clock, when the miller had finished his
work, having loaded the sack of flour and that of bran onto
the cart, he set out on his way home. But the road on the
way back was no longer a downward slope, quite the
reverse...Half way up he was so tired, exhausted, and
covered in perspiration that he had to stop for a moment
to get his breath. A pity he did so.

The weight of the cart began to pull it down the slope,
and for all his efforts to stop it, Charlie, his feet slipping
in the gravel, was carried down to the bottom with it.

Fortunately at that moment the vicar passes. "What
are you doing here, Charlie?" he says; "are you resting?"
"Yes, vicar, I'm getting my breath back, because I'm
worn out and can go no further. I have tried to get up the
slope but can't manage it. I got half-way up, but when I
stopped to draw breath, the cart rolled back."

"But is there no kind soul to give you a hand?"

"I only wish there were! But you're the first person
to come by."

"Let me help you then," replies the vicar, and pulling
up his long cloak with one hand, he begins to push with the
other behind the cart.

At last they reach the top, and just beyond Pio Fire's
house, in front of the church, they stop, weary, exhausted,
and soaked in sweat, to recover their breath.

"By Jove, Charlie," says the vicar, panting, "you
were right to tell us you couldn't manage it. It's too great
a weight for you. I don't know what your mother was
thinking of, to send you to the mill with such a large sack.
Couldn't you have asked her to give you a few kilos fewer?"
"I did ask her!"

And the vicar, interested: "And what was her reply?"

"She said I wasn't to worry, because I would certainly
meet on the way some nincompoop who would give me a
hand. A good thing she was right."

Gino Cencigh
(from <u>Aghe che passe,</u> 1971)

APPENDIX 2

PROSA   POPOLARE *

Las zizilos

Lu Signúor al ero su la crúos che 'l penavo de tri oros.
In chestos tri oros al vevo un gran mac di zizilos che in
ché volto es portavo la plumo blancio, soro di Lui ch'i
fasevo dut un gran davoi cu las alos par condolesi.

Lu Signúor al mûr su la crúos. Al è vegnût un gran
teremot, scurît lu saríali e cu lu teremot son viertos las
tombos dei antics.

E encio las zizilos es àn gambiât colúor da plumo
che di blancios 'e son stados dutos neros e dopo 'e son
stados simpri neros.

Lu Signúor al à vulût dâ chest segnâl che 'e àn
assistût 'e so muart cun tant doul.

A oro di vuio 'a si à duc' un gran riguart di fâ del
mâl a di chesos bestiutos, ch'al dîs, che 'e puarto dis-
gracios in fameo cui cu las danegio.

From <u>Collina</u> (D. Zorzut)

---

* For the difference between these tales and
No. 18, see Introduction, p. 34.

APPENDIX 2

FOLK - TALE

The swallows

The Lord was on the Cross where he had been suffering
for three hours. During these three hours he had over
him a great flock of swallows, who at that time had white
feathers, and who were making a great to-do with their
wings as a mark of condolence.

The Lord dies on the cross. There came a great
earthquake, the sky was darkened, and with the earthquake the tombs of the ancient dead were opened.

And then the swallows changed the colour of their
wings from white to black, and since then they have always
been black.

The Lord wished to give this sign that they had been
present at his death with such grief.

From this time on people take great care not to harm
these little creatures, because it is said that anyone who
harms them brings misfortune on his family.

From <u>Collina</u>* (D. Zorzut)

---

* A village high up in the Carnic Alps north of the River
  Degano (Canal di Gorto). Cf. the Romagnol tale of how
  the robin got its red breast.

APPENDIX 3

TRANSLATIONS INTO FRIULAN

1. La letare di Pauli a chei di Rome, 1, 8-13

E prin di dut 'o soi agrât al gno Diu midiant di Gjesù

Crist sul cont di duc' vualtris, par chel ch'a contin de

vuestre fede in dut il mont. Par me po, Diu ch'o servis

cun dut il gno cur predicjant il Vanseli dal so Fî, al è

testemoni che jo no moli di ricuardâus, domandant simpri

tes mês prejeris di podê vê la furtune, se Diu al ul, di

rivâ adore di vignî a cjatâus. Parceche 'o propit gole di

viodius par fâ a miegis cun vualtris cualchi don di Diu che

us tegni su, al ven a stai par consolâsi a muse un cul

altri par vie de fede ch'o vin compagne, vualtris e jo.

    No uei, fradis, che no saveis ch'o ài vût tal cjâf

unevore di voltis di vignî a cjatâus, ma no ài podût fin

cumó.

Pre Checo Placerean (1972)
(Don Francesco Placereani)

2. Il fî bintar (San Luche xv.11-32)

Un om al veve doi fis. E il plui zovin al dîs a so pari: "Dami
la part che mi tocje di ce che tu às". Al à finit cul dividiur ce
ch'al veve. Il fî plui zovin, pôs dîs dopo, al vent dut e al va
lontan, e lì al à mangjât fur dut ce ch'al veve, vivint come un
bintar. Cuant ch'al veve finît dut, 'e capite une grande miserie
di chês bandis, e lui al scomence a patî la fan. E lant a cirî si
met sot di un di chês bandis che lu mande in campagne a menâ
a passon i purciz. E lui al vares bramât di jemplâ la panse cul
glant ch'a mangjavin i purciz, ma nissun no j' n' dave.

Alore tornât in sè, al dîs: "Ce tanc'fameis di gno pari che
àn pan che ur vanse, e jo culì 'o mur di fan. Mi cjapi su e 'o
voi di gno pari e 'o j disarai: 'Pari, 'o ài pecjât cuintri il cil
e in face tô! No soi degn di jessi tignût par to fî; tratimi come
un dai tiei fameis'."

Si cjape su e al va di so pari. Al ere ancjemò lontan cuant
che so pari lu viôt, s'ingussis, al cor a cjapâlu a bracecuel e
lu busse. Ma il fî j dîs: "Pari, 'o ài pecjât cuintri il cîl e in
face tô; no soi degn di jessi tignût par to fî." Il pari, impen,
al dîs ai siei servidors: "Su, puartait il vistît plui biel e vis-
tilu; meteigi l'anel tal dêt e sandui tai pîs; cjapait il vigjel
ingrassât e copailu; mangjin e gjoldin, parceche chest gno fî
al ere muart e al è tornât a vivi, al ere piardût e lu vin cjatât". E a' jan scomencât a fâ fieste.

Il fî plui vecjo al ere in te braide. Cuant che, tornant, al
fo dacis la cjase, al sint a sunâ e a balâ. Al clame un servidor
e j domande ce ch'al ere. Chel j dîs: "Al è tornât to fradi, e
to pari al à copât il vigjel ingrassât parce ch'al è tornât in
salut". Alore j è vignude la fote e nol oleve jentrâ.

So pari al è saltât fur a preâlu. Ma lui al dis a so pari:
"Viôt tros agn ch'a son ch'o ti servis e che no ti ài mai disu-
bidît e tù no tu mi às dât mai nancje un cavret par ch'o fases
un pocje di ligrie cui miei amîs. Ma cuant ch'al torne a cjase
chest to fî, ch'al à mangjât dut ce ch'al veve cu lis sdrondinis,
tù tu j às copât un vigjel ingrassât".

Alore lui j dîs: "Tù tu sês simpri cun me e dut ce ch'al è gno
al è to; ma si scugnive fâ fieste e gjonde, parceche chest to fradi
al ere muart e al è tornât a vivi, al ere piardût e al è stât cjatât".

3. La prejere di nestri Signôr (San Mateo vi, 9-13)

Pari nestri che tu sês in cil, ch'al sei santificât il to non, ch'al
vegni il to regno, ch'e sei fate la to volontât come in cil ancje
in tiare; il pan che nus covente danusal uè, e perdoninus i nestris debiz, come ancje nô ju vin perdonâz ai nestris debitors,
e no stâ metinus te tentazion, ma libèrinus dal trist.*

                                    Pre Checo Placerean (1970)

* i.e. il djaul.

BIBLIOGRAPHY

Language

Ascoli, G.L.   Sull'idioma friulano (Udine, 1846)
   "   Saggi ladini, in Arch.glott.ital.,
                         Vol. I (Torino, 1873)
   "   Italia dialettale, in Arch.glott.ital.,
                         Vol. VIII (1880)
   "   Il dialetto tergestino, in Arch.glott.
                         ital., Vol. X
Battisti, C.   Storia della Questione ladina
                         (Firenze, 1937)
   "   Il Trentino (Novara, 1915)
   "   Article "Friulan" in Enciclopedia
                         italiana
Bianchini, J.   Gramatiko de Friula lingvo (by instal-
                         ments in "L'Esperanto", Itala
                         Esperanto-Federacio, 1922)
Blanch, V.G.   Linguaggio friulano (San Daniele, 1929)
Boehmer, E.   Bibliografia friulana (Romanische
                         Studien VI, Bonn, 1885)
Contini, G.   Letteratura dell'Italia unita (Firenze,
                         1968), p. 1028 (See above Introd.
                         p. vi, note 2)
Devoto, G. and
   Giacomelli, G.   I dialetti delle regioni d'Italia
                         (Sansoni, 1972)
Elcock, W.D.   The Romance languages (London, 1960),
                         pp. 478-481

Francescato, G. Fonologia friulana (Ce fas-tu?,
                 1951-2, pp. 5-11)
"   Dialettologia friulana (Udine, 1966)
"   Saggi sul vocalismo tonico friulano
                 (Atti dell'Accademia, Udine
                 1957-60)
"   Uno studio sulla dialettologia del Friuli
                 (Congrès internat. de dialectologie
                 gén., 1965)
Frau, G.   Individualità linguistica del friulano
                 (off-print of Clape cultural
                 Aquilèe from Corriere del Friuli
                 of 1 March 1974)
Gartner, Th.   Rätoromanische Grammatik (Heilbronn,
                 1883)
"   Handbuch der rätoromanischen Sprache
                 und Literatur (Halle, 1910)
Gortani, G.,
  Gallia, A. and   Studii sul dialetto friulano (1863;
  Mussafia, A.   reissued, Udine 1966)
Iliescu, M.   Le frioulan à partir des dialectes
                 parlés en Roumanie (Paris, 1973)
"   Saggio di morfologia friulana, in "Studi
                 linguistici friulani" 11 (1970)
Karli, J.R.   Delle antichità italiche, Vol. IV
                 (Milano, 1790)
Lazzarini, A.   Vocabolario scolastico friulano-
                 italiano (Udine, 1930)
Lüdtke, H.   Inchieste sul confine dialettale fra il
                 veneto e il friulano, in "Orbis"
                 VI (1957)
Marchetti, G.   Lineamenti di grammatica friulana
                 (Udine, SFF, 1952)
Merlo, C.   Saggi linguistici (Pisa, 1959) (for the
                 Questione ladina)

Parodi, E. G.   Due parole sui Ladini (Estratto da
                       "Nell'Alto-Adige") (Milano,
                       1922)
Pellegrini, G. B.   Tra friulano e veneto a Trieste (Con-
                       grès int. de dialectologie gén.
                       1964)
    "   Criteri per una classificazione del
                       lessico "ladino" (Studi linguis-
                       tici friulani, I, 1969)
Pellis, Ugo   Sul dialetto friulano (Pagine istriane,
                       Annata vii)
Pirona, G. A., and
  Corgnali, G. B.   Il Nuovo Pirona (dizionario) (Udine,
                       1935)
Pisani, V.   Si può parlare di unità friulana? (Atti
                       del Congresso di Linguistica e
                       Tradizioni popolari, Udine,
                       1969, pp. 54-56)
Porta, G. B.   Grammatica friulana pratica (Udine,
                       1922)
Rohlfs, G.   Struttura linguistica dell'Italia (Leip-
                       zig, 1937)
Salvator, L.   Zärtlichkeitsausdrücke u. Koseworte
                       in der friulanischen Sprache
                       (Prague, 1915)
Salvioni, C.   Italia e Ladinia (Milano, 1918)
Schneller, C. H.   Die romanischen Volksmundarten in
                       Südtyrol (Gera, 1870)
Tellini, A.   Tesaur de lenghe furlane (Bologna,
                       1922-3)
Trabalza, C.   Dal dialetto alla lingua (Paravia, 1917)
Zannier, G.   El Friulano (Montevideo, 1972)

Literature

Full bibliographies and critical introductions are given in
the excellent Anthologies of Bindo Chiurlo and Gianfranco
D'Aronco:

D'Aronco, G.   Nuova Antologia della letteratura
                       friulana (Udine, 1960)
Chiurlo, B.   Antologia della letteratura friulana
                       (Udine, 1927)

Among later and other works not noted there are the
following:

Cencigh, G.	Aghe che passe (short stories and poems) (Udine, 1971)
Chiurlo, B.	Laudi sacri in Friuli nei secoli xiii e xiv (Patrie dal Friûl, 22 Feb. 1908)
Corgnali, G. B.	Scritti di B. Chiurlo (Ce fas-tu?, 1944, pp. 331-343)
"	Un Testo friulano del Cinquecento: Il Travestimento del 1º Canto dell' Orlando Furioso (Udine, 1953)
Fabris, A.	A passe la scalmane (Comedie in tre az) (Udine, 19--)
"	Morosèz, dispièz, confèz (Scenis in furlan) (Udine, 1952)
"	Trapulis and Ambulatori in vile (Comediis) (Udine, 19--)
"	Par lui and Par un ûf and Adio sopis (Comediis) (Udine, 19--)
Faggin, G.	La letteratura ladina del Friuli negli ultimi trent'anni (Estratto dalla Panarie, dic. 1971)
"	La lingua friulana e le sue "chances" (La Panarie 16, 1972)
"	Alla scoperta di un poeta friulano dell' 800: Nicolò di Steffaneo (La Panarie, dic. 1972)
"	Un catechismo friulano del 1770 (Udine, 1972)
"	La cise in flôr (6 poets) (Udine, 1972)
Feruglio, A.	Attraverso la prosa friulana (Ce fas-tu?, Dec. 1928)
"	Fufignis, Prime e seconde dozene (Udine, 1923 and 1925)
"	Lis flabis plui bielis (Udine, 1944)
"	Lis parabulis di Nestri Signor Gesu Crist (Udine, 1943)
" (Titute Lalele)	El Lunis (Udine, 1926)
" " "	Viaz a Vignesie (Udine, 1944)
" " "	Lunari pal '53 (Udine, 1953)
Gironcoli, F. de	La plòe ta pinède (Udine, 1972)
Lea D'Orlandi	Proverbi friulani (Udine, 1960)

Leicht, M.   Prima, seconda, e terza centuria di
                    canti popolari friulani (Venezia,
                    1867)

Malattia, G.   Villotte friulane moderne (Maniago,
                    1922)

Marco, P. Someda de La buteghe dal barbîr (Comedie in
                    un at) (AGF, Udine, 1950)

  "   A l'oselade and Une Scarpute
                    (Comedies) (AGF, Udine, 1949)

Percoto, C.   Scritti friulani (with preface by Chiurlo)
                    (Tolmezzo, 1929)

Placerean, C.   Il Vanseli di N. S. Gjesù Crist (Vol. 1 of
                    the N. T.) (Udine, 1972)

  "   I Faz, Lis letaris dai apuesti, e
                    l'Apocalisse (Vol. 2 of the N. T.)
                    (Udine, 1972)

  "   Pe unitât di glesie tal Friûl (Udine,
                    1972)

Rausch, F.   Geschichte der Literatur des Rhäto-
                    romanischen Volkes (Frankfurt,
                    1870) (includes a genealogical
                    tree of Raeto-romantsch dialects,
                    which is reproduced in La Panarie
                    of June, 1972, p. 13)

Smaniotto, C.   El palisson dal martar (Tre az furlans)
                    (AGF, Udine, 1948)

  "   Il vecio Nadâl (Fantasie par fruz in
                    dos parz) (Udine, 1926)

Virgili, Dino   La Flor (Antologia) 2 vols. (Udine,
                    1968)

Zaneto   Poesiis (Udine, 1963)

General

Bergamini, G.   Affreschi del Friuli (Udine, 1973)

Bettiol, R.   Memorie di vita friulana (Gorizia,
                    1971)

Cavalcaselle, G. B. La pittura friulana del Rinascimento
                    (Vincenza, 1973)

Chiurlo, B.   La funzione storica del Friuli (Lecture,
                    1917)

  "   Caratteri etnici del Friuli (Patrie dal
                    Friûl, 21 Sep. 1915)

Clape culturâl Aquilèe   Friûl-popul e lenghe (Udine, 1972)
D'Aronco, G.   Bibliografia della musica popolare
                           friulana (Milano, 1950)
      "   Manuale sommariodi letteratura popo-
                           lare italiana (Udine, 1961)
      "   Le fiabe di magìa in Italia (Atti dell'
                           Accad. di Scienze, lettere e arti
                           di Udine, 1954-57, pp. 49ff.)
      "   Gli elementi magico-religiosi nelle
                           forme d'arte popolare (ib.1951-
                           54, pp. 195-216
      "   Sull'origine della villotta friulana
                           (Estratto da Atti del vii. Con-
                           gresso Naz.d.tradizioni pop.,
                           Sept. 1957)
Ermacora, Ch.   Vini del Friuli (Udine, 1957)
Garzoni, L.   Canti friulani (with music) (Carisch,
                           Milano)
Gortani, L.   Tradizioni popolari friulani (Udine,
                           1904)
Gramatiche, Vocabulari ed Eserciçis di lenghe internaçional,
                           Esperanto, pai ladins furlans
                           (S. Vito al Tagliamento, 1935)
Leicht, P.S.   Breve storia del Friuli (Udine, 1930)
Marchetti, G.   Il Friuli - uomini e tempi (Udine, 1959)
Marco, P. Someda de   Notoriato friulano (Udine, 1958)
Menis, G.C.   Storia del Friuli (SFF, Udine, 1969)
Ostermann, V.   La vita in Friuli (Udine, 1940)
Paschini, P.   Cenni storici sulla Carnia (Tolmezzo,
                           1925)
      "   Storia del Friuli (Udine, 1953)
Salvi, S.   Le nazioni proibiti (Firenze, Vallecchi,
                           1973)
Tellini, A.   Sentimenti ed Affetti nella poesia
                           popolare...del Friuli (Nozze
                           Gaspero-Rizzi e Vittorina
                           Tellini, 1924)
Tessitori, A.   Monografia storica delle mummie di
                           Venzone (1848)
      "   Monografia storica-scientifica
                           (Udine)

Magazines etc.:   Pagine friulane (1888-1903); Patrie dal
Friul (1875-1965); Ce fas-tu? (1920-   ); Il Tesaur (1949-
1960); La Panarie (1924-49, 1968-   ); Int furlane (1963-
   ); Corriere del Friuli (1973-   )

INDEX

ROMAGNOL: LANGUAGE AND LITERATURE
D.B. Gregor

Uniform with FRIULAN, this book aims to put Romagnol squarely on the literary map of Europe by printing texts (and versions in English) from Aldo Spallicci, Enzo Guerra, Vincenzo Strocchi, Cino Pedrelli and other important writers in the dialect of Romagna. With a complete grammar of the language.   US$13.50   UK£4.00

THE AEOLIAN ISLANDS
Philip Ward

The Lipari archipelago northeast of Sicily is the mythical home of Aeolus, god of the winds, and Vulcan, god of the smithy. In this engaging volume of history and travel, Philip Ward describes Lipari, Salina, Vulcano, Panarea, Stromboli, Filicudi and Alicudi. Profusely illustrated.
US$6.50   UK£1.95

THE HIDDEN MUSIC
Östen Sjöstrand

In the "Oleander Modern Poets" series, Robin Fulton introduces and translates some of the most remarkable Swedish poetry to have emerged since World War II. Sjöstrand's poetic credo has been compiled by Staffan Bergsten.
US$3.50   UK£1.05

PINCERS: A ONE-ACT PLAY
Philip Ward

A journalist and an M.P. meet a sculptor in his studio for their annual reunion. But the occasion is not what it seems: "how cleverly we little scorpions make pincers for ourselves! ... once a year we hold the pincers". Mimeographed. In the "Oleander Dramascripts" series.
US$1.25   UK52p

UNDERSEAS POSSESSIONS: SELECTED POEMS
Hans-Juergen Heise

One of the most important German poets to emerge since the war, Heise was born in East Germany in 1930 and now lives in West Germany. Ewald Osers, recently awarded the Schlegel-Tieck prize, has translated some forty recent poems by Heise for the first book of Heise versions to appear (here with the original German) in English.
US$3.50   UK£1.05

JUST PICK A MURRICANE? by
N. E. Chantz
is "ticklingly funny" according to a British newspaper.
The most misleading introduction to the American language ever misguidedly published, we challenge you to
define ziparoos such as beadle-eyeded, cankered, dennis,
Euston, foam and Gladicea.   US$1.25   UK30p

TOURING CYPRUS
Philip Ward
Another standard travel book by the author of "Tripoli",
"Sabratha", "Touring Iran" and "Touring Lebanon". The
London 'Times Literary Supplement' hailed Philip Ward's
new guide as "a valuable book... it omits nothing and is
sensibly arranged. Philip Ward writes well and amus-
ingly about the history of the island. He is particularly
knowledgeable on the Byzantine frescoes... Just what the
tourist wants".   US$6.00   UK£1.40

PREHISTORIC ROCK ART OF THE LIBYAN SAHARA
Angelo Pesce and Manfred Fürst
Magnificent colour photographs with an authoritative text.
In association with Edizioni del Grifone, we have also
published Angelo Pesce's COLOURS OF THE ARAB
FATHERLAND, COLOURS OF LIBYA, and WAU AN-
NAMUS: A CENTRAL SAHARAN VOLCANO.
                        Price to be announced

COME WITH ME TO IRELAND
Philip Ward
A hugely enjoyable ramble through the midlands, coast-
lands and islands of Europe's most exotic country: its
Celtic language and art, its pre-Christian customs and
archaeology, its timeless conversation and stories everywhere he stopped. This is not the instant Eire of the
travel posters but the sound and scent of the land itself,
and the rich humour of the people who live there.
                        US$6.50   UK£1.95

THE LIBYAN REVOLUTION
Meredith O. Ansell and Ibrahim M. al-Arif
A detailed source-book of legal and historical documents
on the September 1969 revolution that ended the rule of
Libya's Idris I. "For students of Near East politics this
is an absolutely essential book" - 'Book Collecting and
Library Monthly'. By the authors of the comparative
LIBYAN CIVIL CODE (US$45.00).   US$22.50   UK£6.00